Edge of Empires

Edge of Empires

CHINESE ELITES AND BRITISH COLONIALS IN HONG KONG

JOHN M. CARROLL

HARVARD UNIVERSITY PRESS

Cambridge, Massachusetts
London, England   2005

Library of Congress Cataloging-in-Publication Data

Carroll, John M.
 Edge of empires : Chinese elites and British colonials in Hong Kong / John
M. Carroll.
   p. cm.
 Includes bibliographical references and index.
 ISBN 0-674-01701-3 (alk. paper)
   1. Hong Kong (China)—History. 2. China—History—1861–1912. 3.
China—History—Republic, 1912–1949. I. Title: Chinese elites and British
colonials in Hong Kong. II. Title.

DS796.H757C38 2005
951.25'04—dc22   2004059693

Contents

Acknowledgments

When I was a youngster in Hong Kong during the 1970s, one day I asked my best friend, a Chinese teenager, if he and his family would like to go with my family to a public demonstration against government corruption. My friend replied firmly that he had no interest in any such activity. People like me, he declared, should appreciate how good conditions were in colonial Hong Kong, especially compared with Mainland China, where most of his relatives lived on daily rations of rice and cabbage. I insisted that he was wrong and that the communist government of China was doing a reasonable job of providing for its citizens, having freed China from the yoke of Western imperialism.

Shortly after, my high school history teacher asked our class to complete a special project. Queen Elizabeth was coming to Hong Kong for the first time; it was to be a historic occasion. The teacher, a Chinese woman, asked us to make a scrapbook of the queen's visit. My Chinese classmates were all excited about the project. Better Queen Elizabeth than Chairman Mao, they insisted. I was less enthusiastic and tried to do a more controversial project, which the teacher rejected.

I mention these memories not to claim some kind of authenticity over my subject, but for the opposite reason. By assuming that Chinese in Hong Kong should feel a certain way about British colonialism and

Chinese communism, I was constructing categories for my Chinese classmates, determining how they should feel and act and defining what I thought being Chinese in Hong Kong ought to mean. But real people rarely fit such neatly defined categories. From the early 1800s into the twentieth century, some Chinese collaborated with the colonial authorities to build and preserve Hong Kong as a special place dependent on not being part of China "proper." Although these people often contributed greatly to building a new, modern China, they had no interest in being politically part of this China.

Many friends and colleagues have helped with this project. Special thanks go to my teachers at Harvard University, especially William Kirby, for providing support at every stage; Philip Kuhn, for reminding me of the importance of the Chinese outside of China; and Akira Iriye, for stressing the international dimensions of Chinese history. I am also grateful to Elaine Mossmann, in History and East Asian Languages at Harvard, and to Kathleen McDermott, acquisitions editor at Harvard University Press. Karl Gerth and Seth Harter read the entire manuscript or earlier versions of it. Other colleagues and friends who offered insightful comments on chapters or conference papers include: David Barrett, Richard Belsky, Carol Benedict, Gardner Bovingdon, Shiwei Chen, Donald Critchlow, Leo Douw, Paul Frank, Pat Giersch, Richard Horowitz, Hui Po-keung, Tak-wing Ngo, Charles Parker, Caroline Reeves, Helen Siu, Jung-fang Tsai, Andrew Wilson, Wen-hsin Yeh, and Margherita Zanasi. In Hong Kong, Elizabeth Sinn and Carl Smith, on whose work I have relied extensively, Ming Chan, Fung Chi Ming, and Lee Pui-tak all helped with materials and ideas. Christopher Munn generously shared his own sources on early colonial Hong Kong. I am grateful to two anonymous readers for Harvard University Press for their constructive comments.

Thanks also are due the staffs at the Harvard-Yenching Library and the Widener Library at Harvard University; the East Asian Collection, Central Collection, and Archives at the Hoover Institution; the Butler and Starr Libraries at Columbia University; the Hung On-Tao Library, Special Collections, and Fung Ping Shan Library at the University of Hong Kong; the Reference Library of the Hong Kong City Hall Library; the Public Records Office of Hong Kong; the Sun Zhongshan wenxianguan in Guangzhou; and the Centre of Asian Studies at the University of Hong Kong. Bernard Luk and Peter

Yeung of the Canada Hong Kong Resource Centre in Toronto kindly provided research support during my brief visit there in May 2003.

The book could not have been completed without financial support. I am grateful for Harvard University's Frederick Sheldon Traveling Fellowship and several generous fellowships from the Harvard University Graduate Society; a Minor Research Grant and a Faculty International Travel Grant from The College of William and Mary; and two Mellon Faculty Development Grants from the College of Arts and Sciences at Saint Louis University. I would also like to thank Wm. Roger Louis and the British Studies Fellowship at The University of Texas at Austin for financial support and camaraderie, and for reminding me how Hong Kong history is also part of British colonial history.

Earlier versions of Chapter 1 appeared in *China Information* 12.1/2 (Summer/Autumn 1997) and in Tak-Wing Ngo, ed., *Hong Kong's History: State and Society under Colonial Rule* (London: Routledge, 1999). I am grateful to the publishers of both volumes for permission to draw on these articles in revised form.

Privileged as I am in having a network of loving and supportive relatives distributed across the globe, my thanks go both to my own family—especially my parents, if not for whom I might never have encountered Hong Kong—and to my many in-laws. Most of all, I am grateful to my wife and daughter, Katie Monteil and Emma Carroll-Monteil, whose visits to Hong Kong, however brief, I hope have convinced them that Hong Kong is worth the time I have spent studying it.

Note on Romanization

As today, most people in nineteenth- and early twentieth-century Hong Kong spoke Cantonese, not Mandarin or *Putonghua*, the standard dialect of China. Rather than convert their names to the more standard but awkward pinyin system currently used in China, I have tried to retain contemporary usage while disrupting the flow of the text as little as possible.

Names of Chinese people in Hong Kong are generally given according to the romanization they used, how they were written in contemporary English-language sources, or how they appeared in quotations. Because much of Hong Kong's early history comes from colonial records and the local English-language press, many personal names are available only in English. Whenever possible, pinyin equivalents are provided in the index. Names of people in China generally follow the pinyin system, except for such figures as Sun Yatsen and Chiang Kai-shek, who are already well known to many readers by other nonstandard romanizations. Treaty names are listed according to contemporary standards (for example, Treaty of Nanking), with pinyin in the index. Place and institution names in Hong Kong are romanized according to either their conventional (though often inconsistent) usage or the way they appear in quotations: for example, Tai Ping Shan, Tung Wah Hospital. The name "Hong Kong" appears in colonial records and other contemporary English-language sources as two words or one (Hongkong); original usages have been retained. With the exception of Canton, as it was written in colonial documents and the local press and would have been known to English-speaking Chinese, place names in China are in pinyin.

Edge of Empires

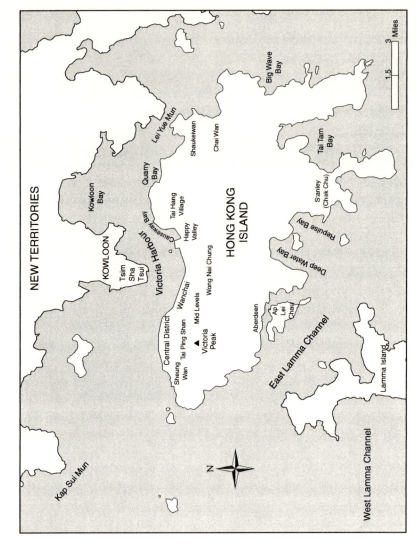

Hong Kong, 1900.

Introduction

*T*YPICAL OF MANY visitors to the British colony of Hong
Kong, Frenchman Marc Chadourne found it an intriguing place, unlike China or anywhere else in Asia. Arriving in the colony's harbor
in the early 1930s, Chadourne was fascinated by how the colony defied
categorizing: "I already begin to recognize all this. It is China—the
howl of her starving pack, her color of spices, her stinking rags, her
insolence, her voracity . . . But this city, that slowly emerges from the
reeking atmosphere, piling up in a marvelous mirage its amphitheater
of buildings, palaces, bungalows, rising vertically with its hanging gardens, its winding roads, its castles in the air, its double peak silhouetted
against the stormy sky—this is not China. It is an English city. It is
Hong Kong."[1] After being driven by taxi through the narrow, shop-
lined streets of Central, the colony's main commercial district, Chadourne arrived at the Sincere Department Store, the first Chinese-
owned department store in Hong Kong and China. "Is this," he
wondered, "another crowd, another race? Gone are the gentlemen in
skull-caps and blue robes; gone the house-wives in little white trousers.
Here there is nothing but Young China—Asia, dressed à la Belle Jar-
dinière."[2]

Orderly streets and roads named after British royalty and colonial
officials, next to busy Chinese markets where many Europeans never
dared to set foot; shops providing every type of traditional Chinese

medicine, along with colonial hospitals supervised by European physicians: such incongruities never failed to impress Western visitors.
Mary Turnbull explains how "Hong Kong, 'Fragrant Harbour' of the
Chinese, has always exerted a fascination for Westerners as an outpost
of empire, a minute enclave enveloped by the vastness of China, an
exotic entrepot pulsating with life and adventure, yet paradoxically a
speck of normality on the brink of a forbidding continent . . . However
dangerous Hong Kong might be for those who succumbed to its temp-
tations, the colony represented order and safety in contrast to the
troubled hinterland, which most Englishmen at the time regarded as
a benighted continent of cruelty and misery, where corrupt mandarins
meted out barbaric punishments, and heathens drowned girl babies at
birth."[3]

Local residents, whether Chinese or foreign, could also be transfixed
by this curious meeting of East and West. In 1948 journalist Su Fuxiang described Hong Kong as truly a "meeting point of East and
West." But Su also explained that although Hong Kong was a cultural
meeting point, its rulers remained English, their subjects Chinese. Because of this unequal balance, a new Hong Kong culture could never
be born. In another article, Su argued that after a century of British
colonialism, Chinese in Hong Kong still could not properly be called
Hong Kong citizens because they did not have the right of representation. Although some Chinese served on the colonial Legislative
Council, Executive Council, and Sanitary Board, they were appointed
by the governor rather than elected.[4]

Hong Kong in History

In this book, I address some of Hong Kong's paradoxes and incongruities by examining Hong Kong as a political and cultural encounter
between a declining Chinese Empire and the ascendant British
Empire. I focus on the relationships between the British colonial elite
and the leaders of the Chinese bourgeoisie. In the century after the
Opium War (1839–1842), upper-class Chinese collaborated with their
British rulers to build a place that these Chinese came to consider
their own. This collaboration resulted not from colonial governance
but from the initiative and endeavor of the rising Chinese bourgeoisie,
whose leaders worked in the spaces opened by colonial inconsistency,

neglect, and, often, incompetence, and shaped by Hong Kong's strategic geographical, political, and cultural position at the edge of the Chinese and British empires. The relationship between the colonial government and this Chinese elite was neither domination nor resistance, but confluence of vision as well as at times conflict of interest. Although the two communities wanted a successful and stable commercial center, the Chinese elite and the British colonialists led largely separate lives and built parallel clubs and associations. Their economic and political collaboration thus coexisted with a system of social segregation.

With historians of China preferring to focus on China "proper" and scholars of British colonialism generally concentrating on Africa and India, until recently the historiography of Hong Kong was limited mainly to two approaches. British historiography usually consisted of hagiographical works stressing the roles of various British governors and civil servants, practically ignoring the Chinese population. The other approach, employed mainly by Chinese Marxist scholars, hardly shed more light on the Chinese community of the colony. It generally dismissed Chinese merchants, for example, as little more than "running dogs" of the British imperialists. For these scholars, Hong Kong had little importance beyond its significance as the spoils of British imperialism, and as a base for the Western imperialists' invasion of China.[5]

In the past fifteen years, however, scholars have constructed a much more nuanced history of Hong Kong. Building on the pioneering work of sociologist Henry Lethbridge and theologian-historian Carl Smith, Elizabeth Sinn and Chan Wai Kwan have shown how Chinese merchant elites achieved social and political prestige, protected Chinese interests under foreign rule, and represented the Chinese community by forming such organizations as the Tung Wah Hospital and the Po Leung Kuk.[6] Refuting the common view of Chinese in Hong Kong as apathetic, willing subjects of the colonial administration, Jung-fang Tsai has argued that the Chinese working classes maintained a long tradition of popular animosity toward colonial rule. The work of K. C. Fok highlights the important contributions of Hong Kong Chinese to the economic development of modern China. Chan Lau Kit-ching shows how Hong Kong was affected by the turbulent conditions in early twentieth-century China. The political turmoil of the early republican period, argues Stephanie Chung, led Hong Kong Chinese merchants to invest in Canton politics to protect their business interests. Christopher Munn's recent study exposes the failure of the early colonial government to transform Hong Kong into the much-anticipated "Anglo-China" where Chinese and European traders would flourish under British liberalism and impartial justice.[7]

A central concern of these works is how the Chinese of Hong Kong adapted to colonial rule and how they survived under an alien, often repressive, colonial regime. While acknowledging the many faults of colonialism, I argue in the present book that, at least for the leaders of the Chinese bourgeoisie, colonial Hong Kong was not such a contentious or bewildering place. The making of a Chinese business elite was inseparably linked with the colonial nature of Hong Kong, and Chinese participation decisively shaped and set the parameters of British rule. Both confluence and conflict characterized Hong Kong's position at the edge of the Chinese and British empires. This combination offered certain opportunities for Chinese merchants to become an organized, self-conscious business elite. To be sure, some of these opportunities were also available to merchants in Chinese cities, such as Canton, Hankou, and Shanghai.[8] But the colonial government's insistence that Hong Kong's historical purpose in the British Empire should be that of a commercial center singled out those Chinese businessmen who impressed the government by helping Hong Kong achieve and maintain this historical ideal. By the end of the nineteenth century, the colonial government saw the Chinese businessmen of the colony not as profit-bound sojourners but as allies in the struggle for order and stability in Hong Kong, South China, and the British Empire.

Contrary to conventional wisdom, I approach Hong Kong as its own cultural-historical place. Although clichés abound of Hong Kong as a site for cultural interaction between East and West and of its important role in modern Chinese history, like Taiwan, Hong Kong has usually been a lens for understanding something else—most commonly "traditional," rural Chinese society as it existed before the communist revolution of 1949. If defined at all, Hong Kong has generally been delimited by its negative qualities: a sleepy colonial backwater overshadowed until 1949 by semicolonial Shanghai; a capitalist paradise without history or culture, where nothing matters but money; a place where the only political values are pragmatism and apathy; and a haven for sojourners and refugees with only a temporary identity. Even the legendary "Hong Kong success story" depends on Hong Kong's negative qualities: before the British arrived in the late 1830s, Hong Kong was nothing but a "barren rock"; prior to the communist revolution of 1949, when entrepreneurs from Shanghai poured into the colony, Hong Kong was just a colonial entrepot with little industry of its own—and the best-known appellation of all, "borrowed place, borrowed time," is based on the assumption that Hong Kong has no real time or place of its own.[9]

Also contrary to conventional wisdom, I argue here that a sense of Hong Kong identity characterized the local Chinese bourgeoisie well before 1949, when the colony was separated from Mainland China by the establishment of the People's Republic of China. The common reluctance to acknowledge a Hong Kong identity before 1949 is closely related to the reluctance to treat Hong Kong as its own place. Part of the reason is political. As Hong Kong has recently reverted to Chinese sovereignty, the emphasis now is often on showing the "Chineseness" of Hong Kong. Another reason is that Hong Kong's population was often so transient. Many of the expatriates and refugees who came to Hong Kong considered it a temporary stop, regardless of how long they actually stayed. Thus, observes Ackbar Abbas, Hong Kong emerges "not so much a place as a space of transit."[10] The common assumption is that a place like Hong Kong where commerce has been so prominent cannot have much of an identity, overlooking how part of what held the Hong Kong Chinese bourgeoisie together as a self-conscious group was its members' commitment to making money. Finally, the recent emphasis on the fluidity, borderlessness, and multiple layers of contemporary Hong Kong identity often detracts from the historical, localized Hong Kong roots of this identity.

As I demonstrate in this work, as early as the late 1800s the leaders of the Hong Kong Chinese business community helped make Hong Kong its own place. The meanings of this place changed over time, but three themes remained consistent: Hong Kong's role in China's nation building; its position within the British Empire; and the official colonial version of Hong Kong's history. These men actively used Hong Kong's strategic position to stress their own identity as a special group of Chinese different from their counterparts in China. Their role in China's nation building demonstrated both their commitment to China and their own uniqueness. Contrasting Hong Kong's development and progress with that of China enabled them to highlight this uniqueness. By participating in such activities as contributing to imperial war funds, organizing ceremonies for visiting British royalty, and attending imperial trade exhibitions, they helped make Hong Kong an active member of this global British Empire. Through dating the "real" history of Hong Kong to its founding as a British colony— as did the official, colonial version of Hong Kong's history—they linked themselves to this history. By stressing the colony's commercial growth, they stressed their own role in this process. Hong Kong's nature as its own place was thus paradoxically shaped by its role as a space of movement of goods and people, its relationship with South China, and its position within the British Empire.

Hong Kong and Colonialism

While many scholars, especially since Hong Kong became a Special Administrative Region of the People's Republic of China in 1997, stress the Chineseness of this former colony, in this book I place Hong Kong within the framework of both Chinese history and British colonial history. Although Hong Kong has been arguably the most important place in China for more than 150 years, it has been such an important place because it was politically not part of China for most of those years. Sun Yatsen, the leader of the revolution that toppled the last Chinese dynasty in 1911, was educated in colonial Hong Kong. The father of modern Chinese law, Ng Choy (better known to scholars of Chinese history as Wu Tingfang), was raised and educated in Hong Kong, where he served the colonial government before moving to China. Hong Kong was the Chinese home of commercial institutions—department stores, insurance, and modern banking— that would later help transform cities like Canton and Shanghai. Until recent decades, most Chinese emigrants went through Hong Kong, while Chinese who returned to China from North America or Southeast Asia almost always passed through Hong Kong. Similarly, remittances from overseas Chinese were invariably repatriated through Hong Kong.

Much of the scholarship on Hong Kong furthermore downplays the colonial presence. For example, a frequent explanation for the colony's remarkable political stability is that Hong Kong realities did not fit classical patterns of colonialism. One study argues that most theories of colonialism tend to emphasize the coercive power of the state or the importance of "segmentation" by race or ethnicity, none of which applies very well to Hong Kong. Because Britain took Hong Kong for trade rather than for territorial control, its acquisition cannot be explained in terms of extracting resources for the metropole. Another study rightly notes that in Hong Kong the British "had no wish, and had made no serious attempt, to spread English civilization to their conquered lands to the extent that they would turn their imperial subjects into yellow or brown or black Englishmen."[11]

Such explanations understate the role of colonialism in Hong Kong's historical development. As Partha Chatterjee notes, "the notion that colonial rule was not really about colonial rule but about something else was a persistent theme in the rhetoric of colonial rule itself."[12] It is an exaggeration to say that "Hong Kong has no precolonial past to speak of," but Ackbar Abbas is right to argue that "the history of Hong Kong, in terms that are relevant to what it has become today, has effectively been a history of colonialism." Although brute force was not used as extensively in Hong Kong as in other European colonies, coercion and military strength were used to wrest the island and Kowloon, the peninsula across the harbor, from China. Hong Kong lacked the resources that would have made territorial gain worthwhile, but the territory nevertheless acted as a base for market penetration and extraction in China. While the colonial government did not enforce separate residential, occupational, and legal status for Chinese and foreigners as rigidly as other colonial regimes did elsewhere, legal discrimination in Hong Kong was both tolerated and encouraged by a government that prided itself on harmony and "impartial British justice."[13]

By minimizing the colonial nature of Hong Kong, these explanations overlook important aspects of the colony's history and society. The Hong Kong colonial government's "positive non-intervention myth" has been discredited. This government used techniques such as modern medicine as instruments of disciplinary power. Although the British did not attempt to convert the Chinese to Christianity as actively as the Spanish did in the Philippines, both early colonial administrators and missionaries saw their mission as promoting civilization, not just in South China but also in Britain and the empire at large. Indeed, much of the potency of the idea of empire derived from its supposed power to rejuvenate both the "backward" colony and the "advanced" metropole. By the mid-1800s, most Europeans considered Christianity, civilization, and commerce to be inseparably linked.[14]

Rather than downplay Hong Kong's colonial nature, we need to ask what role colonialism played in Hong Kong's history. In his recent study of the role of class and status in British imperialism, David Cannadine assesses the various schools of colonialism and their critics. Scholars who focus on the metropole are accused of being neocolonial; those who focus on domination versus independence, however, are accused of falling into simplistic dichotomies and binary contrasts, and of stressing coercion and conflict rather than collaboration. The postmodernists and postcolonialists are accused of writing bad prose, having a weak grasp of history, and overestimating the power of colonial rule.[15]

Cannadine's summary reflects how criticism of recent trends in colonial studies has become a small industry. Much of this criticism is leveled against Edward Said's "Orientalism," which argues that Western representations and images of Asia and the Middle East constructed a discourse based on "the ontological and epistemological distinction between the 'Orient' " and a way of "dominating, restructuring, and having authority over the Orient." Critics contend that Orientalism was not a coherent system of power. Rather, it was as much a sign of weakness, fear, and confusion on the part of colonial rulers. The Orientalist assumption of colonial dominance and hegemony ignores the sometimes fragile, ephemeral, and limited nature of colonial rule.[16]

Revisionists are also critical of the work of the Subaltern Studies Collective, which focuses mainly on India, particularly on "the failure of the nation to come to its own." Although it contests as "elitist" both colonial and bourgeois-nationalist histories, critics claim that this school exaggerates the impact of colonialism on colonial societies and fails to employ any new research materials or provide new theoretical insights.[17] Critics also complain that even subaltern studies no longer focuses on the subaltern, and that it has shifted from social analysis to textual analysis and from studies of underprivileged groups to critiques of colonial power-knowledge. "By the end of the 1980s," writes Raj-narayan Chandavarkar, "Subaltern Studies had begun to leave the sub-altern out."[18]

Given that the most recent approach to colonialism, postcoloni-alism, is inspired by both Orientalism and subaltern studies, it too has been criticized, sometimes even by theorists considered "post-colonial." Influenced also by poststructuralist, postmodernist, and psy-choanalytical theory, postcolonialism emphasizes the importance of difference, representation, and textuality. Like Orientalism and sub-altern studies, it frequently assumes that colonialism mattered more than anything else in colonies, making colonialism *the* determining period in a colonial society's history.[19] Like subaltern studies, post-colonialism is based mainly on the case of India, which becomes the basis for understanding colonialism everywhere else. This "loose use" of "postcolonial," Aihwa Ong contends, "has had the bizarre effect of contributing to a Western tradition of othering the Rest." Its em-phasis on binary contrasts, argues Anne McClintock, "re-orients the globe once more around a single, binary opposition: colonial/post-colonial."[20]

We need more than theoretical criticisms or defenses of Orien-talism, subaltern studies, and postcolonialism; we need more local his-tories that both engage and challenge these approaches. In my study of Hong Kong, I try to avoid grand claims about the "colonial project," a construct that often glosses over historical and geographical differences.[21] Rather than making ahistorical generalizations about co-lonialism, this book looks at one colony over a period of some one hundred years. By considering both intentions and results, I suggest that historical narratives of colonialism must be based also on uncer-tainty. Like Orientalism, postcolonialism has been more successful in showing colonial intents rather than revealing their effects on colo-nized peoples.[22] From the earliest days, colonialism in Hong Kong was mired in insecurity: economic and social problems, troubled re-lations with Chinese authorities in Canton and Beijing, tensions be-tween the British Foreign Office and the Colonial Office, and tumul-tuous conditions across the border in South China. In the present book, I show how the colonial government failed to make Hong Kong into the great "Emporium of the East" envisioned by British officials. I explore the fissures in British colonial rule that left room for local

Chinese elites. The gulf between government and governed, the government's failure to provide adequate medical facilities for its Chinese subjects, and its inability to provide a secure business environment all helped Chinese merchants obtain recognition by providing services to the local Chinese population and the government. Similarly, organizing festivities in honor of British royalty and contributing to British imperial and war funds helped the same merchants gain status from the colonial government. Colonies were not just about exploitation; they were also about how people learned to work within the cracks.

This book also acknowledges the many complexities of subalternity, which in Hong Kong was based on a complicated relationship between race and class. Whereas Orientalists and postcolonialists see colonialism as grounded in racial difference and "otherness," David Cannadine argues that this emphasis on race has come at the expense of social structure: at least for the British, empire was predicated foremost on class and status. But why must colonialism be based on either race or class, rather than on both? Assessing some of the problems in applying subaltern studies to Chinese history, Gail Hershatter observes how the contrast of dominant versus subaltern overlooks the "multiple, relational degrees of subalternity": a person might be dominant at times, subaltern at others, depending on the situation and context. Like subaltern studies, postcolonialism often simplifies the relationship between dominant and subaltern.[23]

Hong Kong was, of course, never comprised solely of Chinese and Britons. Like the treaty ports that dotted the coast and waterways of China, and like most every other city in the British Empire, the colony was multi-ethnic. Apart from the British and the Chinese there were Eurasians (who decreased in number toward the late 1800s but became more prominent in business and political life), Indians (especially the Sikhs and Muslims who served in the police force, and the peripatetic Parsi traders whose once-powerful commercial and philanthropic presence would decrease in the early 1900s), Portuguese from old families in the colony of Macau, the Jewish Sassoon and Kadoorie families, other Europeans, Armenians, and Americans. Each of these groups interacted with others in ways that defy any rigid categorizing.

The complexities and layers of subalternity can perhaps best be seen in the Hong Kong Chinese bourgeoisie. Its leaders were subordinate to the British bourgeoisie, even though the former often had more money and controlled a larger part of the Hong Kong economy than did the latter. Although these Chinese could buy expensive homes on the Peak, Hong Kong's exclusive hill district, they were prevented by law from living in these homes. The Chinese business elites were dominant over the local Chinese community, even though they lost much of their hegemony in the twentieth century; they saw themselves as different from—even superior to—Chinese in China. Some in China, however, considered that the Hong Kong elite were obsessed with making money and were less than fully Chinese because they live in a British colony.[24] Although Chinese were excluded from the highest levels of government in Hong Kong (a Chinese was not appointed to the Executive Council until 1926), and although the Europeans sometimes identified more closely with the colony's Indian traders, colonial officials realized that peace and order in the colony always depended on these "loyal Chinese." British officials often insisted that the Chinese of Hong Kong were incapable of any meaningful political representation but generally considered that such Chinese were somehow more civilized than many of the empire's other nonwhite subjects. Furthermore, these Chinese often saw themselves as members of a worldwide community of overseas Chinese who were financially and culturally superior to many other Asians. A 1947 article on the Chinese in Hong Kong showed that a self-perceived racial superiority was not just the privilege of colonizers. Reminiscent of colonial anthropology, it contrasted the "lazy, less civilized" Malays with the "astonishingly patient and hard-working" Chinese whose "blood and sweat" had built the vibrant European colonies in Southeast Asia.[25]

Despite their admirable intentions of overcoming elite-centered history, proponents of subaltern studies often believe in the existence of a more "authentic" native, and that the lower one's social class or the greater one's repression, the greater one's "authenticity." This often leaves out "hybrid" elites, who are seen as less authentic. Scholars of subaltern studies also assume that resistance is the most important feature of colonialism. Yet as Frederick Cooper writes, "much of the resistance literature is written as if the 'R' were capitalized." Resistance is expanded until "it denies any other kind of life to the people doing the resisting."[26] Proponents of subaltern studies often assume that colonized people have a moral duty to resist their oppressors and, because of this moral obligation, try to resist in various ways. In this book, however, I suggest that such a moral obligation may or may not exist.

I also show that Chinese in Hong Kong were partly responsible for creating the colonial discourse that justified and celebrated British rule in Hong Kong. Orientalism, subaltern studies, and postcolonialism often tend to homogenize and essentialize not only colonial rule, but even the West itself, often producing a form of monolithic "Occidentalism" that ignores the ways indigenous peoples helped create Orientalist, colonial discourse.[27] The present book reveals how Hong Kong Chinese contributed to the "Hong Kong legend" of a colony running smoothly under British free trade and impartial justice. The strike-boycott of 1925–1926 demonstrates how the Chinese bourgeoisie stressed the differences between chaotic Canton and orderly Hong Kong, and between "loyal" permanent residents and the rest of Hong Kong's Chinese population. Hong Kong Chinese also helped construct the official, colonial view of Hong Kong history as beginning with the British occupation.

Colonialism is based on the perverse notion that some races or nations are naturally suited—indeed, chosen—to rule others. But colonialism itself was a "phenomenon of colossal vagueness." It meant different things to different people, in different places, and at different times. For many Chinese in Hong Kong, colonialism was more of a liberating force than an oppressive one. Eager to escape the economic depravity and political turmoil of nineteenth- and twentieth-century China, most Chinese came to Hong Kong because of its economic opportunities and political stability, a fact that both colonial officials and Chinese residents in Hong Kong constantly emphasized. But reassessing the role of colonialism should not be confused with defending colonialism, European or otherwise, in Asia or elsewhere. As historical anthropologist Nicholas Thomas writes, the goal of reexamining colonialism is "not to rehabilitate imperial efforts, but to understand how far and why they were (and are) supported by various classes and interest groups." When looking at the relationship between the colonial state and Chinese society, we must take into careful account the choices and alternatives that the colonial setting offered and China did not.[28]

Finally, and perhaps most important, emphasizing binary contrasts and insurmountable cultural differences ignores the possibility of any dialogue between East and West. Colonies were not always places of tension and failed communication. Viewing colonial histories primarily as cultural clashes obscures patterns of collaboration and accommodation, and it assumes that colonial encounters were always fraught with overwhelming unfamiliarity, bewilderment, or incompatibility—"the most complex and traumatic relationships in human history." Focusing on the "fatal impact" of colonialism, with its emphasis on the shortcomings of an uncaring yet intrusive colonial state often overshadows gaps between intentions and results, and between projection and performance. As Thomas puts it, "the dynamics of colonialism cannot be understood if it is assumed that some unitary representation is extended from the metropole and cast across passive spaces, unmediated by perceptions or encounters."[29]

Colonialism in Hong Kong was based as much on similarities and affinities as on "otherness" and difference. Despite the distance between the Chinese and European communities, their leaders quickly learned how to cooperate on issues of mutual concern. In February 1848, for example, more than twenty Chinese merchants joined a group of European traders in a protest against ground rents.[30] Chinese merchants, British merchants, and colonial officials were all interested in the expansion of capitalism in Hong Kong and China. All agreed that the cure for an ailing China in the late nineteenth century was commerce and political liberalism. All were concerned about order and stability, not just in Hong Kong, but also in China (especially in South China during the turbulent republican era after the 1911 revolution). Although exclusive social clubs and associations kept Chinese and British in Hong Kong apart, they were nevertheless a mutually understandable form of social status.

The Hong Kong Chinese Bourgeoisie

The term "bourgeoisie" is used loosely in this book. Like the Shanghai bourgeoisie studied by Marie-Claire Bergère in her now-classic book on the Golden Age of the Chinese bourgeoisie, the term here refers to "an urban elite connected with modern business."[31] It includes entrepreneurs, compradors, bankers, industrialists, and professionals such as lawyers and physicians—all members of the new business class emerging from the colony's commercial growth and from Chinese and international trade in the late nineteenth century. "Bourgeoisie" denotes both a process and a fluid category with no legal boundaries. Being a member of the bourgeoisie was as much a matter of self-consciousness and self-perceptions, social institutions, and participation in the public sector as it was of economic status. Thus this book focuses less on the business networks of the bourgeoisie than on the multifaceted process of "embourgeoisement": the creation of an upstanding civic status in the colonial setting; a commitment to the social, cultural, and economic development of the colony, especially through the establishment of voluntary associations; and an obligation to maintaining peace and order in Hong Kong.

The Hong Kong Chinese bourgeoisie shared a common bourgeois culture and identity. Like the bourgeoisie in Europe, the bourgeoisie of Hong Kong constituted a "social stratum bound by common values, a shared culture, and a degree of prosperity based on property and earned income."[32] The leaders of the Hong Kong bourgeoisie claimed to represent the interests of their colony. They were conscious, indeed proud, of their contributions to economic development in Hong Kong and China. They were careful about the people with whom they associated, how they conducted their professional and social lives, and how they presented themselves to the rest of society. As elsewhere, the bourgeoisie was united by a strong sense of itself in regard to other classes. In Hong Kong, this bourgeoisie identified itself against a wide array of "others," including the Chinese bourgeoisie in China, the local European bourgeoisie, and the Chinese lower classes of the colony.

As Hong Kong has recently returned to Chinese sovereignty, this study has both historical and contemporary implications. Apart from deepening our understanding of a crucial period in Hong Kong, Chinese, and British colonial history, it challenges standard assumptions about Chinese nationalism and so-called Chineseness, both inextricably linked with the colonial nature of this Chinese city outside of China "proper." It also questions the common assumption that nationalism inevitably pits colonized peoples against their colonizers. Indeed, rather than driving the Chinese bourgeoisie and the colonial government apart, the idea of a powerful, modern China united them. The leaders of both the Chinese bourgeoisie and the government believed that what was good for China was good for Hong Kong (though in the 1920s they were at odds with what leading political forces just across the border thought was good for China). This book may also help explain why the relationship between state and society was so much better in colonial Hong Kong than in the Republic of China (both on the Mainland before 1949 and then on Taiwan), not to mention in the People's Republic of China.

The title of the book, *Edge of Empires*, takes into account both the similarities and the differences between the Chinese and British empires. Although historians have generally been reluctant to acknowledge China as a colonial power, several recent studies have exposed the remarkable parallels between China during the Qing Dynasty (1644–1911) and the early modern European empires. Laura Hostetler shows that, like imperial France and Russia, the early Qing state used cartography and ethnographic representation for empire building, while its settlers colonized parts of the empire by displacing indigenous peoples.[33] James Millward argues that even though China suffered from European imperialism in the nineteenth century, the Qing was also an expansionist empire that helped establish the boundaries of present-day China.[34] And James Hevia reveals some of the similarities between the imperial discourses of the Qing Empire and the British Empire.[35] The gap between the Qing and European empires, argues Hevia, lay not in the "methods of organizing and ruling empires," but in differences in "military and commercials technologies."[36] In the end, however, it was precisely because China and Britain were not the same types of empire that Hong Kong became the place that it did: when the British arrived on the scene in the late 1700s as part of an expanding empire, the Qing Empire was already in decline.

1

Colonialism and Collaboration: Chinese Subjects and the Making of British Hong Kong

*H*ONG KONG PRESENTS another example of the elasticity and potency of unrestricted commerce which in my judgment has more than counterbalanced the barrenness of its soil, the absence of agricultural and manufacturing industry, the disadvantages of its climate and every impediment which could clog its progress. Its magnificent harbor invites the flags of all nations which there is nothing in its legislation to repel. Its Laws give no privileges to any, but afford equal security to all, and I am persuaded the equity with which Justice is administered is beginning to produce a most salutary effect on the minds of the Chinese people."[1] In this glowing report, John Bowring was only slightly exaggerating Hong Kong's progress. The fourth governor of Hong Kong, he may have overstated the "salutary effect" of British free trade and justice on the young colony's subjects, but he was not painting an unreasonably rosy picture of the colony's progress since its founding in 1841. In less than twenty years, Hong Kong had grown from an island of tiny fishing villages to a major commercial center. It had endured epidemics and typhoons, piracy and crime, and an economic depression that nearly prevented it from becoming the "Great Emporium of the East" envisioned by its founders. Most important to a colonial administrator, the British colonial state itself—a mere island in a sea of Chinese residents—had survived these crises unscathed.

The efficacy of British colonial rule was Bowring's answer to a puzzle that continues to intrigue scholars: Hong Kong's extraordinary political stability, especially the amicable relationship between an alien colonial state and the overwhelmingly larger Chinese population. E. J. Eitel—missionary, educator, civil servant, and early historian of the colony—attributed this relationship to British free trade, impartial justice, and education. A political scientist who visited the colony on the eve of the Second World War stressed the colonial government's "consistent policy of conciliation and co-operation." Free-market economists cite the *laissez-faire* policy of the colonial government. One sociological study argues that the government's policy of social noninterventionism reduced the potential for conflict. Other scholars credit the traditional political apathy of the Chinese and the local Chinese elite's support for the colonial regime. A recent summary of British colonial rule in Hong Kong ascribes Hong Kong's stability to a relatively expeditious, judicially fair government with "a record of non-intrusion probably second to none in the modern world," concluding that the absence of any serious demand in more than 150 years for the colony's return to Chinese rule is evidence that Hong Kong Chinese "voted with their deeds and feet."[2]

The explanations cited above have many strengths, but by downplaying the colonial nature of Hong Kong—a tendency that characterizes much of the scholarship on Hong Kong—they place three limitations on our understanding of the historical relationship between the British colonial state and its Chinese subjects. First, their emphasis on the government's noninterventionism often ignores the intrusive power of the state, and their focus on harmony and cooperation overlooks the legal and racial discrimination that plagued Hong Kong. Second, although these theories help explain how the relationship between state and society was maintained, they do not show how this relationship first emerged and changed over time. Finally, they do not say very much about the Chinese people involved in the making of colonial Hong Kong or what the colonial situation had to offer them.

This chapter examines one aspect of Hong Kong's stability by tracing the historical roots of the relationship between the leaders of the Hong Kong Chinese bourgeoisie and the colonial government. Following Ronald Robinson's work in the 1970s on British West Africa, historians have shown how the colonial state was not simply a function of European expansion; rather, it depended on the indigenous peoples who helped build the new economic, social, and political infrastructures. Indeed, argues Frederick Cooper, European colonists introduced not so much "colonialism" as a "series of hegemonic projects" that required help from local elites.[3]

The first Chinese merchants of the British Empire's eastern outpost, Hong Kong, were not passive victims of colonialism. Nor did the imposition of British colonial rule cause the dramatic rupture or traumatic break that postcolonial scholars often decry. Many of the successful early Chinese businessmen in Hong Kong came from a tradition of cooperating and with foreigners, either in South China or in other European colonies in Asia. These were, for the most part, not members of an indigenous population forced to accept the presence of the new rulers; rather, they chose to follow the British to Hong Kong, which offered lucrative opportunities for collaboration. Although Hong Kong had its share of contestation, tension, and conflict between Europeans and Chinese, this was relatively minor compared with the collaboration that would eventually help build Hong Kong into a thriving commercial center.

In early Hong Kong, colonialism not only required collaboration with a local elite, it also helped create a local elite. Although the British did not attempt to create a local bourgeoisie as actively, for example, as did the Japanese after annexing Korea, the making of the Chinese business class was inseparably linked with the colonial nature of the island.[4] By rewarding such men with privileges—for example, land grants—and offering them lucrative monopolies, the government helped foster the growth of a local Chinese business elite. By enforcing separate business and residential districts for Chinese, the colonial government provided them with a domain in which to flourish (though this did not always work to the government's advantage). Hong Kong did not merely continue patterns of collaboration; it intensified and institutionalized them.

Hong Kong and the Canton Delta Region: Early History

Although the once "barren rock" of Hong Kong Island would eventually become famous as a "capitalist paradise," less is known about the island before the British occupation began in 1841. Chinese historical records before the Qing Dynasty frequently mention Kowloon, the peninsula across the harbor, as the place where the emperor of the Southern Song Dynasty sought refuge after China fell to the Mongols in 1276. Throughout the Ming Dynasty, settlers from southern Guangdong and Fujian, the two prominent coastal provinces of Southeast China, migrated to Kowloon. Some of these settlers moved across the harbor to Hong Kong, but the island remained mostly unpopulated, with only a few villages scattered along its southern coast. The 1830 gazetteer for Xin'an (New Peace) County, to which the island belonged, mentions several areas of the island, including a Hong Kong Village, but the island did not get its name until the late 1830s. An assistant magistrate visited the island occasionally from Kowloon to collect land taxes and to register fishing vessels; local headmen or village elders were in charge of local government. In the early nineteenth century the island was the stronghold of the infamous pirate Zhang Baozai, who used the island's peak as a lookout for his buccaneering exploits. When the British arrived in the late 1830s, the island was but a remote outpost in the Chinese Empire, speckled with a few tiny fishing villages.[5]

This rocky island, however, is part of the larger Canton Delta, a commercial region with a long tradition of overseas and intra-Chinese trade. For centuries, Chinese merchants had used the coastal ports of Xiamen and Canton for shipping goods between China and Southeast Asia. In 1557 Chinese authorities allowed Portuguese traders to establish a permanent settlement at Macau, the small peninsula southwest of Hong Kong that soon became the emporium for a "hemispheric exchange of commodities." Chinese goods, such as silk, tea, and porcelain, shipped from Macau to Europe in Portuguese galleons, in exchange for silver from the mines in Japan and the Americas. European missionaries used the settlement as a base for recruiting Chinese Christians. British ships made their way into Chinese waters in the 1630s, and in 1654 the Portuguese allowed the British East India Company (EIC) to land in Macau.[6]

After the Qing ban on overseas trade was lifted in 1684, Europeans became increasingly ambitious to pursue trade with China. British merchants used Macau as a headquarters from which to trade in the harbor at Huangpu, the riverine island about ten miles from Canton. Both Chinese and foreign merchants had been trading in the area for many years, but it was not until 1771 that the EIC was allowed to open a post in Canton, which the Qing government had declared in 1759 the only legal port for overseas trade.[7]

Under what became known as the Canton System, or Cohong System, international trade was conducted through a group of Chinese merchant houses licensed by the Qing government. Known as the hongs and organized into the Cohong in 1720, these companies monopolized trade with foreign merchants, collected customs taxes for the Qing government, and acted as guarantors for the foreign merchants. Western merchants traded in Canton from October to March, confined to "factories," or "manufactories," rented from the Chinese merchants and named after similar centers in British India, where the EIC's agents, or "factors," operated. Although the foreigners complained about the restrictions and conditions in Canton, these inconveniences were secondary compared to the fortunes that could be made in silk, porcelain, tea, and, later, opium. William Hunter, a trader for the American firm of Russell & Co., recalled fondly his days in the factories: "from the novelty of the life, the social good feeling and unbounded hospitality always mutually existing; from the facility of all dealings with the Chinese who were assigned to transact business with us, together with their proverbial honesty, combined with a sense of perfect security to person and property, scarcely a resident of any lengthened time, in short, any 'Old Canton', but finally left them with regret." By the early 1840s almost one hundred foreign hongs, as the European trading houses, too, came to be known, were trading on the South China coast. Half of these were British and one quarter Indian, mainly Parsi.[8]

Although British interest in a trading base on the China coast dated back almost as far as the British presence in the Canton Delta, neither the choice of Hong Kong nor the idea of a colony was seriously considered until the early nineteenth century. In 1815 an EIC official in Canton called for Britain to establish a base on the eastern coast of China, as close as possible to Beijing. After 1821, when Canton authorities drove the illegal opium trade from Huangpu, British traders set up shop in Hong Kong. In August 1834 Lord Napier, British superintendent of trade, suggested that a small British force should take possession of Hong Kong to secure European trading rights in China. James Matheson, of Jardine & Matheson, the largest British hong, echoed to commercial groups back in Britain the desire of his fellow merchants in Canton to protect British trading interests. Although several islands were considered more attractive choices, British traders in Canton preferred Hong Kong, with its deepwater harbor, sheltered from typhoons and easily accessible from both China and the open sea. On 25 April 1836 the *Canton Register* declared: "If the lion's paw is to be put down on any part of the south side of China, let it be Hongkong; let the lion declare it to be under his guarantee a free port, and in ten years it will be the most considerable mart east of the Cape . . . Hongkong, deep water, and a free port for ever."[9]

The Roots of Collaboration: The Opium War

The British "lion's paw" was eventually put down on Hong Kong Island during the Opium War of 1839–1842. The causes and course of the war, ostensibly a conflict over the contraband trade in opium but as much about trading rights, diplomatic representation, and British imperial arrogance, have been studied extensively elsewhere.[10] Although he would go down in history for later dismissing Hong Kong as little more than "a barren island with hardly a house upon it," British Foreign Secretary Lord Palmerston declared his intention to seize Hong Kong soon after war broke out between Britain and China.[11] On Monday, 25 January 1841, in accordance with the short-lived Convention of Chuenpi, Captain Edward Belcher landed with a small group on the northern shore of the island and raised the Union Jack at what became known as Possession Point. The next day the naval commander of the British expeditionary force, Gordon Bremer, took formal possession in the name of the British crown. British traders won their coveted deep harbor and free port as part of the Treaty of Nanking, which—apart from imposing a huge indemnity on China, ending the Cohong monopoly, and opening five Chinese ports to foreign trade and residence—ceded Hong Kong Island to Britain "in perpetuity."[12] The British christened the north part of the island Victoria, after their queen.

Britain's new claim to this rocky island did not guarantee a prosperous port and colony. Chinese cooperation assisted both the British victory in the Opium War, which led to the cession of the island, and the early development of the infant colony. Chinese sources from this period frequently castigate the Chinese "traitors" who enabled the growth of early Hong Kong: guides, provisioners, builders, and artisans. The term "traitor" had been "hung as a crude label of infamy around the neck of collaborators" since the Song dynasty, but it enjoyed new popularity during the Opium War, when Qing officials sought scapegoats to blame for the defeat by the British. Some officials even attributed Britain's strength not to its military might, but to its treacherous use of "Chinese traitors." However exaggerated, these concerns were reasonable, for the British war effort depended on collaboration. The British had great difficulty obtaining supplies in the early part of the Opium War, especially during their unsuccessful, short-lived occupation of Zhousan (known to Europeans as Chusan), a small island in the Yangzi Delta where the local Chinese refused to cooperate. The important role played by these so-called traitors can also be seen from the British acknowledgment of Chinese cooperation. In June 1841, the new British superintendent of trade, Captain Charles Elliot, argued that the British crown had an obligation to retain Hong Kong, not only for commercial and strategic interests but also "as an act of justice and protection to the native population upon whom we have been so long dependent for assistance and supply."[13]

Although the Opium War intensified and dramatized the role of Chinese collaborators in the British "opening" of China, the basic patterns of collaboration had already been worked out earlier in what Dian Murray calls the "water world" of South China and in Southeast Asia. Many of the people of the region whom Elliot referred to as "natives" were Tankas, a minority ethnic group living along the South China coast. These "egg families" had long been assimilated into Han Chinese culture but lived in communities of boats, making their livelihood from fishing, shipping, and provisioning. As part of his attempt to emancipate the "mean people," in the early 1700s the Yongzheng Emperor had abolished the regulations prohibiting the Tankas from taking the civil service examinations, marrying other Chinese, or settling on land. But local Cantonese, who referred to themselves as locals, or Punti, continued to despise the Tankas as outcastes. Like other fisherfolk, the Tankas often turned to piracy, especially when economic conditions were rough. With no established gentry, and often beyond the reach of the Qing state, the Tankas constituted "a subculture that lay largely outside of government control." From the earliest days of the foreign presence in Canton, Tankas had traded with foreign merchants, even though the Qing government prohibited this on pain of death. William Hunter described these Tanka boat people as "perhaps unequalled by any others in the world. They are not only active and intelligent, but good-natured and obliging, and seem anxious to get on as quickly as possible." Working from bumboats, small vessels used for peddling goods to ships anchored in the harbor, the Tankas provided British vessels with fuel and other supplies. After the settlement of Hong Kong, the British rewarded the Tankas with land in the new town of Hong Kong.[14]

One Tanka who benefited particularly from this arrangement was Loo Aqui, an influential merchant and landowner in early Hong Kong. Little is known of Loo's background, except that he was a bumboatman from Huangpu who rose to prominence through piracy and provisioning foreign vessels. During the Opium War, Guangdong authorities secretly invited Loo to Canton, offering him an official title to help stir up trouble in Hong Kong. As leader of several secret societies, Loo promised to provide support to China from within Hong Kong. Instead, Loo returned to Hong Kong; for provisioning the British forces, he was rewarded with a large plot of valuable land in the Lower Bazaar, where much of the Chinese population would eventually settle. Soon Loo became one of the colony's wealthiest and most powerful Chinese residents.[15]

Constructing and Contesting Space: Chinese Builders and Contractors

Just as Chinese collaboration was crucial in the founding of Hong Kong, the building of the colony continued to rely on a network of collaboration between British and Chinese. Colonialism meant creating new conceptual and epistemological spaces, but it also meant building new physical spaces—from residential, commercial, and government buildings to entire cities and towns. As in many other European colonies in Asia, this construction was carried out by Chinese builders and contractors.

When the British took control of Hong Kong in late January 1841, the north shore of the island was mainly unoccupied. The island's Chinese land and water population was probably less than 5,000.

However, Captain Charles Elliot's proclamation on 2 February 1841 that Hong Kong would be a free port attracted "a great influx of natives," who settled in huts on the beach and the overlooking hillsides. In February 1841 shiploads of foreign merchants and missionaries began to arrive from Macau. Jardine's built a temporary godown, or warehouse, on the north shore of the island. By late March, an array of shanties, sheds, and makeshift godowns and residences began to punctuate the northern landscape of the island. As a British engineer recalled, "with such extraordinary celerity were these building operations carried on, that, in the course of two months, the native town, Victoria, which had before presented to the eye scarcely anything but streets and rows of houses, formed of the most crazy, perishable, and inflammable materials, now boasted at least a hundred brick tenements, besides a spacious and commodious market-place . . . a stone jail, a wide, excellent road, drains, and bridges, wherever necessary, and an official residence for the presiding magistrate."[16]

By late 1841, after the first official land sales that summer, the island had more than fifty permanent houses and buildings.[17] A French naval officer compared the small island to a busy anthill. The English-language *Canton Press* wrote in December that "the bazaar is well supplied at cheap rates, and workmen and artizans as well as the materials for building are plentiful." In February 1842 Henry Pottinger, plenipotentiary and superintendent of trade, moved the British superintendency of trade from Macau to Hong Kong. Pottinger soon reported: "the impetus given by the removal [was] quite remarkable." In only one week, "highly respectable and affluent Chinese Merchants" were "flocking" from Canton and Macau to settle or open branches in Hong Kong. The colony's population was "moderately [but incorrectly] estimated" at more than 25,000, while "extensive and solidly built" buildings were "springing up in every direction." The *Canton Press* observed in the same month "great bustle and preparation" for building piers and godowns along the waterfront. New government buildings included a magistracy, post office, land and record office, jail, and "several other barracks either finished or building." After praising the Chinese shopkeepers for having "evinced much good taste in their buildings," the *Press* predicted that the Lower Bazaar—the "China town at Hongkong"—would be among the "most striking features" of the new settlement. The new town also boasted numerous shops, brothels, gambling houses, and tailors, linked by a few rough roads. By March, the total island population was more than 15,000, with some 12,000 Chinese, mainly artisans and laborers. Soon the first Chinese market was built in the Lower Bazaar. The Europeans settled in the main town and along the waterfront.[18]

By mid-1843, warehouses dotted the waterfront, and present-day Central District was already becoming the commercial center of the island. A British visitor noted in June 1843 that most of the Chinese shopkeepers in Macau had moved to Hong Kong, "flying like rats from a falling house."[19] Robert Fortune, an English botanist and adventurer who visited the island in 1843, wrote that "a very large proportion of the Macao shopkeepers have removed their establishments to the Hong Kong; the former place being useless since the English left it." When Fortune returned in December 1845 he marveled at the "noble new government buildings . . . excellent and substantial houses . . . for the [foreign] merchants . . . a large Chinese town . . . a beautiful road, called the Queen's Road . . . lined with excellent houses, and many very good shops." These "new houses and even new streets had risen, as if by magic."[20]

All this development did not, of course, happen "by magic." Chinese contractors and builders completed all major construction work in Hong Kong. As Osmond Tiffany, an American visitor, later recalled, "go where you would your ears were met with the clink of hammer and chisels, and your eyes were in danger of sparks of stone at every corner." Buildings were "run up and finished with magic ease; one day the cellar would be dug, and the next the roof was being finished." Even more impressive than the pace of this construction was "that such numbers of the Chinese were at work, that, like bees, the hive was soon ready for honey."[21] In contrast, in the summer of 1841 a lack of laborers and craftsmen had delayed site clearance and building construction for the new town.[22] In April 1846, Governor John Davis explained to Colonial Secretary William Gladstone that the construction of private and public works in Hong Kong "could not have taken place except for the ready command of the cheap and efficient labour of the Chinese."[23] Few, Chinese contractors, however, were familiar with Western building techniques, often submitting estimates that were far too low. When the contractors could not complete the projects as agreed, they were imprisoned for not fulfilling their contracts; others, realizing how much money they would lose and fearing imprisonment, simply fled the island. The situation became so desperate that in January 1845 plans were made for a contractors' union, leading the *Friend of China* to fear that "we will very much be at the mercy of our labourers; and unless we submit to their extortions building and public improvements may for a time be suspended."[24]

Studies on the strategic use of space have made scholars more sensitive to the nature of physical space in colonies. Timothy Mitchell reminds us that external structures can express power relations. The rebuilding of Cairo in the nineteenth century "was designed to give the appearance of a plan." This was "not merely a device to aid the work of urban reconstruction but a principle of order to be represented in the layout of the city's streets and inscribed in the life of its inhabitants." French colonial governments used urban culture extensively as the foundation of their policy. In Morocco, according to Gwendolyn Wright, urban planning combined French and local architectural styles to establish and maintain social and political order. Similarly, Brenda Yeoh has demonstrated that the colonial authorities of Singapore tried to use "uniform, well-demarcated public spaces" to influence the public behavior of their Asian subjects "towards order and propriety."[25]

Participating in the construction of these colonial spaces could also bring great wealth to indigenous collaborators. As in other colonies, the contractors who did well in early Hong Kong were those with prior experience working for foreigners. Tam Achoy, a particularly successful contractor, was one of the most prominent members of the Chinese community in early Hong Kong. Originally from Kaiping County in Guangdong, Tam came to Hong Kong in 1841 from Singapore, where he had been a foreman in the colonial government dockyards. Tam built some of the most important buildings in the colony, including the P&O Building and the Exchange Building for Dent & Co., one of the largest European hongs, which the government later bought in 1847 to house the colony's first Supreme Court.[26]

Furthermore, colonial urban environments were sites of both discipline and resistance, conflict and compromise. As in other colonies, Europeans in Hong Kong often related physical space to behavior. Edward Cree, a British naval surgeon, noted that Chinese residents used "huts and shanties" for "drinking booths and gambling booths and every kind of debauchery." The *Canton Press* cautioned in 1842 that the progress of the "China town at Hong Kong" depended on street widths and "sanatory [*sic*] regulations."[27] The French naval officer who had compared Hong Kong to a busy anthill remarked that "the Chinese people, naturally vicious in their search of enjoyments, can give loose to their propensities and passions, so that the cafés, eating and drinking shops, gambling houses, opium booths, &c., have already fully occupied the space allotted by the authorities."[28] Matsheds and other temporary structures were considered "subversive of good order and security by promoting a vagabondage population." Thus colonial officials were always happy to see the Chinese taking the initiative in public works, as in building privies.[29]

Even more so than in other colonies, given the island's limited land for building, space in Hong Kong could be highly contested. Describing the firecrackers, lanterns, and "grotesque figures" hanging from Chinese houses along Queen's Road during a ceremony to prevent a typhoon in October 1843, the *Friend of China* complained: "Let the Chinese amuse themselves, that is all fair, but the legs and health of the English Colonists should not be put in jeopardy by those devotees, firing cannons, pistols, guns, and worse than all, abominal [*sic*] crackers on the public highway."[30] European residents also frequently criticized the government for allowing Chinese like Loo Aqui to run "houses of disreputable women" in or near European neighborhoods. In December 1844 the colonial surveyor general insisted that Loo's brothels in the Lower Bazaar should be "replaced by buildings more suitable to the neighbourhood."[31] One Sunday in July 1848, a spectacle of "Jugglery, Buffonery, &c., &c.," performed by a "company of strolling vagabonds from the Chinese provinces" and "accompanied with much noise from crackers and the discordant musicale instruments" at Loo's theater outraged European colonists. The Europeans demanded that the Chinese "be required to build a theatre beyond the limits of the town, where they may enjoy themselves, without outraging the feelings of others."[32]

European residents and colonial officials often complained that the Chinese were not using land properly. Flimsy wood structures built close together were proof that the people did not understand that certain open spaces were needed to reduce the risk of fire and "for the free circulation of air."[33] This contestation never escaped the attention of the local press. In February 1842, the *Canton Press*, while criticizing the pretentious architecture of Hong Kong, jokingly suggested that the Chinese contractor who built the government's Record Office had "blazoned a sly hit at his obtuse and barbaric employers."[34]

Wealth and Power: Colonialism and Its Collaborators

Why were men like Loo Aqui and Tam Achoy so willing to help the British? Nineteenth-century European historians generally saw the Chinese in early Hong Kong at best as sojourners and at worst as the "scum of Canton." Chinese historians, in contrast, have tended to view Chinese in Hong Kong and Southeast Asia as either helpless victims duped by foreigners or as unfilial scoundrels who abandoned their families and homeland. This rhetoric, however, masks the more important question of what the colonial situation offered to Chinese who chose to live under alien rule. If, as Ronald Robinson argues, the colonial invaders "imported an alternative source of wealth and power," what were these sources in early colonial Hong Kong?[35]

Land grants constituted one important source of wealth. The new government used these to reward those Chinese who had helped the British secure and develop the island. For his services during the Opium War, Loo Aqui received a plot of valuable land in the Lower Bazaar. He was later able to obtain, through other grants or purchases eased by his connections to the colonial regime, many more lots in the Lower Bazaar. Soon Loo was running a market, gambling house, theater, and several brothels. Rev. George Smith, who became the first Anglican bishop of Hong Kong, recalled a visit to Loo's home in November 1844: "He possesses about fifty houses in the bazaar, and lives on the rent, in a style much above the generality of Chinese settlers, who are commonly composed of the refuse of the neighbouring mainland." An 1845 government report described Loo as "now the most influential and wealthy of the native residents—formerly an obscure bum-boatman."[36]

Similarly, working for the British helped make Tam Achoy a leader of the local Chinese business community. For his services to the British in Singapore and Hong Kong, Tam was also granted land in the Lower Bazaar. Tam soon bought out his neighboring landholders, blocking off a significant piece of waterfront property for himself and quickly expanding these holdings to include a profitable market in the Lower Bazaar. The transition from landholder to large businessman was easy for Tam. When Hong Kong became the major port of departure to North America and Australia in the late 1840 and 1850s, Tam was one of the main brokers and charterers of emigrant ships. He also ran a general merchants company.[37] In 1865, Tam leased a wharf to the new Hong Kong, Canton, and Macao Steamboat Company, a European firm that ran steamships in the Canton Delta. Because of his wealth, Tam was known to foreigners in the colony as the "Nabob of Hong Kong."[38] In 1857 the *Friend of China* called him "no doubt the most creditable Chinese in the Colony."[39]

Apart from land grants, the early colonial regime introduced other measures that made the colony attractive to Chinese willing to settle there. Scholars of all political stripes have stressed the role of free trade in Hong Kong's economic development. This economy, however, was neither free nor, at least in the early years, impressive. An elaborate system of monopolies and farms, usually offered at public auction, regulated the production, preparation, and retail of commodities such as opium and salt. Liquor and tobacco were licensed and taxed. Ironically, it was from these same types of regulations and monopolies that the British had insisted the Opium War and the "imperialism of free trade" would liberate China. The farms, which accounted for 10 to 25 percent of the government's annual revenue, were almost always held by local Chinese merchants or contractors. The advantage was mutual. For the government, the farm system was an easy way to collect taxes without having to intervene too much at the local level. Because the farms replaced preexisting systems, they showed British control over the young colony. Finally, the system helped build a local Chinese elite that the government hoped to influence. For Chinese, the system provided the prospect of not only becoming very rich and influential in local society but also having some political influence since the government always relied on farmers' advice when making farm policy.[40]

The largest and most durable of the farms and monopolies was the opium farm, which in the nineteenth century could make up almost one quarter of the government's annual revenue. Indeed, explains Christopher Munn, "the opium trade and Hong Kong are so obviously intertwined that it is hardly possible to consider the early history of the colony without some reference to the drug: the colony was founded because of opium; it survived its difficult early years because of opium; its principal merchants grew rich on opium; and its government subsisted on the high land rent and other revenue made possible by the opium trade." Thus when Loo Aqui acquired the opium monopoly from his partner, Fung A-tae, he guarded his new possession carefully. Until the 1850s, the main Chinese markets were also run by monopolies leased for five-year periods. In 1844, when the government relocated the Chinese residents of the Middle Bazaar to the hillside of Tai Ping Shan, Loo petitioned the government for permission to open a market in the new settlement and purchased the management of the market for five years. A similar situation existed for salt. In September 1845, for example, a merchant named Losin secured the salt monopoly while Kam Teen Sze won the stone quarry farm. In March 1845 the government announced a short-lived plan inviting bids to operate sedan chairs in Victoria. In June it invited bids to operate the ropewalk in the Wong Nai Chung valley area. The operation of gambling houses, abattoirs, and privies was also auctioned or granted to bidders. Although none of the other monopolies were as lucrative as the one on opium, they enhanced wealth in the new colony.[41]

The growth of a Chinese business elite also benefited from the colonial government's efforts to reserve lucrative real estate for Europeans. In the first years, most of the Chinese lived in the Lower Bazaar, the Upper Bazaar (sometimes called the Middle Bazaar), or the hillside at Tai Ping Shan. In September 1841, A. R. Johnston, acting plenipotentiary, made land grants at rates below market price to Chinese who had supplied the British fleet before and during the Opium War. Although the early land sales had been designed to keep Chinese away from the valuable waterfront properties, the Chinese were able to stay in the Lower Bazaar. Chinese were also encouraged to settle in the Upper Bazaar, where land was again sold at modest rates. By summer 1843, however, colonial officials had decided that the more ramshackle Chinese shops and houses were taking up valuable land. The colonial land officer proposed the construction of a European-style town in Wong Nai Chung. Only European and Parsi shops would be allowed in the main section of the new town, with a smaller

Chinese town to the south. European warehouses would have marine access while bazaars for the "paltry Chinese shops," for which sea frontage would be "far too valuable," would be permitted only at certain locations.[42]

These plans never materialized, but the same relocation program in 1844 that enabled Loo Aqui to purchase his market monopoly created a Hong Kong "Chinatown," where no Europeans, except for police officers, could live. The relocation allowed a local Chinese leadership to grow, independent of the colonial government. The government had a hard time administering the area, where official regulations such as registration of land sales went unchecked. More successful landowners like Loo Aqui were able to buy up the properties of others, producing a small group of wealthy property owners. Thus by rewarding Chinese with privileges such as land grants and monopolies, and by enforcing separate business and residential districts for Chinese, the colonial government helped foster the growth of a Chinese business elite in Hong Kong and gave it a domain in which to flourish.

Not only did the colonial situation help the growth of a Chinese business elite, it also enabled men excluded from the traditional order in China to re-create aspects of this order in Hong Kong. As a Tanka, Loo Aqui was barred from any gentry functions in China. By working for the British in Singapore, Tam Achoy had violated Qing prohibitions against overseas emigration. In British Hong Kong, however, these prohibitions meant nothing. Because the colonial government, which neither understood its new Chinese constituents nor took much interest in their welfare, did not attempt to fill the vacuum left by the departure of the old gentry class after the British takeover, new landowners and merchants filled the old gentry functions. In 1847 Loo and Tam built the Man Mo Temple on Hollywood Road, in the heart of the Chinese community, on a plot of land originally granted by the government for a Chinese school.[43] Although its ostensible purpose was to worship the Gods of Literature and War and to observe religious festivals, the temple soon became the main social center for Hong Kong's Chinese population, regardless of their regional or occupational affiliations. By controlling the center of Chinese religious and social life, men like Loo and Tam became leaders of the colony's Chinese community. According to a later source, soon after the establishment of the Man Mo Temple, Loo and Tam used the temple as an informal courtroom, resolving legal disputes and generally managing the affairs of the Chinese community in Hong Kong.[44] Although no records of this tribunal survive, the Man Mo Temple seems to have evolved into the self-managed, informal government of the Chinese community.

Thus in Colonial Hong Kong, even outcastes could become respected leaders of the local Chinese community. Tam Achoy was also a trustee at two other temples and a well-known philanthropist. In 1847 he donated £185 to the colonial treasury for building a Chinese school in the Lower Bazaar. The *Hong Kong Register* described Tam that year as "probably as respectable and intelligent as any man of his class in the Colony."[45] In September 1852, Tam was again one of the chief donors to a subscription for building a Chinese hospital, an earlier one having been destroyed by fire the previous winter.[46] Dr. Henry Julius Hirschberg of the London Missionary Society, who organized the fund-raising, reported that "one Tam Ah-Choy, a rich building contractor, had been several times a looker-on in the Hospital, and although, said he smilingly, 'you had no vaccine matter to vaccinate my child, still I give you this (fifteen dollars) with the greatest pleasure'."[47] In 1856, after several particularly damaging fires along Queen's Road, Tam helped form a Chinese fire brigade, equipped with an American-made engine and later named the Tam Achoy Engine Company No. 1. In 1861 he led the Chinese community in contributing to a retirement fund for the colony's harbormaster.[48]

In the new colonial environment, Loo Aqui also became a prominent member of the Chinese community. Although he was widely rumored to be involved in crime, Loo also had a reputation for helping "those who were in distress, in debt or discontented." He too was a chief contributor to the Chinese hospital fund. Dr. Hirschberg recorded that Loo "received me most friendly, and in very good english [*sic*] said to Lee-Kip-Yye, a Chinese broker who went with me to collect the money, 'Do not trouble that gentleman to come here again, I send you the money (fifteen dollars) to your house to-morrow morning', and then turning so to me he said: 'a very good cause, Sir, a very good cause', and then took my hands and shook them most heartily according to English fashion." When the *China Mail* published its list of all the subscribers to the hospital fund, along with their occupations, Loo Aqui, formerly a lowly bumboatman, was now simply listed as a "Gentleman."[49]

Collaboration Institutionalized: The Compradors

The early experiences of Loo Aqui and Tam Achoy exemplify patterns of collaboration between Europeans and Chinese that preceded the Opium War. The career of Kwok Acheong, a Tanka boatman who had also helped the British during the Opium War, represents one form of postwar collaboration that would become intensified and institutionalized in China and especially in Hong Kong: the comprador system. In 1941 an author in a volume commemorating Hong Kong's centenary as a British colony explained how the origin of the comprador system was "really very simple." Westerners came to China to trade, but they did not know the local languages, customs, or business conditions. Thus when foreign companies wanted to sell or buy something from Chinese firms, they went to a comprador; when Chinese firms had something to sell to foreigners, they went to the same comprador.[50]

Simple or not, the comprador system was crucial to the rise of Sino-foreign commerce in modern China. Named after the Portuguese word for "buyer," the comprador system originated in the late Ming dynasty but came to prominence in the early 1800s. When the Canton System was abolished in 1842 after the Opium War, compradors replaced the hong merchants as the main intermediaries between Chinese and Western traders.[51] Some Western company officials became so dependent on their compradors that they were hardly aware of how their businesses in China functioned below the highest levels of operation.[52] By the end of the nineteenth century, compradors were among the richest men in China—not just in the treaty ports but in all of China. Two compradors would become especially famous for their great wealth. One was the comprador for Jardine's in Shanghai in the 1890s, one of the richest men in China. The other was Robert Ho Tung, the Eurasian comprador for Jardine's in Hong Kong from 1883 to 1900, and the wealthiest man in the colony.[53]

Hong Kong was especially important for the growth of the comprador system because most of the foreign firms that did business in China were located in the colony. The system was strengthened even more when foreign firms came from Canton during the Second Opium War (1856–1860). Just as the compradors in treaty ports such as Shanghai were crucial in the formation of the modern Chinese bourgeoisie, the compradors in Hong Kong were vital for the development of a local Hong Kong Chinese bourgeoisie. By the 1860s, compradors were the richest Chinese men in Hong Kong. Kwok Acheong, who settled in the colony after the British took over, joined the Peninsular and Oriental (P&O) Steam Navigation Company in 1845 and soon became its comprador. Some twenty years later he started his own steamship company and competed with the European-owned Hong Kong, Canton, and Macao Steamboat Company. In 1876 Kwok was the third-largest taxpayer in the colony, behind Douglas Lapraik & Co., a local shipping giant, and Jardine's. By 1877 Kwok owned thirteen steamships, making him not only a successful local Chinese businessman but also a regional shipping magnate.[54]

The compradors' interests depended on continued collaboration with foreigners. But in Hong Kong, compradors represented more than economic collaboration. They would help pave the way for a relatively smooth relationship between the Chinese of Hong Kong and the colonial government, and the European community at large. Although he spoke only pidgin English, Kwok Acheong was known for getting on well with foreigners. He was consulted frequently by the colonial government on matters relating to the Chinese community until his death in 1880. Kwok's obituary in the *Hong Kong Daily Press* described him as a man of "great cheerfulness and urbanity in his social relations" who "agreed well with and was much respected by foreigners."[55] The earliest compradors could usually speak only pidgin or a smattering of English, but their sons, educated at missionary schools, the government Central School, or in Britain, became bilingual and bicultural. Comprador positions in Hong Kong were often hereditary: one family might keep the same post for generations.[56] Thus a group of prominent local families known for working closely with foreigners evolved. By collaborating with European merchants, the compradors showed that they could be "proper," "modern" Chinese businessmen, especially when they became wealthier than the European merchants for whom they worked.

As in China, compradors in Hong Kong gradually used their fortunes to become social leaders. But Hong Kong's colonial nature made this easier than in China. Unlike in China, the compradors' backgrounds were never viewed pejoratively. Money talked even louder in Hong Kong, where commerce never had any negative connotations and had been encouraged since the first days of the colony. Moreover, the colonial situation left the Chinese population with no political representation. As the compradors became richer and more powerful, they also became more influential in the social affairs of the Chinese community in Hong Kong, often serving as intermediaries between the colonial government and the Chinese population. Promoting the unity of local Chinese merchants by founding various merchant associations, the compradors helped convince the government that the colony's Chinese merchants were capable of becoming a cohesive, "responsible" class rather than a group of profit-hungry sojourners. Like other wealthy Chinese merchants in Hong Kong and in Southeast Asia, they often contributed greatly to public welfare back in their native districts in China. But even more significant was the role the compradors played in local community affairs and social welfare. The *Daily Press* praised Kwok Acheong for being a "liberal subscriber to all charities" and acting "handsomely to those in his employ." His funeral procession in April 1880, one of the longest the colony had seen, took over one hour to pass.[57]

Patterns of Collaboration

Embedded in the founding of Hong Kong are several intertwined patterns that eventually defined its future as a colony. First is the active role of Chinese collaboration. In neighboring Canton, where the loss of Hong Kong provoked great animosity and resentment, the colony was viewed as the "citadel of British imperialism" well into the twentieth century.[58] But colonialism in Hong Kong was not imposed upon a passive Chinese population. Nor did it involve slaughtering or driving out large numbers of indigenous peoples. Rather, colonialism attracted many merchants, contractors, and laborers from the mainland. Without Chinese help, there might well have been no colony.

Colonization was a continuation of early patterns of collaboration, but it also intensified and institutionalized some of these patterns. The making of a nascent Chinese bourgeoisie was inseparably linked with the colonial nature of Hong Kong. The opium monopoly, for example, "linked imperial processes with local trading systems and played an important role in creating Chinese capital and strengthening Chinese elites."[59] Compradors became instrumental to the growth of Sino-foreign commerce throughout the Chinese treaty ports, but nowhere else would they became as important a part of local society as in Hong Kong.

From the outset until the last days of empire, colonialism was an experiment, with rules often made up along the way. Plans did not always work as expected. Although the government's segregationist policies helped create a local Chinese business elite, they also created an enclave that, out of government control, would be ripe for piracy and crime. Whereas the various farms and monopolies represented collaboration between the colonial government and its Chinese collaborators, "the co-option of elites was a slow and clumsy process, troubled by conflict and mutual distrust."[60] As lucrative as the farms and monopolies were, they were never as profitable as the government hoped. Although the opium trade was fully legal, colonial officials worried that the farmers sold opium for less than they could, misused their colonial privileges, and corrupted the colonial judicial system and police force. At the other end, farmers often had a hard time protecting their farms from other local Chinese competitors. In the mid-1880s opium farming would go to rival Chinese merchants from another British colony, the Straits Settlements in Malaya.

Finally, Hong Kong's historical development was based as much on the weaknesses as on the strengths of the colonial state. Hong Kong's early experience supports recent analysis that expands the colonial framework to examine how a colonial regime both exploits and cooperates with its subjects, often as the rulers try to compensate for the weaknesses of the colonial state. Challenging the common notion of an all-powerful colonial state, Nicholas Dirks suggests that because colonialism was "predicated at least in part on the ill-coordinated nature of power," rulers were always aware of the limitations of colonial power. This awareness of the limitations of colonial power explains the Hong Kong government's need to reward collaborators, such as Loo Aqui and Kwok Acheong, for their service in the Opium War: a token of gratitude, but also an attempt to ensure that collaborators kept working for the right side. For no one in Hong Kong—not even the British, with all their self-confidence and supremacy—could guarantee how long British rule would last.[61]

2

A Better Class of Chinese: Building the Emporium of the East

CHINESE COLLABORATION helped transform Hong Kong from an island of fishing villages into the latest addition to a powerful British Empire that spanned the globe. But despite the colony's early promise, Superintendent of Trade Henry Pottinger's vision of Hong Kong as "the great emporium of the East" did not immediately materialize. The entrepot trade was slow to develop, and Hong Kong at first seemed little more than a colonial outpost and opium center. In July 1842 the *Canton Press* lamented that the early land sales and poor trade conditions had left the Chinese buyers "as poor as rats, the dollars they had being laid out to erect houses, and the same may be said of the few European residents here; they are all sellers, none buyers."[1] Disease was endemic. In May 1843 almost 25 percent of the British garrison died of malaria. Piracy was rampant and crime was equally bad on land. Few large Chinese merchants from South China came to trade in Hong Kong, while the small, often parasitic, Chinese business elite did little to enhance the colony's economic prospects.

Given Hong Kong's economic success in the long run, a few years of depression, disease, and piracy may seem insignificant. Hong Kong's early economic history nonetheless speaks to current debates about colonialism, particularly the argument that criticizes postcolonialism for downplaying the material side of colonialism and, especially, the role of capitalism. Alijaz Ahmad suggests that "we should speak not so much of colonialism or postcolonialism but of capitalist modernity, which takes the colonial form in particular places and at particular times." Asking why Third World postcolonial critics have been given such respectability in the First World academy ("The Postcolonial Aura"), Arif Dirlik argues that the answer lies in the way postcolonialism and its practitioners have repudiated "a foundational role to capitalism in history."[2]

Returning capitalism to the discussion of colonialism is long overdue, for colonialism was the "midwife that assisted at the birth of capitalism." But focusing on the role of capitalism has its own pitfalls. It assumes a linear path of development: capitalist accumulation and colonial conquest and consolidation, moving at a parallel pace, unhindered by recessions, mutinies, rebellions, or other setbacks to colonial projects. It gives too much credit and foresight to the colonial state, ignoring crucial factors not directly related to either capitalism or the colonial state—natural disasters and social unrest, for example—and forgetting that both colonialism and capitalism were based as much on failure as on success, on trial and error. Finally, focusing on the role of capitalism places too much emphasis on the Western colonial metropoles. As Frederick Cooper and Ann Laura Stoler argue, "imperial elites may have *viewed* their domains from a metropolitan center, but their actions, let alone their consequences, were not necessarily *determined* there." The experience of early Hong Kong shows the importance of capitalism in the economic growth of the colony, but it also shows how the British colonial state had little to do with this growth.[3]

Hong Kong Founders

In July 1844, Colonial Treasurer Robert Montgomery Martin reported that the climate, landscape, and trade conditions of Hong Kong were so bad that the British government should abandon the island. "A sort of hallucination" had seized the European merchants who had invested in home building based on an expectation that Hong Kong would "rapidly out-rival Singapore, and become the Tyre or Carthage of the eastern hemisphere." Martin complained that there "seemed to be the greatest possible desire to spend a large part of the Chinese indemnity on this wretched, barren, unhealthy and useless rock, which the whole wealth, talent, and energy of England would never render habitable, or creditable, as a colony, to the British name." The island's commercial prospects were apparently extremely bleak: "There does not appear to be the slightest probability that, under any circumstances, Hong Kong will ever become a place of trade." Refuting claims that Hong Kong might become another Singapore, Martin insisted that "the geographical, territorial, and commercial advantages which have contributed to the prosperity of Singapore, are totally and entirely wanting, and can never be created at Hong Kong." Even the colony's famously deep harbor was not worth the expense and trouble: "I can see no justification for the British Government spending one shilling on Hong Kong."[4]

Martin had been in Hong Kong for only a few weeks and suffered from poor health, for which he eventually resigned his position. According to John Davis, who was governor from 1844 to 1848, Martin's charges were "exaggerated and partial," written "under a feeling of strong prejudice, founded in apprehension for his personal health, regarding which he is remarkably sensitive, and on account of which he has had more leave of absence than any individual in the service." Davis would later report that many naval officers called Hong Kong the "finest harbour in the world." The colony had made considerably more progress in population and revenue in its first six years than had Singapore. Some sixty years later, a guide to Hong Kong and the Chinese treaty ports declared that "the progress of events has shown Mr. Martin to be a false prophet, for Hongkong is now the pivot upon which the trade of South China turns."[5]

Although Martin may have been overly pessimistic, many contemporary observers shared similar sentiments. "It is," wrote the *China Mail*, "a subject of wonder, why, where so wide a choice was open, our negotiators should have selected such a sterile and wild unlovely land as Hong Kong." Botanist Robert Fortune predicted that "viewed as a place of trade, I fear Hong-kong will be a failure." The Rev. George Smith, later Bishop of Victoria, concurred: "Even in a commercial point of view, it is the opinion of the best judges in such a manner that Hong Kong is never likely to realize a small part of the expectations cherished on its first acquisition."[6] In August 1845, thirty-one of the colony's British merchants memorialized the colonial sec-

retary in London, insisting that the island had no commercial potential. Alexander Matheson, head of Jardine & Matheson, told the
British House of Commons in May 1847 that, had they not already
invested so much money in land and buildings, most English firms
would have already withdrawn from Hong Kong years ago.[7]

British officials had hoped the colony would attract Chinese merchants from Macau and Canton and thus be transformed into the
trading center of South China. What went wrong? Part of the problem
was that the Treaty of Nanking, which ceded Hong Kong to Britain
in 1842, diverted trade away from Hong Kong. The treaty opened
five Chinese ports and stipulated that only junks from these five treaty
ports—with special permits issued by Chinese officials for each
voyage—could come to Hong Kong. Junks entering Hong Kong waters without such permits were to be seized by English officials and
turned over to Chinese authorities at Kowloon. Although no evidence
proves that either Chinese or British authorities systematically enforced these provisions, Chinese officials allegedly charged exorbitant
prices for the special permits.[8] Commenting on the colony's "dull"
trade, the *Friend of China* maintained in October 1843 that "some
strong Celestial influence is certainly in action to prevent the Junks
and Native Craft resorting to this Port." And because the larger foreign firms maintained offices in both Hong Kong and Canton, major
Chinese merchants went to Canton and avoided Hong Kong.[9]

Another reason the colony did not attract Chinese merchants was
that it offered no economic advantage. Because trading at the Chinese
treaty ports was cheaper, British merchants preferred to buy directly
from China rather than in Hong Kong. In 1845 the German missionary Karl Gützlaff, who served as the colony's "Chinese" secretary
to the superintendent of trade, explained that "it is vain to expect that
vessels from the ports which are open to British enterprise should
come down to Hongkong for a cargo, when they can buy the goods
they want at their own doors for nearly the same price."[10] Chinese
merchants preferred to use British ships for importing and exporting
goods to and from Southeast Asia because they were faster, safer, and
cheaper than their own junks. Although this benefited British shipping
companies, their ships bypassed Hong Kong.[11] Martin lamented that
"after three years and a half's [sic] uninterrupted settlement there is
not one respectable Chinese inhabitant on the island." One wealthy

opium trader, Chinam, had built a house and freighted a ship in Hong Kong, but he soon returned to Canton where he died of a fever and cold contracted in the colony.[12] In April 1846, Gützlaff explained: "no man possessing a considerable property has ventured to engage in the Hong-Kong trade, or to establish a house on the island." When Chinese "men of substance" were asked why they did not want to trade under "a free government, with full protection of their property," they invariably replied that trading was more advantageous at Canton or the other treaty ports.[13]

Chinese merchants had another reason to avoid Hong Kong: Chinese authorities in Canton used various restrictions to discourage Chinese traders from coming to the colony. Martin explained that had the Canton opium trader Chinam survived his illness, "he would have been prohibited returning to Hong Kong, the policy of the mandarins on the adjacent coast being to prevent all respectable Chinese from settling at Hong Kong, and in consequence of the hold which they possess on their families and relatives." Many colonial officials shared Martin's conviction that Canton authorities tried to deport to Hong Kong "every thief, pirate, and idle or worthless vagabond," both as a way to get rid of criminals and to undermine the stability of the colony. The result was a "Bedouin sort of population, whose migratory, predatory, gambling and dissolute habits, utterly unfit them for continuous industry, and render them not only useless but highly injurious subjects in the attempt to form a new colony." Martin reported that even Gützlaff, the secretary "whose prepossessions are strongly in favor of the Chinese," had confirmed that " 'the moral standard of the people congregated in this place (Hong Kong) is of the lowest description'."[14] Indeed, Martin argued, Hong Kong was viewed on the mainland as "a spot where adventurers and reckless characters may make something out of the English, and where burglars and robbers may resort with impunity, and live upon the profits of their villainy."[15] Rev. George Smith, usually more charitable than colonial officials, described the Chinese population of Hong Kong as consisting mainly of the "lowest dregs of native society" and "of the lowest condition and character." Robert Fortune claimed that the "town swarms with thieves and robbers."[16]

There is no way to confirm these assessments of the early Chinese community. Chinese government sources from the period, eager to portray any Chinese in Hong Kong as unscrupulous traitors, are often even more critical than their colonial counterparts. But by all accounts the European population had more than its own share of unsavory characters. In Britain, the island was seen as a haven for European outlaws, deserters, reckless adventurers, and speculators. The *Economist* noted in August 1846: "Hong Kong is nothing now but a depot for a few opium smugglers, soldiers, officers and men-of-war's men."[17] Robert Fortune wrote that whereas in the earliest days of the colony the foreign population had consisted of "generally most upright and honorable men," by 1845 the foreign population formed a "very motley group." Oswald Tiffany, an American visitor, recalled that "scapegoats and scoundrels from the purlieus of London, creatures that only missed Botany Bay by good fortune, were to be found in the town of Victoria, lording it over the natives, many of whom were more respectable and respected than they had ever been or ever could be."[18]

Regardless of the character of Hong Kong's early residents, the colonial situation could not attract the type of Chinese merchant necessary to develop the colony's economy, much to the dismay and disappointment of local officials. Although by April 1844 about twenty thousand Chinese were in Hong Kong, the colony still had very few large Chinese firms. "The ships in Hong Kong are of the most wretched order," observed Osmond Tiffany, "there being no rich natives on the island." The lack of large Chinese merchants in Hong Kong is evident in the fact that few Chinese bought land in the colony. In a public land auction in 1843, only two of the thirty buyers were Chinese. In another public auction on 22 January 1844, only one or two of the buyers were Chinese. In 1850, none of the twenty largest land lessees was Chinese.[19]

The most important reason that Chinese merchants were reluctant to come to Hong Kong was security: the colonial government could not provide a safe business environment. From the earliest days of the colony until the 1860s, the island was surrounded by pirates. In December 1841, the *Canton Press* reported that piracy continued "to give uneasiness to the native population, and the efforts of the British authorities to put them down, have hitherto been but partially successful." Osmond Tiffany described "a savage set of villains cruising about the mount of the river, who will plunder, if not murder, anyone at the first opportunity. They often go in fast boats with their crews concealed, run alongside of unwary craft, and board them in a moment."[20] Pirates kept spies in Hong Kong, who reported the departure of junks for the Chinese ports with such precision that the junk crews dared to leave only in a strong wind, when they might outrun the pirates, or in large squadrons for safety.[21] In June 1844 a force of 150 pirates plundered a waterfront warehouse.

Governor John Davis wrote to Admiral Thomas Cochrane and Qing Imperial Commissioner Qiying in early 1845 that "the trade which ought to resort to this colony in native junks and boats is comparatively paralysed by the armed vessels which infest and almost blockade the narrow passage of the Lyemoon on the East and the Capsingmoon and other channels on the west."[22] In September of the same year the British Admiralty approved a short-lived plan by Chinese merchants to arm two vessels, manned by Chinese crews and commanded by British officers, to patrol and combat piracy in the surrounding waters. Threats of a giant pirate attack put the entire island on emergency alert during the summer of 1854. By June, the population was in a state of alarm. The compradors and shopkeepers had sent their families home or were preparing to do so. Although the attack never materialized, extra fortifications were placed at both approaches to the harbor, and an auxiliary police force was added.[23]

In October 1854 Wong Aloong and a group of other boat masters trading in Hong Kong petitioned the colonial government to dispatch a steamer to end piracy, which they claimed had greatly harmed their business. The petitioners warned that if the government did not help ensure peace and order, they would no longer be able to come to the colony, and that local merchants would suffer. In the same month the headman of the Lower Bazaar asked that a steamer be sent to crack down on piracy. In less than one month three vessels had been seized by pirates. Fewer than half of the boats previously trading in Hong Kong now dared come to the colony, forcing up rice and wood prices. Unless the government took action, these boats would stop visiting the colony altogether.[24] The same month Lieutenant Governor William Caine reported that a wealthy merchant named Low Sew Kwong had hired armed boats to guard his vessel as he moved his family and valuables from Shunde County to Hong Kong. Low's vessel survived most of the trip, only to be attacked by pirates as it entered Hong Kong waters. In September 1855 John Bowring, who was governor from 1854 to 1859, concluded that the piracy plaguing the colony was "interfering ruinously with its comforts and its prosperity."[25]

The colonial government could not suppress piracy without help from the Chinese government. Contemporary colonial records reveal officials' frustrations toward what they considered to be a lack of cooperation from Chinese authorities.[26] In 1853 George Bonham, governor from 1848 to 1854, complained that piracy had become so rampant that it was impossible for the government to suppress it alone. But the colonial government could do little to control crime within Hong Kong itself. Martin reported that "the European inhabitants are obliged to sleep with loaded pistols; frequently to turn out of their beds at midnight to protect their lives and property from gangs of armed robbers, who are ready to sacrifice a few of their number if they can obtain a large plunder." J. M. Tronson, a British naval officer who visited the island and later came from Bengal to command the British garrison, recalled that "a part of the city named Tai-pin Shan, is inhabited by the Coolies, and by refugees and scoundrels from all parts of the empire . . . Some of the outcasts prowl about the island, and commit various depredations whenever they meet with defenceless people."[27]

The presence of men like Loo Aqui also discouraged Chinese merchants from coming to Hong Kong. Although he was popular for his charitable activities, Loo was also widely known for criminal activities, such as smuggling, piracy, and encouraging corruption among the police force. The *Friend of China* frequently blamed piracy on Loo and his "Lower Bazaar Clique."[28] Rev. George Smith wrote that Loo "was said to encourage disreputable characters by the loan of money, and in various ways to reap [from] the profligacy and crime." In November 1861 William Tarrant, editor of the *Friend of China* and a former colonial official, recalled: "Sea King" Loo had been "monarch of all he surveyed on the water about Hong Kong prior to our taking possession." Loo's presence "had much to do with keeping people of better character from settling, or even visiting the place."[29]

The tactics Loo used to control his opium monopoly were equally intimidating. Reverend Smith described that, accompanied by Chinese or Indian police, Loo "was in the habit of visiting the native boats and private houses, in order to seize every ball of opium suspected of being sold without his license." The *Canton Press* complained that, even in

British Hong Kong, men like Loo were able to "exercise almost despotic sway among their countrymen, whom they squeeze in exactly the same manner as the mandarins are said to do elsewhere." Loo, the *Canton Press* wrote, "squeezes the Chinese who come to settle at Hongkong, that is they are obliged to pay him taxes for being permitted to exercise their calling." The *Friend of China* described the boat that "Potentate Aqui" used to police the opium trade as "to all intents and purposes a PRIVATE revenue cruiser; acting in every respect as if she had been commissioned by the Executive of Hongkong." Enjoying the protection of the colonial police, Loo carried "the commerce of the colony at his belt."[30]

The extent to which Loo protected his opium farm was neither unusual nor illegal. The farm system was used throughout the colonies of Southeast Asia and the Chinese treaty ports. Opium's status as a monopoly commodity required constant supervision at every level of production and sale, guarding supply, and policing illicit competition. Because the aim of the farm system was to make as little work as possible for the colonial government, farmers had their own police force and network of informers, which had wide powers of search and seizure that were sometimes abused.[31]

But Loo's use of force and intimidation to protect his opium farm supports the main point of this chapter: that criticizing postcolonialism for failing to deal seriously with politics and economics ignores the way colonial policies could backfire. Loo's "inquisitorial power for enforcing his monopoly over the timid Chinese," explained Smith, was "sufficient to check and discourage respectable natives from settling at Hong Kong." It was to protect Loo's monopoly, the *Friend of China* wrote, "that the interests of the colony have been sacrificed—that the native traders have been driven away—that the foreign merchants are now abandoning the island." Men like Loo had so much influence that "respectable Chinese" had assured the *Canton Press* "it would be altogether impossible for them to settle at Hongkong."[32]

Not only did Loo's oppressive control of his opium farm prevent Chinese merchants from coming to Hong Kong, the colonial government was unable to assure Chinese merchants that it was committed to keeping the island. Many Chinese feared that Hong Kong might be returned to China. In July 1842 the *Friend of China* regretted that a plot of land granted for building a Chinese temple still remained vacant. "The sole reason alleged for the delay is, that the Chinese fear the island will be restored, and themselves left to their fate." Even after Imperial Commissioner Qiying issued a proclamation in 1843 that Chinese who had served the British forces would be pardoned, the lack of confidence in Britain's willingness and ability to retain Hong Kong diminished its appeal to Chinese merchants. Many Chinese continued to fear the consequences of the Qing prohibitions against emigration. In July 1844 the *Canton Press* reported that a Chinese merchant working for the British commissariat in Zhoushan had been abducted and beheaded by the authorities.[33] In November an anti-British placard called for all Chinese residents to leave the colony, hoping that China would drive out the British barbarians. Although in April 1845 Qiying forbade Chinese in Canton and Hong Kong to molest foreigners, in January 1846 two more anti-British placards appeared in one day: one condemning Canton authorities for being soft on foreigners; the other, an anti-British declaration by "all the people of Guangdong." During the Second Opium War, the viceroy of Canton had placards placed on street corners throughout the colony, calling on all loyal Chinese to rise up against the English barbarians by poisoning or stabbing them or by burning their property.[34]

Overseas Chinese Emigration and the Taiping Rebellion

If the colonial state and British capitalism could not attract enough Chinese merchants to develop Hong Kong's economy, what eventually brought about the colony's transformation? Traditionally, British historians have argued that the growth of Hong Kong's Chinese population was occasioned by the colony's offer of liberal government and free trade. Chinese scholars, in contrast, have stressed that population growth in Hong Kong depended almost completely on happenings in China. The reality lies somewhere between these positions. Attracting enough Chinese merchants (and their wealth) to Hong Kong required not only the rise of Western capitalism and imperialism but also domestic turmoil in China. This combination of push-pull factors resulted in several massive waves of Chinese emigration, which eventually transformed the colony into the major commercial center that its founders had envisioned.

The rise of Western imperialism and the development of capitalism worldwide encouraged Chinese emigration in two ways. First, the opening of Canton and other treaty ports to foreign trade disrupted local economies. Foreign imports, such as British cotton, competed with Chinese products in the markets of Canton—a regional center of textile production and export since the Ming dynasty. Chinese junks lost out to larger, faster foreign vessels. By the late 1840s Canton had lost its hold on both tea and silk trades, causing unemployment throughout Guangdong.[35] Second, the abandonment of slavery by England, France, and some parts of the United States encouraged a demand for cheap labor for Western capitalist ventures—from the mines and railroads of the American West, Canada, and Australia, to the tin mines and rubber plantations of Malaya.[36]

In 1849, one year after gold was discovered in the Sacramento Valley, the first shipload of Chinese laborers came through Hong Kong, en route to California. In December 1850, colonial official W. H. Mitchell wrote that "the Colony's prospects are by no means discouraging . . . The Chinese population about to spring up on the west coast of America must not be forgotten, and for this Hongkong will be the Chief Port of Supply." Between January and June 1850, some 10,000 tons of shipping (mainly silks, lacquered ware, floor matting, camphor trunks, fireworks, sweetmeats, tea, sugar, molasses, wrought granite, wooden houses, planed lumber, and curios) had been loaded in Hong Kong and shipped to California.[37] With this growth of overseas trade came new Chinese labor and talent. In April 1851, Governor George Bonham reported an increase in the Chinese population, mainly artisans from Canton working in the California trade.[38] Three years later, Bonham noted that the colony's "commercial prospects are slowly but certainly extending and assuming a character of greater permanency."[39]

Proving Mitchell's predictions about the colony's prospects, Hong Kong became the major transit point for both free and contract Chinese labor in the 1850s. The harbormaster reported that in 1852 alone 34 ships filled with Chinese workers, mainly from the Siyi and Sanyi regions, sailed from Hong Kong for California.[40] Many other workers went to Peru and the West Indies.[41] In November 1854 the first shipload of Chinese emigrants from Hong Kong arrived in Kingston, Jamaica, and from 1848 to 1857, almost 25,000 Chinese left Hong Kong for Cuba. When gold was discovered in Australia in 1851, more workers went there via Hong Kong. In June 1854 the *Hong Kong Register* reported that in the first half of 1854, 15,548 Chinese left Hong Kong for New South Wales and California.[42] John Bowring, who succeeded George Bonham as governor, noted in October 1855 that 14,683 Chinese had already left Hong Kong in 1855, almost 10,000 of them to California.[43] In 1857 almost 18,000 workers left Hong Kong for Australia. Bowring reported in 1859 that in 1858 almost 14,000 more Chinese had left for Australia or California.[44]

Chinese emigration during the 1850s was the greatest contributor to Hong Kong's commercial prosperity, and both European and Chinese merchants benefited. Chinese scholars have argued that Chinese emigration and the "coolie" or "pig" trade (named after the manner in which the workers were transported) benefited mainly colonial governments and foreign merchants.[45] That, however, is only half of the story. Chinese were involved in the trade at almost every stage: labor recruiters in Chinese villages; crimps, contractors, and other middlemen in Hong Kong and other ports; interpreters and overseers aboard the ships; and labor brokers and shipowners in Hong Kong.[46] Two of the largest coolie brokerage companies for California, Wo Hing and Wo Hang, were both Chinese-owned, the former by Li Sing, one of Hong Kong's most prominent Chinese merchants. Tam Achoy, the contractor who had helped the British build their new colony, was also one of the main labor brokers and charterers of emigrant ships. Chinese emigration was big business, building or enhancing the fortunes of many Hong Kong merchants, both Chinese and foreign.

Not easily disentangled from the rise of Western imperialism and global capitalism, the other cure for Hong Kong's economic woes began in the early 1850s, when many Chinese merchants came to Hong Kong to escape the chaos and destruction of the Taiping Rebellion. Although the rebellion and its suppression cost more than 20 million lives in China, devastated the Chinese countryside, and wiped out cities, it had the opposite effect on Hong Kong. In June 1855, Chief Secretary William Mercer reported that the Chinese population had risen from 37,536 in 1853 to 54,072 in 1854, even while emigration to California and New South Wales continued. The "influx of people flying from the troubles" resulted "directly and indirectly from the confusion which has prevailed in the City of Canton and its neighbourhood."[47] In 1855 the number of Chinese in Hong Kong reached

70,651—a figure that is especially remarkable when we consider that in 1855 some 14,683 people left the colony. Similarly, the Chinese population rose from 74,041 in 1858 to 85,280 in 1859, even though 10,217 people left Hong Kong in 1859. In one of the most dramatic periods, from 1858 to 1862, the population increased by approximately 65 percent.[48]

The rise in the Chinese population of Hong Kong during the Taiping hostilities increased the colony's prosperity, which then attracted more wealthy Chinese. Even after the conditions on the mainland improved, the influx of immigrants continued. The average value of landed property and rent in June 1855 was 60 percent higher than in June 1854.[49] James Johnson, an American naval officer who visited Hong Kong in May 1857, found the colony's main street, Queen's Road, filled with "a constant stream of humanity with its eddying tides, pouring, tossing, and rushing in every direction over its surface." Shops were crowded "with myriads of human beings whose busy hands were plying with wonderful dexterity and unremitting efforts, their various implements of trade." The town was full of stores "containing every variety of article manufactured in Canton and the interior towns, excit[ing] the curiosity and admiration of the stranger."[50] In August 1857, Governor Bowring reported that the Chinese of the colony were "all concurring to render Hongkong one of the most prosperous and progressive of Colonies under the protection of the British flag."[51] By March 1858 Bowring wrote that it had become "impossible to walk through our Streets without observing a marked improvement in the domestic comforts as in the dress of the people."[52] The following March, Bowring reported huge increases in the value of lands and houses over the past five years, noting that "the growth of a superior character of Chinese houses is one of the most marked and pleasing signs of improvement. There can be no doubt of the present opulence of many of the Chinese settlers who came penniless to the Colony, and who from labourers and fishermen have become Shopkeepers; from Shopkeepers, Merchants and Shipowners." Sanitary conditions had also improved, Bowring explained: "Chinese habits are difficult to change or even to modify but there is no comparison between the general cleanliness of Hongkong and that of any Chinese City which I have ever visited."[53]

Wang Tao, the pioneer journalist who worked in Hong Kong with

Scottish missionary James Legge, once described Hong Kong as a place where the "hills all around are rather bare of trees, and nothing but water meets the eye." When Wang first arrived, "merchants generally wore short jackets and put on a cotton overcoat when the weather got cold. The women paid little attention to their dress. Even the singsong girls wore plain cotton when entertaining their visitors, and rarely wore jewellery of any sort." But Wang later observed that, "drastic changes are now taking place in the way of life in Hong Kong. People are beginning to pursue luxury . . . Sartorial splendour has supplanted the plainer styles of the past. At fashionable social gatherings, some spend tens of thousands of dollars on a single dinner. Bright lamps burn through the night, and loud music is heard until the small hours. Hong Kong's prosperity now exceeds that of [Canton], and it is all the result of fate and chance."[54]

With this influx of Chinese, and the enhanced financial position of the Chinese community, came an increase in the number of Chinese hongs. In 1858 Hong Kong had only 35 hongs, but by 1859 more than 65 Chinese firms were large enough to be considered hongs.[55] In 1845 the number of small Chinese family trading houses was 78; by 1867 it had risen to 1,775. In 1867, just three years after the Taiping Rebellion was crushed, the number of Chinese general merchants in Hong Kong had risen to more than 70 from fewer than 10 in 1846.[56]

The combination of the Taiping Rebellion and the growth of Chinese communities overseas did more than save Hong Kong from an economic depression; it changed the island's basic reason for being. Hong Kong was transformed from a colonial outpost into the center of a transnational trade network stretching from the China coast to Southeast Asia and then to Australia and North America. Because the Chinese population in these overseas communities required Chinese goods, such as tea, sugar, dried foods, rice, and rattan, exports soon rose. The growth of the Hong Kong Chinese population also meant a greater demand for Chinese products, which coincided with the development of the entrepot trade to deal with the needs of the new overseas Chinese communities. Since the overseas communities were generally made up of Chinese who had fled first to Hong Kong, where they had maintained extensive business contacts, many important trade connections were forged.

At the heart of this giant trade network were the *Kam Shan Chong* and *Nam Pak Hong,* the large Chinese import-export firms that acted as middlemen for trade between the overseas Chinese communities and China. The *Kam Shan Chong* were firms that traded mainly with the overseas Chinese communities in Australia and North America, while the *Nam Pak Hong* traded with northern Chinese ports and the Nanyang region of Southeast Asia. At first, these firms usually dealt in Chinese herbs and medicine, peanuts, rice, beans, tea, liquor, dried fish, preserved foods, silk, and sugar. But by the late 1850s, more than one quarter of the colony's trade was in the hands of such Chinese merchants.[57] In March 1859 Bowring marveled at how the Chinese merchants' "relations with foreign countries are everywhere spreading and they carry on their transactions with many of the subordinate ports which are little known to or visited by foreign merchants."[58]

Overseas emigration and exports also made Hong Kong into a major shipping center of South China and Southeast Asia. New services, such as fitting, repairing, and provisioning emigrant ships, boosted the colony's economy. Emigration furthermore helped build business connections between Xiamen, Macau, and Canton, whose ports provided both emigrants and provisions. New professional services arose to cater to the emigration trade—marine, fire, and property insurance, law firms, and large international banking institutions—while many smaller Chinese "native" banks and moneychangers handled remittances from overseas Chinese.[59]

Li Sing and the Li Family

Hong Kong's position as a space of transit and connections paradoxically shaped it as a place of settlement. Although most of the Chinese who came to Hong Kong during the 1850s and 1860s were in transit to Southeast Asia, Australia, or North America, many stayed in Hong Kong. The Taiping Rebellion and the rise of overseas Chinese communities created a new class of wealthy Chinese in Hong Kong, where they became settlers rather than sojourners. Among the new immigrants were wealthy Chinese who brought their families, capital, entrepreneurial skills, and business connections. Although their extensive business operations expanded far beyond South China, Hong Kong nonetheless became their home base. As much of the new capital en-

tering the colony went into real estate, soon a group of large merchants and landowners arose. In 1854 Bowring wrote that the prosperity of the colony had "created a class of Chinamen daily becoming
more influential and more opulent to whom we may look for future
cooperation."[60]

Examples of this new class of Chinese are the Li brothers from
Xinhui district in Guangdong, who came to Hong Kong in the early
1850s. In 1854 Li Sing and his brother Li Leong bought a vacant lot
in the Upper Bazaar. Soon they were operating a moneychanging and
lending business. In 1857 they bought another lot and started the Wo
Hing firm, probably the largest broker of emigrant labor and charterer
of emigrant ships. By the mid-1860s the family's holdings included
real estate and interests in the gambling and opium monopolies. In
1876 Wo Hing was the eleventh-largest taxpayer in the colony. As
head of this successful family, Li Sing became one of the colony's most
prominent merchants. In 1876 he was the twelfth-largest taxpayer in
the colony, only two places below the Hongkong and Shanghai
Banking Corporation. He founded the Wa Hop Co., which laid a
telegraph cable from Hong Kong to Canton. Li was also the first
Chinese to form fire and marine insurance companies in Hong Kong;
he founded both the Tseoung On Fire Insurance Company and the
On Tai Marine Insurance Company. Li Sing died in May 1900, leaving
property valued at more than 6 million Hong Kong dollars to be
divided among his eight sons.[61]

Hong Kong was, of course, not the only place where Chinese merchants sought refuge during the Taiping Rebellion. They also fled to
Hankou and Shanghai, bringing their wealth and cultural tastes. By
end of the rebellion, many of these men had come to consider these
cities as their home.[62] But three features made Hong Kong different
as a place of settlement. First, many of the Chinese who came there
settled for the long term. Second, settling in a British colony was not
the same as settling in a Chinese city with a strong foreign presence.
Many of these merchants identified strongly with colonial Hong Kong
and the British regime. During the Second Opium War, for example,
Li Sing's family sided with the British since it had so many financial
interests in Hong Kong, even hiring Chinese mercenaries to fight for
the foreign powers in Tianjin. For its efforts, the family received part
of the war indemnity, including some pieces from the Imperial

Summer Palace in Beijing. Third, Chinese merchants in Hong Kong operated within an even larger commercial arena than did their counterparts on the mainland. Many of these men had strong business connections extending from South China to Southeast Asia, Australia, North and South America, and the West Indies. By the 1860s, for example, the Li family's holdings included a short-lived trading company in Borneo.

With the arrival of men like the Li brothers, a new Chinese business elite had emerged by the late 1850s. The early businessmen of Hong Kong had derived most of their income from landholding and trade with Canton. Many of these new businessmen, however, were both real estate magnates and leaders of the overseas Chinese trade. They were also beginning to move into trades previously dominated by Europeans, such as insurance, shipping, foodstuffs, telegraph communications, and mining enterprises in China and Southeast Asia. The Chinese business community also saw several important demographic changes. In the early years, Chinese merchants had lived and conducted their business mainly in the Chinese sections of town, leaving their families in their home villages or in Canton. By the late 1850s, however, Chinese businessmen were beginning to buy or rent property from European owners in the more desirable parts of the main town previously occupied by Europeans. Merchants were increasingly bringing their wives and families to the colony. In 1844 the ratio was approximately 5 Chinese males to every female, but by 1865 it had shifted to about 2.5 males to every female.[63] For these new Chinese businessmen, the colony was no longer just a temporary home and a place to get rich fast.

Confidence Restored: New Foreign Investment

The Hong Kong government realized that the Chinese merchants were largely responsible for the colony's new prosperity. In May 1863 Governor Hercules Robinson reported to the Colonial Office that "it is the Chinese who have made Hong Kong what it is and not its connection with the foreign trade."[64] Hong Kong's new economic growth, moreover, benefited local European merchants and attracted new foreign investment. Naval officer James Johnson marveled at the "handsome and spacious residences" on Queen's Road belonging to

European and American merchants.[65] Several new European banks were opened in the late 1850s and early 1860s, while Portuguese firms moved to Hong Kong from Canton and Macau. The American firm of Heard & Co., which had its main office in Canton, opened a branch office on Queen's Road in 1850. In 1857 Douglas Lapraik, who had begun his Hong Kong career as a watchmaker's apprentice, co-founded Hong Kong's first dry dock at Aberdeen, which later merged with the neighboring Hope Dock as the Hong Kong and Whampoa Dock Co. In 1860 Lapraik started a steamship company that ran the South China coast. He also founded the Hong Kong Hotel Co. in 1866. By the time of his death in 1869, Lapraik owned a fleet of seven steamships.[66] It was also during the 1860s that building and repairing ships began to be an important business, run mainly by Europeans. The Aberdeen Docks were begun in the early 1860s, while the Union Dock Co. began to build docks at Hung Hom in Kowloon.[67] The Hongkong, Canton, and Macao Steamboat Company, formed in October 1865 mainly by Douglas Lapraik, bought several American steamers. Shipping between Hong Kong and Canton and the United States and Australia began to increase. By the mid-1860s the number of European and American ships entering and leaving the harbor may have exceeded that of all of Great Britain.[68]

The clearest indicator of foreign investors' confidence in the colony's economy, sparked by the infusion of new Chinese capital, can be seen in the founding of the Hongkong and Shanghai Banking Co., Ltd. in July 1864. Until the late 1840s all local banking facilities had been provided by larger British firms, such as Jardine's and Dent's. Several joint-stock companies opened branches in Hong Kong in the early 1850s, but most Western banks in Hong Kong and China were branch offices of Anglo-Indian banks, such as the Chartered Bank of India, Australia, and China, established in 1853 in London by a group of East India merchants, shipowners and members of Parliament. Because these institutions were controlled from India or England, their directors had little knowledge of local conditions.[69]

The impetus for forming the new bank came when Thomas Sutherland, superintendent for the P&O Steam Navigation and self-made tycoon, learned that the Bombay-based Bank of China was planning to open up a branch in Hong Kong. The branch would finance trade between Hong Kong and the Chinese and Japanese treaty ports, but it would offer only 5,000 of the 30,000 shares in Hong Kong and the Chinese treaty ports. Within a week, Sutherland had drawn up a prospectus for a new bank. Though most of the bank's capital came from Dent's and Jardine's, the bank's provisional committee and subsequent directorate included representatives of the main European, American, and Parsi firms in Hong Kong. This was a clear indication of the foreign merchants' confidence in the colony, and the founding of the new bank was widely seen as a sign of the colony's new prosperity.[70] Local Chinese capital was important from the start, and the bank would become the leading bank on the China coast for more than fifty years.[71]

Colonialism and Development

British historians, colonial officials, and visitors have generally attributed Hong Kong's economic growth to British liberal institutions and laissez-faire economic policies. In 1872, Scottish photographer John Thomson wrote that "Hong-Kong used to enjoy the reputation of being the kind of place—distant, disagreeable, and very hot—to which one's worst enemies ought to be consigned. It was truly a vile place at one time—the resort of pirates and the worst class of vagabonds of the south of China." But "under the liberal and enlightened governments" of Britain, the colony was "gradually throwing off its old bad habits." In his memoirs, Governor William Des Voeux recalled his first impression of Hong Kong when he arrived in October 1887: "what a monument of British enterprise!" E. J. Eitel, missionary, educator, and early historian of the colony, once wrote: "the genius of British free trade and political liberty constitutes unmistakenly the vital element in the historic evolution of Hongkong."[72] Almost one hundred years later, omitting both Chinese emigration and the Taiping Rebellion, G. B. Endacott attributed Hong Kong's economic growth mainly to "British liberal economic policies, particularly free trade, and a strong laissez-faire spirit in administration which aimed at keeping the ring clear for free enterprise under the law administered impartially to all without fear or favour."[72]

None of these, however, was sufficient to make Hong Kong the "great emporium of the East" envisioned by its founders. What we have seen confirms for the early years what recent work on twentieth-century Hong Kong history has argued: the role of the colonial state in Hong Kong's economic development has been exaggerated. Colonialism could even hinder Hong Kong's economic development, as it did by discouraging industrialization before the Second World War.[73] Failed attempts in the 1960s to restructure Hong Kong's industry were the fault of both the colonial government and the Chinese industrial elite, which had been, as Alex Choi puts it, "domesticated by the colonial state." In the 1970s the strategy of flexible, labor-intensive, small-scale manufacturing that enabled the colony to prosper came not from the government but from what Kim-ming Lee calls the "guerrilla tactics" of local Chinese manufacturers.[74]

Why did the early colonial regime not try harder to make Hong Kong more attractive to Chinese businessmen? To be sure, the rules of both colonialism and capitalism were much newer when the British first occupied Hong Kong than, for example, when the Japanese tried to create an industrial bourgeoisie in Korea.[75] Hong Kong's early experience almost seems indirectly to confirm the worn image of the colonial government as a laissez-faire regime, just as this image is finally being erased.[76] The early government, in fact, played an interventionist role from the outset by rewarding collaborators and offering land grants and monopolies (see Chapter 1). Nor does the fact that the British government had no grand design for either Hong Kong or China adequately answer the question. British interest in a trading base on the China coast dated almost as far back as the British presence in the Canton Delta region. Once coercion and military strength were used to wrest the island from China, Hong Kong was to be Britain's administrative, commercial, and military center in East Asia— and a means to help Britain open China's markets and free its people from centuries of tyranny, excessively regulated commerce, and economic stagnation.

Early colonial administrators saw their mission in Hong Kong as promoting both commerce and civilization in South China. Whether they were unwilling or unable to achieve this mission remains unclear. In the long run, Hong Kong's commercial success did not depend on its colonial administrators. Governor John Bowring once described Hong Kong as "naturally a refugium peccatorum for the scum of Canton and the large Cities of Southern and Western China." He warned that Hong Kong's "adjacency to the continent will always make it the receptacle of outlaws, vagabonds and criminal offenders, and the migratory and shifting character of a large portion of its population will long be a source of trouble and anxiety."[77] Ultimately, however, Hong Kong's proximity to China would help make the colony the "Great Emporium of the East" envisaged by its founders. In the immediate years after the 1911 revolution, Chinese entrepreneurs opened new factories in the colony, a trend repeated periodically in the republican period.[78] The chaotic years of the 1920s brought both labor and capital to the colony. Many of the new immigrants were wealthy Chinese, and in 1923 alone the government received 3.5 million Hong Kong dollars in premiums on new land leases. The Japanese invasion of China in 1937 further drove up the colony's Chinese population, sometimes by as many as five thousand people per day.[79] Among the new immigrants were prosperous Shanghai businessmen who established factories in Hong Kong. By the late 1930s the number of Chinese-run factories in Hong Kong may have exceeded two thousand, employing more than one hundred thousand people. Similarly, after the Second World War and the Communist victory in 1949, emigrant Shanghai entrepreneurs helped rejuvenate Hong Kong's economy so much that the government admitted that the infusion of Shanghai capital and business experience gave the colony a ten- to fifteen-year head start over the rest of East Asia.[80] Indeed, Hong Kong's legendary economic success perhaps had less to with its status as a British colony than because, at least at crucial points in Chinese history, it was not part of China.

3

Strategic Balance: Status and Respect in the Colonial Context

*F*RIENDSHIP BETWEEN NATIONS, like friendship between persons, grows only where there is mutual respect and give and take." When the scholar Lo Hsiang-lin wrote this in 1963, he was emphasizing the role of Hong Kong as a center for cultural "interchange" and "confluence" between "East" and "West"—specifically, between China and Britain. Lo may not have shared with European colonial historians their confidence in the superiority of Western culture, but his characterization of Hong Kong as a cheerful meeting of East and West was similar to theirs. In 1895 E. J. Eitel described how Chinese and Europeans in Hong Kong had been brought closer together by the "extremely slow process of amalgamation which depends more on the silent influences of English education, English speaking and English modes of living." The "mighty spirit of free trade" had "fused the interests of European and Chinese merchants into indissoluble unity." The establishment of British Hong Kong resulted from "the inchoative union of Europe and China, by the subordination of the latter to the former, and this by means of free trade coupled with enlightened and humane local government."[1]

More recent studies of Hong Kong's history have generally been less convinced of this "unity" described by Eitel, let alone of the "enlightened" or "humane" nature of colonial rule. Whereas Lo saw Hong Kong as place of confluence, recent studies stress conflict and unrest, the colonial government's neglect of its Chinese subjects, and the oppressive nature of the colonial regime.[2] As reflected in the title of one collection of essays, the emphasis is now on how Hong Kong survived despite its "precarious balance" between China and Britain.[3]

In contrast, focusing on the case of Chinese merchants in the late nineteenth century, I argue that these merchants survived and thrived not *despite* but *because of* Hong Kong's "precarious balance": its strategic position at the geographical, political, and cultural borders of the British and Chinese empires. Colonialism in Hong Kong did not always work as intended—nor was colonialism necessarily so bewildering and disruptive. Spaces in British colonial rule left room for local Chinese elites. As elsewhere, colonialism in Hong Kong had different meanings for different people; its significance lies not in what it was intended to be, but rather in what it became.

The Gulf Between Government and Governed

A wide gulf separated the colonial government and its Chinese subjects in early Hong Kong. Despite its importance in the British Empire, Hong Kong remained largely absent from what Thomas Richards calls the "imperial archive."[4] Whereas in India learning local languages was the necessary first step in an extensive network of "investigative modalities," most British officials in China and Hong Kong apparently did not share this concern.[5] Like China, Hong Kong occupied a very small place in the British national consciousness or in British imperial historiography. The colonial government generally made little attempt to understand its Chinese subjects, their society, or their customs. Shortly after his arrival in Hong Kong in 1859, Governor Hercules Robinson complained that no senior colonial officer in his new administration could read or write Chinese. When Robinson offered financial incentives to encourage officers to study Chinese, only three responded to his offer.[6] Not until 1861, some twenty years after Hong Kong became a colony, did the British make plans for training (including Chinese language instruction) cadets for the Hong Kong Civil Service.

The gulf between government and governed can be attributed to several factors. Because the British had no grand design for Hong

Kong, policies were often made on an ad hoc basis. Most colonial officials were sojourners with no intention of staying for more than a few years. As today, Hong Kong was a heavily policed city, with legal punishments for Chinese almost always higher than for Europeans. Describing the early Hong Kong government as a "regime of intimidation," Christopher Munn has estimated that a Chinese person in early Hong Kong stood a "one in ten chance" of appearing in court before an English magistrate.[7] As in China, contact with the state was to be avoided whenever possible.

The gulf between colonial state and Chinese society cannot be blamed on the colonial government alone. By siding with the British during the opium wars, some Chinese showed their intention of staying in Hong Kong, but many others did not have such plans. Like many European officials and merchants, most Chinese in Hong Kong came there as sojourners, leaving their families and business interests in China. Many were unsure how long Britain would be able to keep Hong Kong. Finally, in a colony with an alien legal system, Chinese residents often preferred to rely on traditional Chinese ideas of social and governmental organization and to "keep to themselves and avoid dealings with the British administration as much as possible."[8]

More important than the cause of this gulf is what it meant for the Chinese merchant elite. Colonial ignorance, indifference, and incompetence created a demand for services that these merchants were in a special position to offer. Through charitable and voluntary organizations, they resolved civil and commercial disputes, provided medical facilities, and created a voice for the Chinese community. By offering such services, local Chinese merchants were able to take advantage of Hong Kong's position at the edge of the Chinese and British empires to enhance their own power and prestige.

The Man Mo Temple and the Tung Wah Hospital

In Hong Kong, the earliest of the charitable and voluntary organizations was the Man Mo Temple, founded in 1847 by Loo Aqui and Tam Achoy. As the Chinese population increased, so did the power of the temple as an informal governing organization. In 1851, in a colonywide effort that cut across regional and occupational lines, local Chinese merchants repaired and expanded the temple. The merchants elected a committee that deliberated disputes among the Chinese community.⁹ The temple's role in mediating local disputes was later taken over by the Tung Wah Hospital.

The establishment of the Tung Wah Hospital was the result of an especially acute gap between government and governed: the colonial government's failure to provide suitable medical facilities for its Chinese subjects, and the Chinese population's prejudice against Western medicine. Although disease and poverty had plagued the colony from its early days, the colonial government preferred to rely on emergency measures.¹⁰ But in 1868 more than 900 Europeans and Indians were admitted to the Civil Hospital for medical treatment, while only about 200 Chinese sought treatment—even though the Chinese population was almost 100,000. The need for a Chinese hospital became especially apparent in 1869, as did the Chinese merchants' ability to establish such an institution. After the death of a Chinese emigrant at an ancestral hall in April of that year, an investigation revealed corpses and dying patients side by side in the hall; the conditions were, by contemporary Western medical standards, dreadfully unsanitary. This caused such a scandal that details of what would otherwise have been dismissed as a "native problem" reached London. Embarrassed, both government and Chinese community leaders were eager to control the situation. A group of Chinese merchants offered to build, at their own expense, a Chinese hospital. By June 1869 a hospital committee composed of about twenty prominent Chinese residents was formed.¹¹ The committee chairman, Ho Asik, was a prominent merchant, landowner, and neighborhood-committee leader. Leung On, comprador to Gibb, Livingston & Co., one of the oldest and best-known British firms in the colony, was actively involved from the start. The hospital was officially opened in February 1872 by Governor Richard Graves MacDonnell.¹²

As the Tung Wah Hospital grew, its offerings expanded: caring for the destitute; sending corpses and remains back to China for proper burial; repatriating kidnapped laborers and women; and running an insane asylum. Equally important were its community services. As the Chinese population increased, the hospital became the cultural and social center of the Chinese community. Soon so many Chinese bypassed the colonial registrar general for the Tung Wah Hospital Committee that the hospital became *the* place for the settlement of civil and commercial disputes. Eager to avoid unfamiliar British law, with its foreign courts and corrupt clerks, many Chinese preferred to have disputes settled by the hospital committee.[13] Although the choice to consult the hospital's committee rather than the colonial legal system is as much an indictment of British justice in Hong Kong as it is testimony to the hospital's success, the Tung Wah nonetheless bolstered the power of the Chinese merchant elite.

The Tung Wah Hospital also became known as the voice of the Chinese community. As Elizabeth Sinn explains, this was the first Chinese association "which could justifiably claim to represent the whole Chinese community."[14] This claim was reinforced by a committee and directorate made up of wealthy Chinese from various dialect, geographical, and social backgrounds. Ng Choy, a hospital director, declared in February 1878 during Governor John Pope Hennessy's ceremonial visit to the hospital that the hospital represented "every class of the Chinese community . . . and, in fact, every trade and profession in this Colony." Ng may have been exaggerating, but until the end of the nineteenth century, the Tung Wah Hospital remained unchallenged as the voice of the Chinese community. When Ng described the governor's visit as the "first instance in the history of Hongkong of a Governor making a formal call on the Chinese on the occasion of their New Year," he was not simply noting the historical nature of the visit. Rather, Ng was announcing that he and his peers deserved such a visit, not just as hospital directors but as leaders of the local Chinese community.[15]

From the perspective of the colonial government, men such as Ng Choy provided invaluable services by managing the Chinese population. As immigration from China increased in the mid-1800s, the government found itself vastly outnumbered. Organizations such as the Man Mo Temple relieved the government by resolving disputes among the Chinese community. In 1853 Governor George Bonham reported that since the founding of the Man Mo Temple, not one civil case where both sides were Chinese had gone before the Supreme Court.[16] The Tung Wah Hospital, too, showed that Chinese elites could be used to manage the Chinese community and to perform functions the government would otherwise have to do. Governor MacDonnell welcomed the proposal for a Chinese hospital from the outset. It was an ideal way to cover up the corpse scandal and to take credit for reducing government expenditures while making the Chinese feel important.[17] Although the Hospital Ordinance of 1870 incorporated a Chinese management committee and conferred considerable power on the directors, it allowed for government intervention to check the board's power and gave the government a supervisory role.[18] As the Tung Wah Hospital's nonmedical work increased, so did its usefulness to the government. During his ceremonial visit in February 1878, Governor Hennessy congratulated the founders for having done "an immense amount of good."[19] The hospital committee also soon proved to be an invaluable ally in mediating strikes and boycotts. Its directors mediated during the cargo workers' strike of 1872 and the hawkers' and rickshaw drivers' disturbances of 1883, and helped end the 1884 anti-French strikes and riots.[20]

The District Watch Force

Whereas the Tung Wah Hospital helped compensate for the colonial government's failure to provide medical facilities for its Chinese population, the establishment in 1866 of the District Watch Force enabled Chinese community leaders to cope with another of the colonial government's shortcomings: its inability to control crime.

A defining theme of colonial rhetoric was that colonialism ensured peace and order, but this was not the case in early Hong Kong. Chinese and European merchants complained about the inefficiency and corruption of the police force, composed mainly of Indians and discharged European sailors, often drunkards who could not even speak Chinese. Longing for an "efficient, stout, active body of men to be our guardians," the *Hong Kong Register* once described the existing European police officers and constables as "men who crawl along their several beats more asleep than awake—their huge ill-fitting boots and shoes apparently a burden to them—men that an active supple Chinaman would distance in a hundred yards."[21] Governor John Bowring summarized the situation in his annual report for 1854:

> The Police is a costly, dislocated and inefficient body, and its reconstruction has long been deemed a most desirable object . . .
> The heads of the Police are Europeans, the secondary officers half castes, Malays, Hindoos, and other Orientals (not Chinese)

and the lowest functionaries principally Chinese. From the im-
perfect acquaintance with Oriental tongues possessed by the
higher officers the intercourse is unsatisfactory . . . while the little
knowledge that the subordinate officers have of Chinese, makes
them by no means the best instruments for carrying out the regulations. As regards the Chinese themselves, the class who we
have had hitherto at our disposal are so universally corrupt that
it is found impossible safely to employ them.[22]

Both European and Chinese business communities quickly learned to
rely on Chinese guards and street detectives. When in September
1850, within a stone's throw of the Central Police Station, a European
was robbed of a gold watch, the police failed to recover the watch or
capture the two Chinese thieves. He eventually resorted to "the only
feasible plan": hiring Chinese detectives, who quickly located both
watch and thieves.[23] Soon all the major foreign hongs hired their own
guards, as did Chinese merchants, because the police patrolled only
the European section of town.

Unlike similar systems in other Asian colonies, the District Watch
was not imposed from above by the government. In early 1866, amidst
rumors that Chinese in Canton planned to burn and loot Hong Kong,
several neighborhood-committee leaders, including Ho Asik and Tam
Achoy, asked Governor MacDonnell for permission to form a group
of guards and watchmen.[24] MacDonnell was only too happy to agree.
The constables would be under the direct supervision of the registrar
general and deal only with the Chinese section of the city, while the
force would be funded completely by the Chinese community.[25] Despite sporadic tensions on issues such as noise from festivals and religious ceremonies, the government saw the force as evidence that
"substantial and intelligent Chinese were prepared to deal with public
matters."[26] By the 1880s the force's duties had expanded to assisting
with government censuses, conducting detective work in the Chinese
parts of the city, and helping the Po Leung Kuk—a charitable organization established in 1880—locate runaway girls and women forced
into slavery and prostitution.[27] The force also helped the government
keep order in the wake of the Chinese republican revolution of 1911
and during the strikes of the 1920s.

In 1891 the District Watch Committee attained legal status through a new management committee appointed by the governor. This might appear to be an example of the government's successful co-opting of a Chinese organization. Indeed, many of the District Watch activities fit neatly with what Bernard Cohn calls the "officializing" procedures that helped establish and extend the power of the modern European colonial state. Although the District Watch was officially proposed by James Stewart Lockhart, registrar general and colonial secretary, the idea came from Wei Yuk, comprador and unofficial member of the Legislative Council.[28] The management committee would consist of twelve of the most prominent members of the Chinese community, including Wei, Ho Kai (barrister, physician, and financier), and Ho Fook (comprador to Jardine and Matheson and well-known philanthropist). Rather than weakening the committee by making it an appendage of the government, the move strengthened the committee by linking it officially to the government.

One result of linking the District Watch Force to the colonial government was that both the Chinese press and annual government reports now mentioned the force's performance as a responsible, self-managed, and self-financed group. In 1893 the acting registrar general noted how the force relied almost solely on voluntary contributions, so much so that the government did not have to provide its annual contribution.[29] In 1895 Lockhart praised the force for helping bring more than 350 cases before the magistrate and for assisting the police during the laborers' riot of 1894. Two Chinese newspapers published weekly lists of these cases.[30] Lockhart also noted that the force had received a grant for its role during the plague of 1894.[31] In 1912 the registrar general reported that the "excitement bred of the Revolution" in China and an "unintelligent passion for politics" had posed an "element of danger" and "opportunity for the unscrupulous." But the "unostentatious work of the gentlemen on the Committee helped in no small degree the observance of the Colony's regulations and the keeping of the peace."[32] In 1916 the committee's "disinterested advice on questions of all kinds affecting the Chinese community" had once again "proved of the greatest value to the Government."[33]

By the late 1910s and early 1920s, yearly administrative reports routinely referred to the "loyal advice and assistance of this important Committee." But the District Watch's linkage to the colonial government did more than bring praise and publicity to the organization as a whole; it also drew attention to individual members. From the administrative report for 1913 we learn about Eurasian comprador Ho Kam Tong's "public-spirited donation" of five thousand Hong Kong dollars toward the cost of building a watchmen's quarters in Kowloon.[34] Yearly administrative reports listed the retiring or deceased committee members and their replacements, as well as the members reappointed by the governor. The report for 1916 noted that four committee members, including Ho Kam Tong, had been reappointed for five-year terms.[35]

Because of its institutionalized linkage to the government, the District Watch Committee quickly became even more powerful than the Tung Wah Hospital Committee. It enjoyed legal status, and its members were later included in the Civil Service List. Unlike the Tung Wah Hospital, its members were appointed rather than elected. These members served for five years and were almost always reappointed—occasionally up to four terms—while Tung Wah appointments were only for one year. By the early twentieth century, the District Watch had grown from an informal police force to an institutionalized advisory council frequently consulted by the colonial government: for example, during the tram boycott of 1912–1913 and the strike-boycott of 1925–1926, and for labor and trade policies. "In reality," concluded political scientist Lennox Mills in 1942, "the Committee is the Chinese Executive Council of Hong Kong and is consulted on all matters affecting them."[36]

Responsible and Organized Merchants

The Tung Wah Hospital and the District Watch Force are examples of how Chinese leaders used the gulf between government and governed to their own advantage. Throughout the late nineteenth and early twentieth centuries colonial officials and European colonists praised these organizations as evidence of "progress" in the Chinese community.[37] Furthermore, the Chinese leaders used Hong Kong's official, colonial history to distinguish themselves from the rest of Hong Kong's Chinese population.

In an attempt to revise the old colonial histories, scholars have begun to question some of the standard explanations for Hong Kong's economic success. Tak-Wing Ngo has demonstrated how the ascription of this success to liberal government and laissez-faire economic policies—"the Hong Kong legend"—is an artifice of a dominant colonial historiography based on political domination. This historiography, he notes, ignores any "activities not sanctioned by the ruling authorities," such as industrial development by Chinese entrepreneurs, while focusing on the entrepot trade under British merchants. Even though Hong Kong's industries were highly developed before 1949, when entrepreneurs came from Shanghai to escape communist rule, the government maintained that Hong Kong's economic success was due to the entrepot trade. This interpretation followed from colonial policy, which dictated that Hong Kong should be an entrepot, even though Chinese industry was the largest employer in the colony. According to this "artifice of 'good policy'," industry became important only when the government decided it was important. Thus, non-European actors were allowed on the stage only when the colonial government deemed it safe for them.[38]

But "the Hong Kong legend" was built on both domination and collaboration; it benefited both the government and the Chinese merchant community. First, the artifice of good policy was as much the work of Chinese merchants as of the colonial government. In 1881—in a "Congratulatory Address by the Chinese People, Gentry and Merchants of the Whole Colony"—prominent Chinese, including Wei Yuk and Leung On, praised Governor Hennessy:

In the four years of Hennessy's rule, we find strict justice and clear impartiality, felicitous benevolence and tenacious earnestness . . . His multifarious labour in removing oppression and fostering loyalty, and all the other measures of his effective government, are too numerous to count up. There is none among us Chinese who does not reverently look up to him as one of the bright spirits; there is none who does not love him as one loves one's parents. The last four years have passed as if they had been but a day . . . His Excellency is designated by us as the merciful prince, and lauded by all far and near as such . . . Our Chinese people, who have been drinking his gentleness and feeding on his goodness, have silently experienced his educating influence beyond measure, and tranquilly enjoyed the shadow of his protection beyond and above all limit.[39]

Although Hennessy enjoyed a special relationship with the Chinese community, such memorials were not uncommon for other governors. When William Des Voeux, perhaps the colony's laziest governor, took temporary leave in February 1890, the farewell address listed all of his accomplishments: in "the short time" of his government he had performed so "many acts of kindness and benevolence" that it was "impossible to enumerate them all"; he had "constantly consulted the Chinese community before enacting new laws or amending old ones" and "made no class distinctions"; and he had frequently consulted and followed the "humble opinions" of the Chinese population.[40] With such flattering praise from the Chinese business community, small wonder the Hong Kong legend has lasted so long!

Second, while the importance of the entrepot trade should not obscure Hong Kong's earlier industrial development under Chinese entrepreneurs, Hong Kong's historical role as a commercial entrepot meant special recognition for those who contributed to this role. Like other European colonists, the British used various criteria to assess other cultures' level of "civilization": technology, cleanliness, religion, and commerce. But nowhere was commerce more important than in colonial Hong Kong, the fundamental purpose of which was to extract revenues and resources from China. Presenting themselves as a cohesive group of successful, responsible merchants committed to the colony's future helped Chinese merchants win the respect of the colonial government.

The establishment of the Nam Pak Hong Kung So in 1868 was a good sign of this commitment. Originally a mutual-assistance association for the various Chinese import-export firms, it became the largest commercial and occupational group in the colony. Apart from managing guild activities and providing banking and insurance services, the Nam Pak Hong ran a uniformed neighborhood watch force and a fire brigade. As in China, these were services both for the neighborhood and for the safety of corporate holdings. Like the philanthropic and charitable activities of the Tung Wah Hospital, they represented an expansion of Chinese participation in the local "public sphere": the community spirit, urban consciousness, and commitment to collective civic betterment that colonial officials hoped to elicit from their Chinese subjects. Like the Tung Wah Hospital, the Nam Pak Hong mediated during strikes and boycotts. Until the founding of the

Chinese Chamber of Commerce in 1896, the Nam Pak Hong "was the closest thing to a Chinese Chamber of Commerce Hong Kong was to have for many years to come."[41]

The entrepreneurship of local Chinese merchants also impressed the colonial government as proof of their commitment to Hong Kong's commercial future. By the late 1870s, the government became increasingly willing to acknowledge publicly the vital role of Chinese merchants in making Hong Kong a commercial center. Chinese merchants became more prominent in government reports, and in considerably more glowing terms. In his report for 1879–1880, Hennessy explained that Chinese now provided more than 90 percent of government revenue. Chinese merchants were moving into trades previously dominated by Europeans: Hennessy observed that "a considerable amount" of European shipping was "now getting into the hands of Her Majesty's Chinese subjects in this Colony," and that a "fleet of Chinese owned steamers" was "now competing with the foreign shipowners." Chinese merchants had also begun to buy commercial real estate from Europeans. In a speech to Chinese community leaders in April 1881, Hennessy remarked that "the great prosperity" of Hong Kong "was due far more to the [Chinese] merchants, bankers and shopkeepers" than to any labors of his own. Addressing the Legislative Council in June, he attributed the colony's economic progress to its Chinese merchants, "clear-headed, shrewd, intelligent and capable of managing business on a large scale."[42]

In another speech to the Legislative Council, in February 1882, Hennessy noted that the government revenues for 1881 were the largest ever. Whereas in 1876 only 8 of the 20 highest taxpayers had been Chinese, in 1881 all but 3 were Chinese. One Chinese businessman had recently bought two "very important lots" on which to build a large sugar refinery, complete with all the latest European equipment. A group of Chinese merchants had even bought a piece of crown land to make a dock capable of handling large British naval ships. Hennessy could not recall "a time when there was more successful enterprise among all the classes alike of the community Europeans as well as Chinese." Some of the more prominent Chinese had also suggested a joint trust fund for the public good, "further indication of the real progress of Hongkong." Hennessy concluded that "as long as they desire to establish themselves and their descendants in the Colony for ever, so long we have a guarantee for loyalty and good order."[43]

Supporting the Empires

From Outcast to Gentry

Loyalty and good order were especially desirable to a colonial government, but they were also important to any government. Hong Kong's position at the edge of two empires doubled local Chinese merchants' opportunities to obtain respect: from both the Hong Kong government and the Qing government. Like its Ming predecessor, the Qing viewed Chinese emigrants with suspicion, barring them from the accepted channels of upward social mobility, especially the civil service examination. It was especially reluctant to relinquish its negative image of the Hong Kong Chinese, who willingly chose to live in a British colony. Given the active role of Chinese collaborators in the British occupation and settlement of Hong Kong, the Qing's position was hardly irrational.

Despite its negative image of overseas Chinese, the Qing became increasingly eager to cultivate a nominal allegiance from them. Especially from the 1850s on, it became more willing to sell official degrees and titles, both to cover the heavy expenses of the campaigns to suppress the violent uprisings that tore China apart in the mid-1800s, and for famine and flood relief. By the late 1800s, overseas Chinese had become a lucrative source of funding.[44] Chinese merchants in Hong Kong were thus in an ideal position to provide services the Qing needed. Donating to Chinese relief funds proved an important way for these merchants to obtain honors. This occurred both on a large-scale basis by large associations, such as the Tung Wah Hospital, and by merchants on an individual basis. Li Sing, one of the original founders of the Tung Wah Hospital and the Po Leung Kuk, was known for financing bridge and dike works in his native district. Other local Chinese founded schools, libraries, hospitals, and charitable organizations.[45] The Qing consequently began to refer to overseas Chinese as "Chinese subjects" rather than the traditional epithet of "Chinese traitors." The Tung Wah became so involved in fundraising for famine and flood relief in China that it often received praise from Chinese officials. Its efforts after the 1877 floods in Shanxi even won a scroll of thanks from the Qing emperor.[46]

The lack of official Chinese diplomatic representation in Hong Kong until 1891, when a consulate was finally opened, meant that local Chinese merchants gained status by serving as unofficial middlemen between the Chinese community of Hong Kong and the authorities in Canton. The Man Mo Temple Committee hosted Chinese officials passing through the colony and arranged sales of official titles and degrees.[47] These informal diplomatic and consular services were continued by the Tung Wah Hospital.

Status from the Qing government also helped Chinese in Hong Kong obtain and affirm leadership as the local gentry. In a plaque presented in 1884, Chinese officials, including Li Hongzhang—the celebrated "Bismarck of China"—referred to the Tung Wah committee members as the Chinese "gentry" of Hong Kong. Titles and degrees also meant special dress, which visibly separated the holders from commoners. The *Government Gazette* reported that during Governor Hennessy's visit to the Tung Wah Hospital in 1878 there were "nearly 300 influential native residents from all classes of the community; and of those present some 50 or 60 were in their Mandarin costumes, some with blue buttons, some with crystal, and some with gold buttons; while a few had the additional honour of wearing the peacock's feather." Among those in uniform were Ng Choy and compradors Leung On, Wei Akwong, and Kwok Acheong. The journalist Wang Tao recalled that the Tung Wah directors held an annual new year celebration, for which they wore "all sorts of fine headgear and gowns, as if they were illustrious officials having an audience with the emperor!"[48]

Hong Kong merchants' donning official robes has generally been interpreted as an attempt to imitate scholar-officials in China. Such dress surely denoted power and authority, separating its wearers as members of a special class.[49] But mimicry is not always an attempt to be the same. Nor is it necessarily a way of showing respect, tribute, or veneration. As Homi Bhabha argues, it can also be a way of evading control. Similarly, Beth Fowkes Tobin argues that "displaying oneself dressed in another culture's clothing can be a form of empowerment as well as appropriation."[50]

For Chinese merchants, dressing in official robes served several functions. Above all, it let them display their commercial success, which came from living and doing business in a Chinese city outside of China. It helped them impress the other Chinese of Hong Kong, many of whom were unsure of Hong Kong's diplomatic and political status. It showed the colonial government that they also answered to another calling. But it also let them flaunt their status to the Qing government: as men outside "the system," they had nevertheless obtained immense power, status, and wealth. Official Chinese dress in a British colony was thus a visible symbol of Hong Kong's complex position at the edge of two empires.

The View from Hong Kong

Aid to China was also important to the authorities in Hong Kong. In a colony so close to the Chinese mainland, order was crucial, both in Hong Kong and in China. Although Hong Kong's prosperity depended on conditions in China, which often brought useful immigrants, their labor, and their capital to Hong Kong, the colonial government generally preferred peace and order in neighboring Canton. Officials frequently blamed conditions in China for piracy in Hong Kong waters and for crime on land. The colonial government was therefore eager for any aid that might help ensure order across the border.

As important as the aid itself was the way in which Chinese merchants provided assistance. Compare the relief efforts of the Tung Wah Hospital and men such as Li Sing in the 1870s with the earlier experience of Tam Achoy. In February 1860, Tam, along with five British subjects, was charged in Hong Kong with organizing "a hostile expedition against subjects of the Emperor of China."[51] As Tam testified, he had received a request from the ranking official of his home district in Guangdong to help put down "a tribe of Hakkas who had forcibly taken possession" of his village and "were committing great ravages throughout the neighbouring country." He had chartered a steamer from comprador Kwok Acheong, fitted it with guns, and hired English sailors. When two of the sailors were killed, Tam was charged with piracy. Tam and the other defendants claimed that they had attacked the Hakka villages because their inhabitants were involved in piracy, and that they were unaware of breaking any law. Tam insisted that he had acted in response to a Chinese official's request, had shown the colonial registrar general written authority from the Qing government, and had not acted out of financial gain. All pleaded guilty, put themselves at the mercy of the court, and received a reprimand.[52] In 1865 Tam supplied the local militia in his home district with Western arms and munitions. Although such actions earned Tam official recognition from the Chinese authorities and a biography in the local gazetteer, the colonial government preferred more orderly forms of aid to China.

British Empire Activities

Local Chinese merchants also impressed the colonial government by participating vigorously in the type of empire activities that have generally been examined only from the perspective of the colonial state. Bernard Cohn observes how early modern European states displayed their power through "theatrical displays" of "ritual performance and dramatic display" designed to ensure the "well-being and continued power of the rulers over the ruled."[53] In India, for example, royal visits aimed to inspire the loyalty of Indian princes and to validate their role in the preservation of the British Empire.[54] But the role of colonized peoples in these activities has generally been neglected.

When British royalty began to take notice of Hong Kong in the second part of the nineteenth century, Chinese merchants were ready to be noticed. During the visit of the Duke of Edinburgh in 1869, Chinese merchants organized a banquet, theatrical performance, and traditional lion dance. In 1879, Chinese donated more than half of the sum collected for the Irish Famine Fund and were the largest individual subscribers.[55] In 1887, on the fiftieth anniversary of Queen Victoria's coronation, Chinese merchants again organized the festivities. Governor Des Voeux recalled that the first party to arrive at Government House was a "large deputation of Chinese, bringing a splendidly embroidered address to the Queen, containing a striking recognition of British justice." The Man Mo Temple Committee presented a tablet engraved in Chinese with the words "Everlasting Prosperity," later affixed to the facade of Government House. Bonfires on the hilltops, European gas lanterns with Chinese and Japanese paper lanterns hanging "literally in millions" from houses on the terraces, and illuminated vessels in the harbor: all "made a spectacle which could hardly be equalled outside of fairyland." The Chinese procession the next day was more than four miles long and consisted of some ten thousand people. With laborers barefoot but all wearing coats or hats provided by Chinese merchants, and four dragons each over 100 feet long, the procession was truly a "mixture of splendour and squalor." The night procession, which included two silk dragons lit up from inside, was over 1 mile long. Although the European colonists had "evidently made strenuous efforts to provide a display worthy of the occasion . . . what was far more striking was the feeling which animated the Chinese." This, Des Voeux concluded, "can hardly be more striking of their appreciation of the government to which they had been subject during Her Majesty's reign."[56] In his annual report, Des Voeux noted that the "British Community fell short of no other in its outward expression of loyalty; but the most striking feature of the occasion was the heartiness with which the Chinese took part in it . . . There can scarcely be better proof that they are, on the whole, satisfied with the rule, of which they have now had some 45 years' experience."[57]

Whether the Chinese merchants were as satisfied with British rule as Des Voeux imagined, they had learned that being part of a global empire provided numerous outlets for recognition. In the celebrations for the 1891 jubilee of Hong Kong's fifty years as a British colony, Chinese businessmen were active members of the Jubilee Committee.[58] Ho Kam Tong, one of three wealthy Eurasian brothers and assistant comprador to Jardine and Matheson, raised money for the widows and children of British troops killed in the Boer War and for the London Tropical School of Medicine. In 1892 and 1907, Ho planned banquets for the visiting Duke and Duchess of Connaught. Ho's brother, Robert Ho Tung, chief comprador to Jardine and Matheson, administered Queen Victoria's Diamond Jubilee Fund and the South African War Fund. During the First World War, Ho Tung donated the cost of two airplanes and several ambulances to the British government. Chau Siu-ki, real estate developer and insurance and shipping magnate, served on the War Charities Committee. Ip Lan Chuen was secretary of the Chinese section of the War Charity Fund. In April 1924, Ip supervised the committee that represented Hong Kong Chinese merchants at the British Empire Exhibition in London.[59] Just as royal visits and representation at empire exhibitions helped put places like Hong Kong on the map for many Britons, they enabled prominent Hong Kong merchants to distinguish themselves, at home and across the empire.

Colonial Education

Hong Kong's education system also helped Chinese merchants become a special class and win the respect of the colonial government. Colonial education has long been condemned as merely a tool of imperialism.[60] Alistair Pennycook has recently argued that British educational policies in colonial Malaya provided "an English-educated elite and a vernacular-educated population better able to participate in a colonial economy."[61] For postcolonialists, education exemplifies the potent disciplinary powers of the modern state. In colonial Egypt, writes Timothy Mitchell, the "order and discipline of modern schooling were to be the hallmark and the method of a new form of political power." Education was designed to shape and discipline both the body and the mind, "from the inside out." Gauri Viswanathan argues that the teaching of English literature masked economic exploitation and political domination in British India. But to other scholars, the emphasis on education as a colonial tool obscures how colonial education was shaped at all levels by interactions between colonizer and colonized, and between metropole and colony. Many Indians, including nationalist reformers opposed to British rule, demanded English education. In West Africa and Indochina, the type and curriculum of education were shaped both by the French colonial regime's designs and by the natives' attitudes toward education. In Taiwan, Japanese education was also influenced by the demands of the Taiwanese elite.[62]

Where does Hong Kong's education system fit in this debate? Colonial education was designed to produce students for the colonial, capitalist economy and to help further Sino-British commercial and diplomatic relations. "The schools," writes Bernard Luk, "sought to produce a bilingual, bicultural elite to function as middlemen between the British traders in Hong Kong and the merchants and mandarins of China." And especially after the turbulent 1920s, the colonial government used the education system to promote traditional Chinese culture against the ideas of nationhood and citizenship so prevalent

on the mainland.[63] But as Alice Ng has argued, colonial education in
Hong Kong was not "an uncritical transfer of content and system from
the metropolitan country." It was shaped by several factors, including
the "social composition and attitude of the local Chinese community."[64]

Rather than focus on the intentions behind colonial education, consider some of the results. Colonial education provided invaluable opportunities, in Hong Kong and in China, for future Chinese businessmen. It enabled boys from the colony and China to learn English,
which was vital for a position in the colonial civil service, with European firms in Hong Kong, or in the Imperial Chinese Maritime
Customs. It built networks that would carry over into their business
careers. It also allowed graduates to compete, often very successfully,
with foreign merchants in Hong Kong and in China. Finally, although
racial discrimination from the European community would persist well
into the twentieth century, colonial education enabled Chinese businessmen to navigate between cultures and to win some degree of acceptance from the European community of Hong Kong.

The last point is especially important. While organizations like the
Man Mo Temple, the Tung Wah Hospital, and the District Watch
Force enabled Chinese merchants to gain the respect of the local Chinese community and both Chinese and colonial governments, they
often had the opposite effect on the local European community. European residents frequently suspected the Man Mo Temple of trying
to control "native affairs," while from the beginning the local English
press resented the Tung Wah Hospital's non-medical work, fearing
that the hospital would become an *imperium in imperio* that might turn
the Chinese population against the government. Whereas the close
relationship between the Tung Wah Hospital and both Chinese and
colonial governments enhanced the image of the hospital among the
local Chinese population, it made the European community suspicious.[65]

The European community's attitude toward these Chinese organizations cannot be separated from its attitudes toward the Chinese population in general. Early Hong Kong society was divided into many
sub-groups that, apart from being connected by the circulation of
goods and labor, often had little contact with each other. Governor
John Bowring lamented in 1858 that "the separation of the native

population from the European is nearly absolute; social intercourse between the races is wholly unknown."[66] Visiting Europeans were frequently shocked by the local Europeans' scorn and disdain for the Chinese, noting how Europeans would beat Chinese coolies with sticks and umbrellas. In 1877 a visiting Englishman complained that British military officers treated Chinese "as if they were a very inferior kind of animal to themselves." When Governor Arthur Kennedy and his successor, Hennessy, began receiving prominent Chinese at Government House, European traders and their wives refused to accept invitations to functions at Government House. Hennessy was considered so "pro-Chinese" that when he left the colony in February 1882, no members of the British business community went to the pier for the traditional farewell ceremony. Leading members of the Chinese community, however, bid the governor farewell, presenting him with gifts and embroidered silk banners.[67]

The British community's prejudice toward the Chinese population was based on a combination of class and cultural, national, and racial superiority. But because the Britons' disdain for Chinese was based on both ethnocentricity and class, they were more accepting of those Chinese who could appear to be less Chinese or who had achieved commercial success—even more so if they could claim both qualities. Britons furthermore generally considered Chinese as superior to other "natives" in their colonies. Comparing them favorably to the Malays, a British merchant in Singapore once described the Chinese, "as a race, quite capable of civilisation of the highest kind. They are at once labourers and statesmen. They can work in any climate, hot or cold, and they have great mercantile capacity." And even among one group of "natives," some were more capable of becoming "less native" than others. Europeans in Hong Kong were often fascinated by wealthier Chinese, especially those who spoke English and, as Lethbridge put it, "showed evidence of some degree of anglicization." An editorial in the *China Mail* from March 1847 catches an early glimpse of this fascination. Commenting on a visit to Hong Kong en route to Canton by Whampoa, a rich Singapore merchant, the writer observes that Whampoa, only thirty-two years old, is already very rich. Moreover, "he is a remarkable man, combining the features and costume of a Chinese, with thoroughly English feelings and a command of the English language to express them."[68]

In 1847 no Chinese in Hong Kong could have charmed the European community the way Whampoa did. When in 1856 Governor Bowring raised the question of more representation in government, including appointing English-speaking Chinese to the Legislative Council as they were in Singapore, he suggested encouraging Chinese to learn English as "the means of access to social distinction."[69] In his response, however, the colonial secretary doubted whether "education has made much progress among the youthful population as to give promise that the next generation will be much superior to the present in moral culture ... The testimony of those best acquainted with them, represent the Chinese race as endowed with much intelligence, but as very deficient in the most essential elements of morality."[70] But by the 1870s and 1880s, a generation of bicultural, wealthy Hong Kong Chinese had evolved, mainly as a result of the colony's education system. When in 1880 the colonial secretary reluctantly approved Governor Hennessy's appointment of Ng Choy as the first Chinese unofficial member of the Legislative Council, he did so partly because of the "educational advantages" that Ng had gained from studying at St. Paul's College in Hong Kong and at Lincoln's Inn in London.[71]

Many of these men were educated at the integrated Central School (later called Queen's College), founded in 1862 as an amalgamation of three pre-existing government schools.[72] From its establishment the Central School was remarkably successful in drawing Chinese students. In 1864 the *Government Gazette* reported that the school continued to "grow in favour with the Chinese" and that applicants considerably exceeded those accepted, even after school fees were charged in 1863.[73] An education at the Central School could mean a good job with a foreign firm, in the Imperial Chinese Maritime Customs, or at the new government schools in China.

Whether they started their business careers in Hong Kong or in China, graduates of the Central School became some of the most successful businessmen in the colony. For example, Yung Hin Pong became the comprador of the Hong Kong branch of the Chartered Bank of India, Australia, and China. Sin Tak Fan, a Eurasian, taught at the school after graduating until 1878, when he became a government clerk and interpreter. In 1880 Sin left government service for the first of a series of positions with prestigious British legal firms.[74]

Wong Kam Fuk became comprador of the Hongkong and Kowloon Wharf and Godown, the managing director of a Chinese steamship company, and co-owner of a cotton-yarn business.[75] Chau Siu-ki founded several important insurance companies and was a powerful banker, shipper, and developer. Lau Chu Pak became comprador to A. S. Watson's, one of the colony's oldest firms; co-founder of the Chinese Chamber of Commerce in 1896; and a director of the Tung Wah Hospital, Po Leung Kuk, and District Watch Committee. Ho Wing Tsun became the comprador of the Hong Kong branch of the Banque de l'Indo Chine. She Posham was the comprador to the Hongkong Hotel. Ng Hon Tsz, comprador to the National Bank of China, was also the assistant manager of the Yuen Fat Hong, one of the oldest and most important Chinese trading houses in Hong Kong, where he was in charge of the firm's foreign business. Wong Lai-Sang joined the Great Northern Telegraph Company of Shanghai. After a decade with the Hong Kong Public Works Department, he worked for a British architect and co-founded his own gasoline-lamp firm.[76]

The best known of the Central School graduates were the Eurasian Ho brothers. Robert Ho Tung, who entered the school in 1873, became an internationally known tycoon. He joined the Chinese Imperial Customs after graduating but resigned in 1880 to become comprador of Jardine and Matheson. A millionaire by the age of thirty, he was a financier, property and steamship owner with interests in shipping and insurance, and import-export merchant. Ho was generally believed to be the wealthiest man in Hong Kong and was associated with practically every large business in the colony, either as shareholder or director. Former chairman of the Tung Wah Hospital Committee, Ho Tung was a renowned philanthropist, both in Hong Kong and in China.[77] His brother Ho Kam Tong was Jardine's assistant comprador, a flourishing businessman, and a committee member of the Tung Wah Hospital. Even more so than his brother, Ho Kam Tong was known in Hong Kong and China for his public service and philanthropy.[78] Another brother, Ho Fook, graduated in 1881 and then joined a Chinese shipping firm in Vietnam. Ho Fook later became assistant comprador at Jardine's, eventually succeeding Ho Tung as head comprador when the latter retired. With his partner, Lo Cheung Shiu, who taught at the Central School for seven years after graduating and then worked briefly in the government treasury as a clerk, Ho Fook owned and managed Ho Fook and Company—a firm that transported sugar between Hong Kong and Chinese ports.[79]

Guides and Directories

One indicator of how far the Chinese businessmen of Hong Kong had "progressed" by the turn of the century is the way they were described in English-language guides and directories to Hong Kong. Whereas earlier works usually omitted any serious mention of Chinese businessmen, by the turn of the century this had changed. Consider, for example, *Twentieth Century Impressions of Hongkong, Shanghai, and other Treaty Ports of China*. This directory, part of a series on the British dependencies, was published in London in 1908 by Lloyd's Greater Britain Publishing Company, Ltd., which had offices throughout the empire. Although the commentary on sport and social life focuses mainly on the European community in Hong Kong, considerable attention is paid to the Chinese business and professional classes.

It is possible to read these directories as attempts to claim the "Far East" and its inhabitants for British readers and to demonstrate Britain's mastery over the world. Beth Fowkes Tobin, for example, argues that even something as seemingly objective as natural-history illustration could be an integral part of the imperial effort to gather information about the world's natural resources and to manipulate them: "The white border and snipped twig of late–eighteenth-century botanical illustration reinforced the idea that a plant could be plucked from one cultural and ecological context and inserted into another with ease and with little regard for negative consequences."[80] Throughout *Twentieth Century Impressions* are illustrations and photographs—the harbor, landscape, buildings, villages, homes, people, statues, and the entire Tung Wah Hospital Committee—all extracted from their natural context and transported to readers in Britain. In one page of photographs, readers are introduced to Ho Fook, his wives, sons, and daughters, and their family home in the Mid Levels.[81]

Such directories may also be read as a reflection of the way Hong Kong society should be organized. In the Hong Kong section of *Twentieth Century Impressions*, for example, we find two categories of brief biographies: "Social and Professional Biographies" of Europeans and

"Oriental Social and Professional Biographies." This separation rein-
forces the point that Europeans and Chinese are, and should be, dis-
crete groups. It also makes clear who is more important. Although the
Chinese outnumber the Europeans, they come after the Europeans in
the directory sequence. Another section, on the "Oriental Mercantile
Community," provides brief biographies of Chinese, Parsi, and Japanese firms.

But what did such guides do for these people? First, they saved
many Chinese businessmen in Hong Kong from historical obscurity
and served as an alternative official history, memorializing the prominent Chinese businessmen of Hong Kong. By distinguishing the
"prominent members of the Chinese community of Hong Kong," the
directories also separate such men from the rest of the colony's Chinese population. Through either family background or hard work,
these men have become celebrated members of Hong Kong society:
for example, Lau Chu Pak—"a native of Hongkong and a member of
a good old Cantonese family." Choa Leep Chee, sugar merchant and
comprador to the China Sugar Refinery, is head of "a good old Chinese family that has been prominently connected with the British colonies" in Singapore and Malaya "for more than five generations." Photographs of the home, business, drawing room, and family history of
Ng Li-hing, the head of Goh Guan Hin, one of the colony's oldest
general merchants, help provide authenticity.

These sources also explain what is required to become a prominent
member of the Chinese community. By celebrating the men's rise to
fame and success, the guides show the correct way to do this. Chau
Siu-ki "owes his position entirely to his own initiative and keen business instinct." Wong Kam Fuk is "a man of shrewd business ability."
"In the management of affairs entrusted to him," Ho Kam Tong "has
always displayed great ability, and has gradually forged his way to the
front." Like his brothers, Ho Fook has "distinguished himself both by
his business acumen and by his activity in the wider sphere of philanthropy and public service." "Hard work and honest endeavour, followed by steady and well-earned promotion," readers learn, "is, in
brief, the record of Mr. Sin Tak Fan." Through his "perseverance and
keen business instincts," Wong Lai-Sang has "gained not only a good
comfortable position for himself but a good reputation among both
Europeans and Chinese." By showing how the men are all members

of the Tung Wah Hospital, District Watch, Sanitary Board, or Pò Leung Kuk, the guides stress the importance of these organizations as markers of status in Hong Kong.

Works such as *Twentieth Century Impressions* portray these Chinese men as members of a group with certain collective standards of success—being bicultural, urbane, and modern gentlemen—even while stressing individual skills and attributes. Choa Leep Chee lives at "Burnside," surrounded by "some hundreds of varieties of English and European flowers." Ho Kam Tong's colonial-style villa has its own Chinese garden. Lau Chu Pak lives in an English-style villa named "Ardmore" and is a "thoroughly up-to-date man, well versed in the customs of Western civilization." Lau has also contributed "a great deal toward establishing cordial relations between his countrymen and Europeans." Indeed, his ability to navigate between cultures is as impressive as his business success. Robert Ho Tung has built many residences in a Chinese-British hybrid style, the "pride of the British Colony and the admiration of the visitor." His own home, the most spectacular of these residences, has the quaint English name "Idlewild" and offers a magnificent view of the colony's majestic harbor. These are also men with the time and money for leisure. Several are avid gardeners and horticulturists. In 1905 Choa Leep Chee's garden at Burnside won the governor's award for the best-kept private garden, an award that went to Robert Ho Tung's garden at Idlewild in 1907. Ho Kam Tong, who loves horticulture and photography, has won many prizes in floral shows and photography contests. Most have some overseas experience. Robert Ho Tung has traveled throughout China and Asia, and twice to North America and Europe. His brother Ho Fook's "outlook has been widened by much travel," including two trips to Europe and one to America.

Furthermore, the guides stress that these prominent Chinese men have all made the best of their English education, to which they owe their success. They all appreciate the benefits of their English education and are eager to ensure that their own children receive the same education. Like their father, the children of Ho Wing Tsun are all receiving "a first-class English education." Ho Fook, who "recognises the advantages which, in a British Colony, naturally follow from a thorough grasp of Western methods," is making sure that his children "shall enjoy these advantages to the fullest extent." And "thanks to his father's clear realisation of the advantages which follow upon such an equipment," Wong Lai-Sang's only son has also been given a "thoroughly sound English education."

Finally, the guides highlight the role that successful Chinese men play in Hong Kong's economy and society. They have all dedicated themselves to the economic and social improvement of the colony. This is especially clear in the case of Robert Ho Tung, who despite health problems remains "one of the most enterprising and public-spirited men in the island." Ho Tung's brothers are also praised for their public spirit. "Whenever a good cause is in need of assistance," whether in China, Hong Kong, or elsewhere in the empire, Ho Kam Tong "is always one of the first to come to its aid." Ho was active in every major philanthropic or charitable organization in the colony and on his own—distributing medicine during the plague of 1894, establishing scholarships at local schools, and providing coffins to poor Chinese families who would otherwise leave their deceased in the streets. During the Boxer "troubles" of 1900, Ho personally traveled to Beijing, where he chartered steamers to evacuate refugees. He also helped families of Japanese soldiers killed in the Russo-Japanese War of 1904–1905. "In fact," readers learn, "he never tires of well-doing."

Regardless of their intent—whether to display the human "holdings" of the British Empire or to illustrate how a colonial society should be organized—these guides and directories distinguished such Chinese from the rest of the colony's Chinese residents. By showing how far some Chinese businessmen had come since the colony's early days, they explained the rules for making it to the top of Hong Kong society. By listing the right organizations and activities, they highlighted the standards of success in colonial Hong Kong and celebrated the men who had contributed so greatly to the colony's economy and society. As the "Who's Who" of Hong Kong, such works would eventually enable the Chinese businessmen of the colony to survive in the historical record, even after the British Empire had faded into the imperial sunset.

~ 4

A Place of Their Own:
Clubs and Associations

$\mathcal{B}$Y THE END OF the nineteenth century, the Hong
Kong Chinese business elite had become a full-fledged bourgeoisie.
Despite their increased wealth and status, however, they continued to
face racial discrimination from the European community. This chapter
looks at how Chinese business and community leaders dealt with one
aspect of this discrimination: their exclusion from the elite social world
of the European bourgeoisie. By establishing an elite network of clubs
and associations, the leaders of the Chinese bourgeoisie created an
equally exclusive social world. By doing so, they strengthened their
own social position, both in relation to the European community, and
among the Chinese population of Hong Kong.

The Rise of the Chinese Bourgeoisie

Bourgeois status in Hong Kong was predicated largely on wealth. By
the end of the nineteenth century, Hong Kong was the center of a
Chinese capitalist expansion that ranged from China to Southeast Asia.
In the late 1880s local Chinese merchants bought shares in the
European-run Hong Kong, Canton, and Macao Steam Boat Company.
By the late 1890s Li Sing and Poon Pong were directors of the firm,
while the Eurasian Sin Tak Fan was the largest non-European share-
holder. As in China, Hong Kong compradors and merchants were

active investors in foreign manufacturing, finishing, and packaging industries, and in public utilities. In many cases, Chinese owned 60 percent of the shares, sometimes more than 80 percent.[1]

Apart from controlling trade with China and Southeast Asia, Chinese began to dominate Hong Kong's industrial sector. In September 1899, Governor Henry Blake wrote that "the growth in number and variety of the manufactures" over the past five years "shows that Chinamen are not too conservative to turn their capital and abilities into [*sic*] new directions." Property was also a critical economic factor for the growth of this class. In 1895 the Hong Kong Land Investment Agency included Li Sing and Poon Pong among its Chinese shareholders. By the early 1900s, Chinese owned the most real estate in Hong Kong. In October 1900, Blake reported to Colonial Secretary Joseph Chamberlain that "the richer Chinese have during the year purchased many residences in Victoria hitherto occupied by Europeans."[2]

The rising economic status of the Chinese bourgeoisie was also evident in the growth of a consumer culture and conspicuous consumption, with advertising now aimed at the Chinese upper classes. Department stores such as the Sincere Company, founded in 1900 by Ma Ying Piu, an overseas Chinese from Australia, and the Wing On Department Store, founded in 1907 by the Kwok brothers, also from Australia, signaled the growth of a bourgeois Chinese commercial culture. Here, Chinese shoppers could purchase almost anything they desired, without having to endure the humiliating looks and disdain they encountered in European establishments such as Lane, Crawford & Co., the premier British department store in Hong Kong.[3]

Yet another sign of the rising power of the Chinese bourgeoisie was the growth of a corporate culture. Newly formed organizations represented the interests of the Chinese business community, such as the Chinese Chamber of Commerce, founded in 1896 by prominent merchants and compradors. The chamber unified the various Chinese guilds and native-place associations, and it represented Chinese commercial interests against the European-dominated Hong Kong General Chamber of Commerce. But it was also founded to promote a modern Chinese business class in Hong Kong. Finally, local Chinese and overseas Chinese founded new banks and financial institutions. Established in 1919, the Bank of East Asia was the first Chinese-capitalized bank traded on the Hong Kong Stock Exchange. The prime movers were Kan Tong-po, comprador to the Yokohama Specie Bank and the National City Bank of New York, and the brothers Li Koon-chun and Li Tse-fong. When new Chinese industrialists turned to these new banks for capital, the Chinese bourgeoisie of Hong Kong had truly come of age.[4]

Self-Perceptions

The leaders of this bourgeoisie saw themselves as a special class, distinct from the rest of the local Chinese population. With the British, they had built Hong Kong from a barren rock into a thriving, stable metropolis. In their calls for economic, political, and social reform in China, these men indirectly reaffirmed their own status as members of a special, privileged class. Like the emerging local bourgeoisies in other British colonies and territories, when Chinese businessmen expressed their conviction that commercialism and capitalism were the cure for China's ills, they were also affirming the distinctive importance of the Chinese bourgeoisie in Hong Kong.[5]

That these men no longer saw themselves as ordinary members of the Chinese population was especially evident in March 1901, when a group of prominent Chinese residents asked Governor Blake to establish a special school exclusively for their own children. The eight petitioners, their occupations, and their backgrounds provide a useful insight into a cross-section of the Chinese bourgeoisie. The first signature on the petition was that of Ho Kai, barrister, physician, financier, and unofficial member of the Legislative Council. A close friend of Ho Kai, and an unofficial Legislative Council member, Wei Yuk was comprador to the Mercantile Bank of India, Ltd. and former chairman of the Tung Wah Hospital. One of the first Chinese to study in Britain, Wei was educated in England and Scotland.[6] The rest of the petitioners also had impressive credentials. Fung Wa Chun, previously comprador to the National Bank of China, was comprador to a large American firm, a successful opium merchant, and co-founder of the Chinese Chamber of Commerce. Chow Tung Shang was the chairman of the National Bank of China, and Uen Lai Chün and Lo Kun Ting were, respectively, chairman and ex-chairman of the Tung Wah Hospital Committee. Tso Seen Wan, a prominent solicitor educated in England, was for some years the only Chinese solicitor practicing in Hong Kong. Like Ho Kai, Tso was well known in the Chinese community, both as a lawyer and an adviser on foreign matters. Wei On, one of Wei Yuk's two sons and also educated in England, was an influential solicitor.[7]

Referring to themselves as representatives of "an important and influential section of the Chinese Community," the petitioners explained the need for "a suitable English School for the education of the children—both boys and girls—of the upper classes of the Chinese resident in this Colony." Praising the government for providing education to the colony's Chinese and foreign residents, they lamented how education for Chinese had been "directed almost exclusively" toward the "lower and lower middle classes" at the expense of the "higher and more thorough training of the children of the more well-to-do classes." Schools such as Queen's College, which some petitioners had attended when it was called the Central School, were "excellent Government institutions in their way." But "the indiscriminate and intimate mingling of children from families of the most various social and moral standing" rendered them "absolutely undesirable as well as unsuitable for the sons and daughters of respectable Chinese families." Given the large increase in the Chinese population of a "higher social status and permanently residing in this Colony," it was time that "some provision be made for a secondary education for their children."[8]

The petitioners couched their request in terms guaranteed to please colonial administrators, showing how well they had learned to work within the colonial situation. Not only were they acknowledging the superiority of English education, but by asking for "commensurate advance" and "equal provision" for the education of Chinese girls, they presented themselves as reformers. Chinese in Hong Kong had "failed to assimilate to any extent English sympathies and ideas" and were "ever backward in responding to the call of public duties." Echoing British conceptions of Hong Kong's historic mission to open China, the petitioners noted how the new school would "not only endow our young men and women with more open minds and greater public spirit" but would also "result in the more cordial co-operation of the British and Chinese nations and closer intercourse between them." The value of education ("one of the best forms of national investment") outweighed the expense and would increase "commercial and industrial efficiency" and promote a "higher level of civic duty." Most important, it would contribute to the "wider diffusion of moral culture and religious feeling" that the colony's Chinese residents so sorely lacked.[9]

Government Perceptions

While the petition says much about the self-perceptions of the Chinese business elite, colonial administrators' comments illustrate how the government saw these Chinese. In his dispatch to Chamberlain, Governor Blake—"remembering that the better classes of Chinese are as anxious as any European to preserve their children from contact with children of a lower class, intimate communication with whom would be prejudicial to their moral character"—supported the proposal. Inspector of Schools A. W. Brewin, who had "long been convinced of the necessity for a school for the better class of Chinese," was duly impressed by the credentials of the petitioners, noting that four of them had been educated in England.[10] Another inspector, E. A. Irving, wrote that although the proposal clearly suggested "class legislation," it was "fully justifiable" because it proposed to "turn out Chinese boys well equipped with the best sort of education and thoroughly in sympathy with modern ideas." Irving felt that "a great deal of the money spent on teaching smatterings to boys who do not pursue their education" was "wasted," and that government policy should be to help Chinese boys who were "willing to receive a comparatively complete education."[11] Like the petitioners, colonial officials considered the new school essential, not only for the preservation of the "respectable" Chinese upper classes of Hong Kong but also for the future of China. Blake predicted that if the school were to attract upper-class children from the mainland who would "probably form part of the official class of the future," the consequences would be "far-reaching and the benefit to this country may amply repay the small outlay that the scheme demands."[12] Although some members of the Chinese community objected, the new school—St. Stephen's College—was built the next year.

The Persistence of Race

Despite their status and wealth, the leaders of the Chinese bourgeoisie faced racial discrimination that permeated Hong Kong society. Some historians have suggested that discrimination in Hong Kong even increased during the first part of the twentieth century. From the beginning, the colony's Chinese and Europeans had generally lived apart, but not until the twentieth century did the government use legislation to preserve residential exclusiveness for non-Chinese.[13] Although racism and discrimination are not easily quantified, Hong Kong's experience seems not to have been unique. As Indonesian colonial cities developed, they also became increasingly more segregated than in earlier times. Across the globe in Kingston, Jamaica, another British colony, spatial segregation developed after the banning of slavery and the rise of a black merchant class.[14]

European parents in Hong Kong went to great lengths to protect their children from the so-called negative influences of the Chinese. In a letter to the *Daily Press* in January 1901, "A Parent" expressed disappointed surprise that Hong Kong had no school for Europeans only, whereas all the Chinese treaty ports already did: "It is impossible to conceive that European lads can benefit morally from intimate contact with Chinese boys." Later that month the *China Mail* asserted that "European children in this Colony have been ruined irretrievably by intercourse with and contamination from the mixed races with whom they have had to associate in the elementary schools."[15] The same year a group of Europeans, including the heads of all the major hongs, persuaded the government to open a separate school for Europeans, arguing that "the education of the European children suffers very much from the fact that Europeans and Asiatics are mixed" and that "constant contact with Chinese, both in class-room and playground must affect the formation of the character of the European boy." Governor Blake, worried about "the deteriorating moral effects of the mixture of the two races in school," found the proposal "highly expedient." Inspector Irving, who had previously served in the Chinese Protectorate in Malaya, wrote that while "I have the greatest respect for the many good qualities of the Chinese . . . I would strongly object to send children of my own to attend a mixed school." Irving agreed that the school should be reserved for "scholars of European British Parentage exclusively." The Kowloon School was originally built and presented to the government by the Eurasian Robert Ho Tung as an English school open to all races, but now the government persuaded Ho Tung to let the school be used only for European students. Ho Tung reluctantly agreed, regretting a decision "so opposed to the spirit which prompted my offer of the school to the Colony." Although Colonial Secretary Joseph Chamberlain worried that schooling along racial lines would become the standard for the colony, he eventually sanctioned the Kowloon British School because the parents demanded it.[16]

In 1908 a Western resident proposed in an English language newspaper that special seats on trams and in parks be reserved for foreigners.[17] Although this resulted only in a heated debate in the local press, segregation was often enforced both informally and legally. In some hotels, Chinese guests could stay only in certain rooms or could not stay overnight. European officers of the Hong Kong and Shanghai Bank were discouraged from marrying non-British women; until the Second World War, no bank officer had married a Chinese.[18] Marriage between European civil servants was not legally prohibited, but it was discouraged: European policemen who married Chinese or Eurasians were not allowed to re-enlist after their contracts expired, while prison wardens and employees in the Public Works Department who married Chinese or Eurasians were not allowed to live in government quarters. In 1912, Governor Francis May boasted that under his administration no European police officers or prison officers were married to Chinese or Eurasians.[19] Chinese and foreign visitors were often struck by the width of the racial divide in Hong Kong.

The Peak of Discrimination

One of the most visible examples of the government-enforced racial divide was the Peak, the exclusive hill district on Hong Kong Island. Perched high above the rest of the colony, the Peak was often compared to Simla, the Indian hill station north of Delhi where the British elite went to escape from the heat and, more important, from the Indians. Complete with its own police station and water supply pumped from below, the Peak had all the features of a quaint English town—English-style homes and villas, clubs, a hotel, a hospital, and an Anglican church—connected to the city below by the Peak Tram, which opened in May 1888.[20] No Chinese, except for the servants, cooks, and drivers in their special uniforms, were to live there. In 1902 this residential segregation became law when the Colonial Office supported an ordinance preserving the Peak district for residents approved by the governor, including Chinese of good standing. Under the 1904 Peak District Reservation Ordinance, however, no Chinese, except for servants, were allowed to live on the Peak. After certain loopholes in the 1904 ordinance became apparent, an ordinance of 1918 guaranteeing that the Peak would remain European survived until after the Second World War.

The determined efforts to reserve the Peak for Europeans illustrate three interrelated points: the often-precarious nature of colonial rule; the need to place the Peak (and Hong Kong) in its comparative colonial perspective; and the importance of hill stations in British colonialism. As Anthony King and Dane Kennedy have argued, the hill stations tell more about British colonialism than their quaint, almost comical, appearances might suggest.[21] According to King, the hill station was a "social physical place" that "both resulted from and helped to maintain the social structure and social behaviour of the British colonial community in India."[22] Similarly, amidst the fears of increased contact with Chinese and rising economic competition from the Chinese bourgeoisie, these movements were attempts to preserve the status and social structure of the elite European community of Hong Kong.

Colonial culture has long been portrayed as one of self-confidence and superiority, an assumption that only recently scholars have begun to question. Dane Kennedy shows how the white settler culture in Kenya and Southern Rhodesia, far from being based on confidence and assurance, "was preeminently the expression of the white community's tenuously held position of predominance in the colonial order. The power to shape and control social identity, to determine the distinctions between themselves and others, was crucial to that predominance."[23] Nor could the facade of colonial superiority mask the consuming fear of the tropics and their physical and psychological effects. Well into the mid-twentieth century, Europeans drew on the latest biological and social theories to argue whether whites could ever thrive in the tropics. Medical manuals often cautioned that whites would lose their health, energy, and cultural orientations if they remained in the tropics too long.[24]

Thus the ostensible purpose of the hill stations was as sanitaria and resorts, grounded in the "ethnomedical beliefs" that diseases such as cholera, malaria, and typhoid occurred less often in the hill regions.[25]

But the hill stations were also designed to help the British remain British. Re-creating colonial hill stations as what Kennedy calls "nostalgic simulacra" helped the British construct a sense of community and identity in their alien environment. Here "the British could restore the physical and psychic energies they needed for their imperial tasks, replicate the social and cultural environments that embodied the values they sought to project, and regulate and reproduce the individual agents who were vital to the continuance of their rule."[26] The stations were also attempts to preserve some semblance of colonial prestige against the rising socioeconomic status of non-whites. In India, fears of contact with upwardly mobile Indians were frequently encoded as concerns about hygiene, sanitation, and disease. Acts and ordinances to preserve the health of white colonists were designed to construct, repair, and maintain racial barriers.

Finally, the hill stations were strategic centers of colonial power and control. Although Hong Kong was never seriously threatened by any domestic uprisings or attacks from neighboring China, the distance from the Chinese provided by the Peak enabled the British to maintain their sense of superiority and control. Even today, a short walk round the Peak offers a panoramic view of Hong Kong Island, the harbor, and Kowloon. Before Britain leased the New Territories in 1898, one could see beyond Kowloon into imperial China. Governor William Des Voeux recalled the view from the governor's residence, "Mountain Lodge": from one veranda was "a magnificent prospect over the China Sea, comprehending a long line of mountainous coast and innumerable islands." Crucial to this sense of superiority and control was the Peak's separation from the Chinese population. As Des Voeux explained, "neither sight nor sound gave any token of human existence, and it seemed difficult to realise that within so short a distance was a dense population." From certain spots on the Peak "could be seen immediately beneath one's feet the whole length of the town of Victoria."[27] From the Peak, a colonial official could see more than just the ships, junks, and sampans in the harbor. He could survey—as if a display of the colony's subjects—the Chinese workers who, forbidden to use the Peak Tram, carried their loads up the steep Old Peak Road; the Portuguese, Jews, Armenians, Parsis, Japanese merchants, and the Chinese and Eurasian compradors, who lived in the Mid-Levels; and, at the very bottom, the Chinese laborers in their tenement buildings.

And who knows how many administrative issues were decided on morning walks in the rarefied air of the Peak?

But without legal enforcement, the Peak could not be maintained as a European reserve any more than the hill stations could in India. As in India, concerns about European health were linked to fears of increased "native" wealth. In May 1904, 80 of the 90 property owners on the Peak petitioned the government to preserve the area for "the exclusive residence of non-Chinese inhabitants." The petitioners hoped to keep the Peak "as a place of residence for themselves, their wives and their children, and the wives and children of their successors." Because of the "vast increase" in the size and wealth of the Chinese population, areas previously inhabited by Europeans were now "mainly in the occupation of Chinese." If more Chinese moved to the Peak, the Europeans would be forced downward, which would be "highly prejudicial to their health." Not only was the Peak "undeniably" the best place for Europeans unused to such a tropical and "unnatural environment," it was the only place in Hong Kong "fitted to be a healthy residential quarter for people accustomed to a temperate climate." To preserve the Peak for Europeans, the government would have to prohibit all Chinese, except for servants, from living there. Such a prohibition would not cause any "hardship" to the Chinese, who were already in their "native climate." It was "for the advantage of a community as a whole" that each people should reside in "the environment to which it is best adapted." But the "future welfare" of the colony, and its "consequent value to the Empire," depended greatly on "the well-being of the European section of the community." The Peak was thus to be preserved as a place where the "rising generation" of Europeans might spend its childhood in the "healthiest obtainable surroundings."[28]

When the proposed bill came before the Legislative Council, Chinese members Ho Kai and Wei Yuk showed little opposition. Ho argued that although the bill had "a decided savour of the nature of class legislation," he was "quite convinced" of its "reasonableness and expediency" because the wealth and well-being of Hong Kong depended greatly on the European community. Although most of the other Chinese leaders saw no objection to the bill, they agreed with Ho and Wei's suggestion of adding a clause giving the governor the right to grant exemptions for Chinese he considered fit to live on the Peak.[29]

Governor May reported that the registrar general had met with the Tung Wah Hospital committee, members of the "leading Chinese Mercantile Firms and Chinese Guilds," and "other influential Chinese." These Chinese had voiced no objections to the bill but had respectfully requested that the government reword the bill to be "less distasteful to Chinese sentiment." The Chinese had shown "their well-known common sense" by recognizing that it was "not an unreasonable measure" and did "not really prejudice their interests." Happily, the governor reported, the ordinance had passed "without evoking friction or ill-feeling."[30] The new ordinance stipulated that no owner or tenant could lease a property or building "to any but non-Chinese or permit any but Non-Chinese to reside on or in such land or building." The only Chinese who received permission to circumvent this rule was the Eurasian Sir Robert Ho Tung, who in 1906 had a European buy several houses for him, then moved one of his wives, Lady Clara, and her children there. By 1917 Ho Tung owned three houses in the Peak district, though he and his family were never completely accepted by their European neighbors.[31]

In September 1917 an alarmed Governor May reported that a Chinese, or his European lawyer, had discovered a loophole in the wording of the 1904 ordinance: a Chinese living in his own house on the Peak could not possibly be "permitting" anyone to live there. Ho Tung's brother, Ho Kam Tong, had also purchased a house, "Lysholt," at public auction. Citing the 1904 ordinance, May asked Ho to sell the house to the government. A well-known philanthropist, Ho agreed to give the profit from the sale to the War Charities Fund. But now Ho was trying to buy another property. Only a few days earlier, Robert Ho Tung had bought two semi-detached homes and planned to make them into one home for his daughter, who would soon marry a Chinese. Other Chinese had expressed interest in similar properties, and Ho Tung was planning to build a large place for his own residence on "the one really good site still vacant on the Peak."[32]

As in 1904, the 1917 controversy was as much about race and class as about health. May explained how wealthy Chinese businessmen, "living with their wives and concubines in semi-European fashion," had been "steadily ousting" the Europeans from the Mid-Levels. The Portuguese had been the first to go, then the other Europeans. As a result, rents on the Peak were rising. If Chinese were allowed to settle on the Peak, they would set a trend of buying homes at "fancy prices far beyond the European purse." These "displaced" Europeans would be forced into the "less desirable and less healthy parts of the Colony." But the problem was more than financial. With more children than ever on the Peak, European parents "bitterly opposed any contact between their children and Chinese children." Wealthy Chinese men would soon bring their wives, concubines, and "numerous progeny" who would be "thrown into daily contact with the European children in the children's playground and the few shady spots to which the Europeans are now taken by their nurses and amahs." Chinese families living on the Peak would have more contact with the less privileged Chinese living below, greatly increasing the likelihood of "the carriage and dissemination of communicable disease." It would be "little short of a calamity if an alien and, by European standards, a semi-civilized race were allowed to drive the white man from the one area in Hong Kong, in which he can live with his wife and children in a white man's healthy surroundings." Furthermore, Ho Kam Tong would be violating the ordinance because he planned to let his wives, concubines, and children live in his new property while he continued to live in a posh new home in the Mid-Levels. May thus asked for permission to give "legal force" to the "obvious intention" of the ordinance by modifying it so that, "except with the consent of the Governor-in-Council, no Chinese may reside at the Peak."[33]

Finally, the residency controversy highlighted the rise of a group of Eurasians who, although biracial and bicultural, remained primarily "Chinese" in the view of the European population. The 1904 ordinance had failed to define "Chinese," thus enabling Eurasians such as Ho Tung and Ho Kam Tong to slip through. To colonial officials and European residents, these Eurasians were "to all intents and purposes Chinese in their habits and customs." May now sought to expand "Chinese" to include Eurasians. He proposed to define the term as "a person of Chinese race on the side of one parent only; or, as an alternative, to refer in the Ordinance to 'persons of Chinese extraction' instead of to Chinese, with power vested in the Governor-in-Council to decide what constitutes Chinese extraction."[34]

As in 1904, the Chinese members of the Legislative Council did not object to the bill. May explained that although they realized the "alternations of the law would be derogatory to the prestige of their race," they did not disagree with the "justice and reasonableness of the proposed legislation."[35] Although the Chinese Chamber of Commerce passed a resolution against the ordinance after some Eurasians called a special meeting of the chamber, the Peak District Bill passed as originally written.[36]

Explaining the Racial Gap

Why did Chinese and Eurasians in Hong Kong not actively protest this racial discrimination? Irene Cheng, Robert Ho Tung's daughter, insisted that the Peak ordinance was "bitterly resented by the Chinese and other Asian residents of Hong Kong."[37] And in 1921 leaders of the foreign community and the English-educated Chinese elite formed the League of Fellowship, the goal of which was to "promote good fellowship within the Colony, irrespective of race, class and creed."[38] But only in 1925, during the great strike-boycott, was there a demand that Chinese be allowed to live on the Peak. And this demand came from the strike organizers in Canton, who could hardly have afforded to live on the Peak even had they been allowed to do so.

Local Europeans usually blamed the Chinese for this racial gap. In 1891 the *Daily Press* explained that "a Chinaman himself is scarcely conscious that he is not on his own soil; he dubs Europeans as 'devils' and 'barbarians' in the streets of Hongkong with the same fervour of conviction with which the people of Canton so dub them in their own streets, and it never occurs to him that on British soil the real foreigners are those who are not British subjects." European historians have generally attributed the persistence of the racial gap to its acceptance by the Chinese population. E. J. Eitel, the colony's early historian, accused the Chinese of "deliberately refusing any identification with the European community." This and other signs of "Chinese clannish exclusivism," Eitel argued, "clearly indicate that on the Chinese side there is, as yet, no desire to see the chasm that still separates Chinese and European life in the colony, bridged over."[39]

This view has gone unchallenged in many English-language histories. Lennox Mills, the political scientist who visited the colony in 1941, concluded that "the racial bitterness which has caused so much trouble in India is not found in Hong Kong, although British and Chinese have separate clubs and, on the whole, social intercourse be-

tween the races is limited . . . perhaps also one may hazard the guess
that the Chinese is too content with the society of those of his own
race to trouble himself with his exclusion from European circles." A
popular recent history of Hong Kong insists that the Chinese were
not particularly interested in taking part in the Europeans' social and
sporting activities: "If the unpleasant sweaty, cheese-eating Westerners
wanted to keep their objectionable habits to themselves, the Chinese
were not complaining."[40]

Chinese historians have taken a different approach. Some of them
accuse the Chinese bourgeoisie of helping their British overlords op-
press the Chinese masses. Most, however, argue that, humiliated by
European oppression and imbued first with Sun Yatsen's anti-
imperialist zeal and later with the revolutionary fervor of the May
Fourth years, the Chinese bourgeoisie strove to break down the racial
walls that separated them from the Europeans.[41]

But none of these arguments adequately explains how the Chinese
elite dealt with the racial gap in Hong Kong. Hong Kong's colonial
situation provided a variety of bourgeois European associations, clubs,
and societies from which to borrow. Like their counterparts in other
British colonies and dependencies around the world, the leaders of the
Chinese bourgeoisie claimed for their own use the attitudes and activities that defined the European bourgeoisie. Yet, by forming their
own exclusive social world instead of trying to join the Europeans'
world, they were able to define themselves in contrast to the European
bourgeoisie and thereby highlight their own uniqueness. Had the
leaders of the Chinese bourgeoisie tried to join the European social
world, they would have remained in a subordinate position. In their
own social world, however, they were the undisputed masters.

European Social Life in Hong Kong

Understanding the Chinese response to European racism and exclusivism requires understanding the social world of the British upper
classes in Hong Kong. Not all Britons, of course, were wealthy. Class
divisions existed, moreover, among the English, the Scots, the Irish,
and the few Welsh in the colony. But wealthy Britons generally tried
to live the life they had enjoyed, or had aspired to enjoy, in Britain.
They built large English-style houses and villas, surrounded by well-

manicured gardens, tennis greens, and croquet lawns. Privileged
British social life in Hong Kong revolved around parties, formal din-
ners on the Roof Garden of the Peninsula Hotel or at the Repulse
Bay Hotel, bridge, clubs, and the annual St. George's and St. Andrew's
balls.

Like their counterparts at home and in other colonies, the British
in Hong Kong were obsessed with sports and team games. "One of
the happiest of the Empire's gifts to the world," writes Jan Morris,
"was the gift of organized sport." Moral improvement, rather than
relaxation or enjoyment, was the ultimate purpose. Sport represented
"an amalgam of ideals: Christianity, Darwinism, nationalism and imperialism." Manly sports like cricket were supposed to help build character. They fostered the necessary moral and physical qualities to help
one in life—teamwork, loyalty, honesty, and fair play—qualities considered especially valuable in the trying conditions of the colonies.[42]

In Hong Kong, sport defined elite status. The British bourgeoisie
of Hong Kong played all the fashionable sports and games of the
genteel British upper classes.[43] Hong Kong had a club for every sport
and a sport for every club: cricket at the Cricket Club, conveniently
located among the office buildings of Central District; tennis at the
Ladies Recreation Club; rowing at the Victoria Sailing Club and
sailing at the Yacht Club on Kellett Island; polo in Causeway Bay; golf
in Deep Water Bay; and hunting in Fanling. Most of these activities
were closed to the Chinese majority of Hong Kong's population. A
symbol of elitist activities, sport enabled the British bourgeoisie to
flaunt and affirm status and prestige, to one another, to the Chinese,
and to lower-class Europeans.

The most important mechanism for affirming status and prestige
was the "gentleman's club" with its strictly limited membership. The
center of British social life, the club was a symbol of both social status
and political domination across the British Empire. Here, "one could
feel like a gentleman among other gentlemen while being served by a
native staff."[44] Especially in Asia and Africa, writes Morris, the club
"was the place where the imperialists celebrated their Britishness, authority and imperial lifestyle." But "wherever they were . . . whatever
made their pretensions, the clubs of Empire had this in common: that
they made the Right People feel more important, and made the
Wrong People feel small."[45]

In Hong Kong the club that separated the right people from the wrong was the Hong Kong Club, founded in 1846 by the heads of the leading British hongs. Although by the late 1800s Chinese served increasingly on the boards and committees of both Western and Chinese commercial firms, none of the major European clubs admitted Chinese. A handsome three-storey building on Queen's Road, complete with reading and dining rooms, bars, guest rooms, a library, nine billiard tables, and a bowling alley, the Hong Kong Club was no exception. The club's rules stipulated terms for the admission of "all persons" and "any gentleman," but it had no Chinese members.[46] Until after the Second World War, the only Chinese who could enter the club were its two hundred or so cooks and servants.

Although European women were also barred from the Hong Kong Club (at an auction before the club moved to its new building in 1897, a rug was offered as having never been stepped on by a woman[47]) these women had their own club. The Ladies Recreation Club (LRC), jokingly known as the "Ladies' Recrimination Club," was founded in February 1884 on a piece of land below the Peak. In 1883 a group of European women wrote to Acting Colonial Secretary F. Stewart requesting "on behalf of the ladies and families of this Colony for the grant, at a nominal rent, of a small piece of ground for the purpose of health and recreation." Reminding the colonial secretary "how limited are the means and opportunities of relaxation on this tropical rock and how greatly the health of both the ladies and children are tried by the length and severity of the summer of Hongkong," the women argued that "the acquisition of a ladies' recreation ground would be a public boon of the greatest sanitary importance in varying the dull monotony of life and inducing the ladies to take exercise so needful in the tropics to the preservation of health, but from which they are debarred by the absence of any suitable place." Justifying the proposal to the colonial secretary, Acting Governor William Marsh explained that "the grantees include English, German, American and Portuguese so that all classes are represented, except Chinese who do not take any exercise."[48] When the *China Mail* reported that "the Ladies of Hong Kong are now in possession of a resort where they can obtain physical recreation of the most health-giving and bracing kind," it meant that the *European* women of Hong Kong had their own club.[49]

The Chinese Response

The Chinese response to colonial British discrimination was not to push for an end to it, but to create an equally exclusive social world of their own. In some ways, this tactic was not new. In the earlier years of the colony's history, the success of Chinese merchants had soon made them into powerful economic rivals of the Europeans. Despite their wealth, they were barred from the same channels of upward social mobility that excluded them later at the turn of the century. Chinese merchants had quickly learned to seek social status by establishing such organizations as the Tung Wah Hospital and the District Watch Force. As the Hong Kong Club was to the Europeans, these institutions had become a means for establishing and reaffirming social rank among the Chinese population.

At the turn of the century, however, the situation had changed in two ways. The new clubs and associations formed by the Chinese bourgeoisie no longer made any claim to be traditional organizations for the Chinese gentry, nor did they seek confirmation from the Chinese government for fulfilling gentry functions. They were based on Western models and often on modern concepts, such as sports. The Chinese business community had also become much more heterogeneous. As the colony grew and its economy diversified, a new generation of Western-trained merchants, businessmen, and professionals emerged. In the late 1880s the colony received a new group of Chinese returning from overseas—the result of restrictive immigration laws introduced by the British Dominions and by the American Exclusion Acts of 1887.[50] Overseas Chinese retailers, such as Ma Ying Piu of the Sincere Company and the Kwok brothers of the Wing On Company, introduced new retail and management techniques to Hong Kong and China. As Jung-fang Tsai concludes, "a younger generation of merchants, businessmen, professionals, and new intelligentsia emerged in Hong Kong, a generation more Westernized than the old elite and more inclined to innovations and new commitments."[51]

The Chinese Club

Barred from the Hong Kong Club, several prominent Chinese and Eurasians formed their own club in 1899: the Chinese Club. Among the founders were the Eurasian brothers Robert Ho Tung (the club's first chairman) and Ho Kam Tong. Another founder, Kwan Sun Yin, was one of the first Chinese practitioners of Western medicine in Hong Kong. Kwan graduated in 1893 from the Hongkong College of Medicine, where he was the classmate and roommate of Sun Yatsen, the founder of the Chinese Republic. Kwan ran one of the largest, most lucrative private medical practices in the colony.[52]

As the Hong Kong Club was the mechanism for reaffirming social prestige among the European community, the Chinese Club became the gentleman's club for the Chinese community. Membership and directorship were restricted to some of the most prominent Chinese and Eurasian businessmen and professionals in Hong Kong. Many members were compradors, such as Lau Chu Pak of A. S. Watson's and Ching King Sing of the German trading house Carlowitz & Co.[53] Ip Shu Kam was comprador for Reiss & Co. His family had been compradors since the early days of the colony and before that during the "factory" days in Canton. Lau Pun Chiu was comprador for the Hongkong Shanghai Bank—by far the colony's most powerful bank (though in 1912 he either mismanaged or absconded with more than seventy thousand Hong Kong dollars of the bank's assets and fled to Shanghai)—a director of the Tung Wah Hospital, and a philanthropist noted for his educational and relief work in Guangdong. Other members came from the new class of legal, banking, and insurance professionals. The Eurasian Sin Tak Fan, three-term club president, was well known in local legal circles as the chief interpreter for Ewens and Harston, one of the leading solicitors in Hong Kong; B. Wong Tape was a New Zealand-educated insurance magnate.[54] As a group, the members of the Chinese Club represented some of the most successful businessmen and professionals in the colony.

The Chinese Recreation Club

While the Chinese Club became the Chinese parallel to the Hong Kong Club, the Chinese Recreation Club (CRC) became the Chinese parallel to the Hong Kong Cricket Club. Like the Hong Kong Club, the Cricket Club was founded in the early decades of the colony and membership was limited to Europeans.[55] Denied admission to the Cricket Club, Ho Kai and Wei Yuk (who had both signed the 1901

Chinese school petition) and several other prominent Chinese petitioned the government in 1912 for a piece of land in Taihang Village
to start their own club.[56]

The decision to form an English-style club revolving around sports,
especially cricket, is of particular importance here. The "old English
and manly game" was played in all the British territories. Anthony
Trollope claimed that cricket identified the English wherever they
went: "Where a score or so of our sons are found, there is found
cricket."[57] Cricket also had great moral implications, providing the
"fibre of moral fabric" that would guide the Englishman through his
adult years. Of all the sports, cricket most symbolized the values that
had made Britain an empire: loyalty to an elected captain, esprit de
corp, and respect for truth and fair play. British colonists were especially keen to show through cricket that they had not degenerated in
the tropics. Cricket also symbolized loyalty to the mother country and
empire unity. Lord Harris, former governor of Bombay, claimed in
1921 that "cricket had done more to consolidate the Empire than any
other influence." The famous Indian batsman Ranjitsinhji, who once
insisted that the British Empire would be a better place if its officials
were all cricket players, wrote that "cricket is certainly amongst the
most powerful links which keep our Empire together." As James
Mangan concludes, "cricket was the umbilical cord of Empire linking
the mother country with her children."[58]

Cricket was not just the most British sport; it was also one of the
most elite sports. Such sports, according to Pierre Bourdieu, derive
their popularity in part from their "distinguishing function" and in
part from the gains in distinction that they bring. Within British communities in the colonies, cricket offered well-to-do colonists a way to
flaunt their status and wealth. As in India, one reason cricket was so
popular among the Chinese upper classes in Hong Kong was that it
indicated class, status, and hierarchy. Even more important than the
sports were the institutions and functions surrounding them. As in the
British clubs, the CRC screening process was rigorous and membership fees were high. Club rules were strict, and an atmosphere of
elegance and poshness pervaded—both on and off the playing field.
Proper cricket and tennis whites were required, while the serving and
eating utensils in the club's dining room were made of silver.[59]

As with the European clubs, the CRC was a mechanism for affirming elite status and prestige. Its directors and members featured some of the best-known (usually Western-educated) Chinese men of the colony. Apart from Ho Kai, who died two years after the founding, and Wei Yuk, there was Chow Shouson. From an old Hong Kong family, Chow was selected in 1873 by the Qing government as one of the first Chinese to study in the United States. He was educated at Phillips-Andover Academy and at Columbia University, until the Qing government recalled the study. After serving as Chinese consul in Inchon, Korea, Chow was appointed managing director of the Chinese Merchants Steamship Navigation Company in 1903 and the Peking-Mukden Railway in 1907. Heavily decorated by the Chinese government, Chow returned to Hong Kong after the 1911 revolution, whereupon he immersed himself in local commerce and industry. Chow was director of many local corporations, including the Hongkong Electric Company, the Hongkong Telephone Company, Hongkong Tramways, A. S. Watson's, and the Bank of East Asia.[60]

Another director of the Chinese Recreation Club, Dr. Arthur Waitak Woo, was a brilliant British-trained physician. After graduating from London Hospital in 1913, Woo held several important appointments at London hospitals, including one previously held only by Britons. After further study in the United States and Europe, Woo worked at Peking Union Medical College for two years. While in Beijing, he was also medical adviser to the ministries of Foreign Affairs and Communications, and personal physician to Chinese president Li Yuanhong. After returning to Hong Kong, Woo opened his own clinic and was appointed lecturer on gynecology and obstetrics at Hong Kong University. A prolific publisher in both British and Chinese medical journals, Woo was a member of medical groups worldwide. In 1928 he became the first Chinese president of the Chinese Medical Association. As with many of the more prominent medical and legal professionals, Woo was extensively involved in Chinese business circles, both in Hong Kong and on the mainland. Lo Man Kam, another director, was a prominent Eurasian solicitor trained in England, legal adviser to the Chinese Chamber of Commerce, and director of several large businesses.[61]

By playing the elite British sports that defined the British bourgeoisie of Hong Kong, the Chinese bourgeoisie proved that Chinese too could be respectable, modern gentlemen who could adopt and

assimilate British culture. Through hosting cricket matches on week-
ends and public holidays against the Hong Kong Cricket Club, the
Kowloon Cricket Club, and the local Portuguese community's Club
de Recreio, CRC members displayed and affirmed their status and
prestige, to each other, to their European opponents, and to the Chinese lower classes. The founding of such clubs does not, however,
mean that bourgeois Chinese were trying to be "more British than
the British." Indeed, the Hong Kong Chinese bourgeoisie never em-
braced the British sports and game culture as wholeheartedly as did
the new local bourgeoisies elsewhere in the British Empire.[62] Trying
to become British would have only kept them subordinate to the "real"
British. Rather, they were trying to be Hong Kong Chinese. For their
club symbol, the founders of the CRC chose two of the eight trigrams
from the *Book of Changes*, surrounded by the laurel wreath used by
British sports clubs. The clubhouse, surrounded by tennis greens, was
a two-storey pavilion that combined Chinese and Western designs.
Apart from enjoying British sports and games, such as tennis and bil-
liards, members could practice Chinese martial arts or play mah-jongg.

The South China Athletic Association

While the Chinese Club and the Chinese Recreation Club were
clearly founded as organizations for elite businessmen, leadership of
other sporting and recreational associations also became signs of elite
status. The South China Athletic Association (SCAA), founded as a
sports club with no elite connections, soon became another means of
confirming elite status. The idea for the SCAA came in 1904 when
students at one of the government English schools organized a soccer
club to compete with other teams in South China. In 1911 the club
won the gold medal in the first all-China sports competition in Nanjing; in 1913 it represented China at the first Far East Games in the
Philippines.[63]

As the SCAA's membership increased, its organizational structure
became more formal. Other sports and activities were added, and
prominent Chinese businessmen were elected to leadership positions.
Board membership of the SCAA soon became a requirement for per-
petuating one's elite status. Besides Chow Shouson, Lo Man Kam, and
Arthur Woo—all members or directors of the CRC—the directors or

honorary directors of the SCAA included the most important Chinese businessmen in the colony. Chan Kam Po, the American-educated director of C. Ah Ying & Company, a large import-export firm and contractor to the Royal Navy, had previously held several important posts in the Chinese government. In Hong Kong, where he was the director or manager of many firms, including the Bank of Canton, Chan was the executive director of the Chinese Chamber of Commerce and a director of the Tung Wah Hospital. Chan was known for his contributions to schools in Hong Kong and Guangzhou.[64] Chau Tsun-nin, an influential, Oxford-educated barrister and businessman, was also a partner, manager, or director of many local shipping and insurance firms. Lee Chi Chung, a member of Sun Yatsen's revolutionary movement in Japan, was treasurer of the local branch of Bank of Canton. Li Yau Tsun was a prominent manufacturer of leather goods, paper, and ice. Li was a member of all the major Chinese committees at some time in his career, and was decorated by the Chinese government for his efforts in flood relief.[65]

The Young Men's Christian Association

Like the South China Athletic Association, the Young Men's Christian Association (YMCA) was originally not an elite organization. Yet it too provided leadership opportunities for bourgeois Hong Kong Chinese when it was introduced in the early 1900s. Although the idea for a local branch came from two visiting Western YMCA officials, the initial funding came from businessman Li Yuk Tong and his brother. Originally from Taishan in Guangdong, Li had gone to California at age eighteen. After running a Chinese pharmacy, he came to Hong Kong, where he founded two general-merchant firms. In 1895 Li went to Canton to open the Canton Electrical Power Company, a flourmill, and a large import-export company. Returning to Hong Kong, he founded some of the first Chinese insurance companies in the colony and helped found several others in Canton and Shanghai.[66]

With funding from businessmen such as Li Yuk Tong, the Hong Kong Chinese YMCA opened in February 1902. Initial prejudice against the association's religious background faded quickly, and by 1903 the association was receiving money from non-Christian Chinese

impressed by its educational work.[67] Like the SCAA, the YMCA was
run by a board of directors composed of prominent Chinese residents.
Directorship also enabled recently arrived overseas Christian Chinese
businessmen, such as Ma Ying Piu, the founder of the Sincere Department Store, to find niches for status affirmation as latecomers.
Born in Xiangshan (later renamed Zhongshan) in Guangdong, Ma had
made his fortune in Australia as a fruit merchant. In 1899 he and a
group of overseas Chinese from Australia and several wealthy Hong
Kong merchants formed the Sincere Company. Under Ma's leadership, the Sincere Company became one of the most famous department stores in Asia, with branches in Canton, Shanghai, and Singapore. A devout Christian, Ma combined traditional Chinese and
Christian moral and social concerns with the corporate ideal espoused
by Western department stores. His department store offered employees Christian and ethical training and classes in English and ac-
counting; it also raised money for charitable causes. Ma was often
sought for his advice on community affairs and was deeply involved
in many educational, social, and religious organizations.[68] Within only
a few years, Ma had evolved from an immigrant entrepreneur to a
leader of the local Chinese business community.

A Hong Kong Chinese Bourgeois Social World

These new organizations did not replace the established institutions
of elite status. Many of their members were already members of the
Tung Wah Hospital, the District Watch, or the Chinese Chamber of
Commerce. Some, such as Ho Kai and Wei Yuk, were members of
the colonial political machinery. Others, such as Ho Tung and his
brother Ho Kam Tong, had obtained elite status by their sheer wealth
and generosity. Often, however, these organizations served as
stepping-stones to the older, more established elite institutions. Of
eight of the South China Athletic Association's early directors, only
one, Li Yau Tsun, had been on the Tung Wah Hospital or Chinese
Chamber of Commerce committees. Within a few decades, however,
most of these men had served on committees for the Tung Wah or
Chamber of Commerce, and several were on the colonial Legislative
or Executive councils.

The formation of such organizations shows that the leaders of the

Chinese bourgeoisie had the ability to appropriate and adapt new models to enhance and perpetuate their own status in a changing era. These new organizations succeeded where the older institutions had not. The older institutions helped establish Chinese merchants as the Chinese gentry of a British colony. But by appropriating for their own use the model of elite English clubs and sports, and the institutions surrounding them, affluent Chinese and Eurasians proved that they too were modern, respectable gentlemen. As they did for the Europeans, elite English sports played an important social function, offering affluent Chinese a new way to flaunt their status and wealth. These Chinese did not idly sit by and accept the discrimination that pervaded Hong Kong society, but nor did they seriously attempt to challenge it. Instead, they created their own exclusive social world. This world was neither fully Western nor fully Chinese; it was a third world: a Hong Kong Chinese bourgeois world.

5

Nationalism and Identity: The Case of Ho Kai

As Hong Kong entered the twentieth century, a new Chinese business and professional class arose. The leaders of this class—many of whom were born and educated in Hong Kong and then trained in Britain—came to see themselves as members of a privileged group, in not only Hong Kong but also the greater Chinese world and the British Empire. Yet, like many Chinese inside and outside China, they became increasingly concerned about the fate of their ancestral homeland. Following a series of skirmishes with Western powers in the late 1800s—and culminating in the humiliating defeat by Japan in the Sino-Japanese War of 1894–1895—China had proved itself incapable of resisting the foreign imperialists.

Among this new class of Hong Kong Chinese was Ho Kai: barrister, financier, physician, and community leader. Because he supported the revolutionary movement in China yet believed that the Western presence was beneficial for China, and because he served the colonial government in Hong Kong, Ho has often been cited as a "collaborationist patriot" forced to choose between Hong Kong and China. But Ho did not seem to identify with that dichotomy. For Ho, whose Chinese nationalism developed in the colonial context, what was good for Hong Kong was good for China. The key to a strong China was a commercially vibrant China. This conviction grew out of Ho's identification with colonial Hong Kong.

Ho Kai in the Scales of History

Although he is not as well remembered as other Chinese nationalists, Ho Kai was part of a small but important group of reformers in Hong Kong and the Chinese treaty ports during the second half of the nineteenth century. In one study of political reformers in the late Qing, Ho Kai's vehement criticism of the Self-Strengthening Movement (1861–1895) is described as "a symbolic turning point in the reform movement." Indeed, many of the political ideas of Sun Yatsen, the father of the Chinese republic, were "at least partially a result of his early familiarity with Ho's theory of popular sovereignty." Some scholars have stressed the radical nature of Ho's political thought. Although—like the constitutionalists Kang Youwei and Liang Qichao—Ho supported the idea of a Chinese constitutional monarchy, he rejected the notion that the Chinese classics had anything to offer China. Instead, he advocated using Western ideals of democracy to accelerate China's political reform. Indeed, Ho is considered so important to the Chinese reform movement that his affiliation with colonial Hong Kong is often overlooked.[1]

Other scholars have been less impressed by Ho and his reformist ideas. Mainland Chinese scholars, for example, often dismiss him as a "comprador reformer" who, because of his own class background, was unable to propose any radical alternatives to feudalism. As an overseas Chinese capitalist, Ho understandably wanted China to become as prosperous as Hong Kong. But his call for increased foreign investment in China would have only ended in disaster. Japanese Marxist scholars have similarly criticized Ho for failing to see beyond his capitalist blinders. In a capitalist world, they say, Ho's insistence that capitalist commercial and industrial development would end foreign influence in China was fundamentally flawed and would only strengthen foreign domination of China's modern economy.[2]

According to this analysis, Ho Kai fits into a broad category of "compradors" centered on compradors and merchants whose connections to foreign capital made them the "seed and embryo" of the group. This category quickly expands to become a giant, reactionary and parasitic Chinese "comprador bourgeoisie." Using their various connections to foreign imperialism, the members of this group shut out the patriotic "national bourgeoisie," increasing foreign domination of China's modern economy, thwarting the growth of an incipient Chinese capitalism, and hindering the development of Chinese nationalism.[3]

This category of "compradors," however, is too broad to be of any real analytical value. Furthermore, it is based on the supposed distinction between "comprador capital" and "comprador bourgeoisie" and "national capital" and "national bourgeoisie." As Yen-p'ing Hao argues, any valid distinction between "comprador capital" and "national bourgeoisie capital" is virtually blurred. Similarly, Marie-Claire Bergère argues that these "superficially obvious" but "artificial" labels, first applied by Mao Zedong and the Chinese Communist Party in the 1920s, fail to convey that "national capital" is "meaningless as an economic term."[4]

Because he served the Hong Kong colonial government and dealt extensively with European merchants, Ho's allegiance to China has also often been questioned. Harold Schiffrin writes that Ho, "for all his patriotism and interest in constitutional government, still bore the burden of a dual allegiance." Ho was "essentially a conditional revolutionary, who could not conceive of activism except when supported by British gunboats." Jung-fang Tsai describes Ho and his friend Hu Liyuan as being trapped in the paradox of "collaborationist patriotism." Some contemporary European observers, who were otherwise impressed by Ho's commitment to British liberalism, wondered about Ho's Chineseness. An 1890 article explained how men like Ho Kai could hardly be considered "genuine natives" because "no Chinaman cares twopence about representation 'in principle'." Ho has thus gone down in history as "a most curious mixture of a Chinese nationalist and . . . a running dog of Western, especially British, imperialism."[5]

Ho Kai was indeed a "curious mixture," but these historical analyses greatly simplify the situation in which Ho lived and operated. They overlook the possibility that Ho did not necessarily see any difference between what was beneficial to Hong Kong, a British colony and Chinese city, and what was good for China, an empire ruled by Manchu monarchs and their Chinese officials. They downplay the way Ho's Chinese nationalism emerged as part of his colonial experience. They misread Ho's concern with order in Hong Kong as being anti-Chinese, and his pride in Hong Kong as being uncritical admiration for British liberalism. By focusing solely on the question of Chinese nationalism, they confound Ho's own financial concerns with concerns toward both China and the Chinese population of Hong Kong. Finally, they overlook how nationalism, like colonialism, may mean different things to different social groups. In short, they oversimplify the problem of identity in turn-of-the-century Hong Kong.

Ho Kai and Hong Kong Identity

Only recently have scholars begun to deal seriously with Hong Kong as a place with its own identity. Most argue that a sense of Hong Kong identity did not develop until after 1949, when the border with the new People's Republic of China was closed, causing Chinese residents to identify more closely with Hong Kong. Several strategic dates provided the catalyst: during the 1967 riots, when Chinese in Hong Kong supported the colonial government against communist agitators and local left-wing groups; in the 1970s, when a sense of Hong Kong cultural identity began to emerge; in the prosperous 1980s, when a locally born cohort came of age; in the early 1990s, when the Tiananmen Massacre and the impending handover in 1997 forced many Chinese to think of themselves first as "Hong Kongese," second as Chinese; or in the late 1990s, when Hong Kong increasingly became defined by its cinema and architecture, and by what Ackbar Abbas calls a "culture of disappearance." Regardless of the exact dates and causes, the emphasis is almost always on the post-1949 period.[6]

But such arguments understate the complexity of the relationship between identity and political or geographical borders. For example, accessibility to Mainland China has increased dramatically for Taiwan citizens in the past two decades. Yet many people in Taiwan, Mainlanders and Taiwanese alike, are increasingly identifying themselves with Taiwan because accessible borders enable them to contrast conditions in China with those on Taiwan. The situation in pre-1949 Hong Kong was quite similar. Easy accessibility to China, especially to neighboring Canton, reminded Hong Kong Chinese of the glaring differences between China and Hong Kong.

Scholars have also generally assumed that Hong Kong identity and Chinese identity cannot coexist. But more recent work on Chinese urban history points to the existence of a multiplicity of identities, even with the rise of specifically urban consciousness and what William Rowe calls "locational solidarity."[7] Similarly, overseas Chinese in Southeast Asia, Wang Gungwu argues, can have "multiple identities." The increased use of postcolonial theory, critical anthropology, and feminist studies reveals the shifting and unstable nature of overseas Chinese identities, showing how a person is a "site of differences." Nor is identity static. Rather, as Stuart Hall argues, it is a process or a production, "never complete, always in process, and always constituted within, not outside, representation."[8]

Scholars have perhaps also focused too much on the "Chineseness" of Chinese in Hong Kong and other colonies, at the expense of other types of identity: settler identity (Ho Kai's family were settlers from Guangdong), creole identity (Ho was a Cantonese born in British Hong Kong), or class identity (he was a businessman). Work on other parts of the British Empire may be of help here. Philip Morgan argues that British identity coexisted with "myriad alternative identities, sometimes complementary, sometimes contradictory, which were locally—but no less powerfully—articulated." Simply put, Britons "had many loyalties, many allegiances." In his study of the great Indian cricketer Ranjitsinhji, Sadatru Sen argues that Ranjitsinhji did not attempt to be "exclusively English or purely Indian." Ho Kai similarly saw himself as not only Chinese but also a British subject. His frequent travels to China reminded him that he was a different kind of Chinese—just as, for example, Australian women's sea voyages "home" to England reminded them that while they were members of the British Empire they belonged to a special category of British subject: Australian.[9]

An emphasis on Chineseness assumes that Hong Kong Chinese identified only with Chinese politics and not with affairs in British Hong Kong. But men like Ho Kai could be actively involved in the politics of both Hong Kong and China. Indeed, it was Ho's involvement with both that would eventually alienate him from the colonial administration. And as Helen Siu has argued, being Chinese and being part of the Chinese polity can be very different. Many Chinese in Hong Kong identified with China as a culture rather than as a state, though they certainly hoped for unity and stability in that state. Finally, the emphasis on Chineseness ignores variations in identity among different members of the Hong Kong Chinese population— for example, between sojourners and permanent residents. Ho Kai often saw himself as being different from other, less Anglicized, Chinese in Hong Kong. During the investigation of the Po Leung Kuk Committee in 1892, he explained to British officials that, "you must always make allowances for Chinese. They do not always give the true reason. They give reasons which are not really true—at least that is so far as my experience goes."[10]

Ho Kai's Hong Kong identity helped shape his views of Chinese nationalism. In the 1901 school petition, Ho Kai referred to himself and other prominent Chinese in Hong Kong as "permanent residents." Like colonial settlers elsewhere, these men defined themselves in contrast to both foreigners and other Chinese. In 1917, for example, the Eurasian millionaire Robert Ho Tung admitted that no part of the Hong Kong population could be described as "purely indigenous." But he contrasted Hong Kong's "commercial and domiciled Chinese community" with both the Chinese lower classes and the colony's foreign residents, the latter consisting mainly of "birds of passage, who pass through on their way to the tin mines and rubber plantations of the Malay States and the Dutch East Indies." It was this Chinese community's "progress and material and intellectual development" that had made Hong Kong so remarkable. "It can no longer be said," Ho Tung insisted, "that the Chinese resort to Hong Kong for sordid motives only." Although "patient industry and frugality" had brought many Chinese "considerable wealth," much of it was "invested in and spent in Hong Kong." How the Chinese owned more than three-fifths of the property in Hong Kong was a testimony to "their faith in the permanent prosperity of the colony, and the safety of domicile under the folds of the British flag."[11]

That many Chinese had come to see Hong Kong as their permanent home became evident in December 1911, two months after the Chinese republican revolution. Ho Kai and seventeen other Chinese petitioned Governor Frederick Lugard for a permanent cemetery for "Chinese permanently residing in Hongkong." The petitioners, who had already located a suitable plot of land on the south side of Hong Kong Island, referred to themselves as "eighteen of the leading Members of the Chinese Community of Hong Kong," all "permanent residents in this Colony" and "most of them British subjects." Petitioning "on behalf of themselves and their fellow countrymen" who had made the colony "their home," they had "no intention of returning to China save for temporary purposes—social, commercial or otherwise." Except for a cemetery for Chinese Christians, none of the existing Chinese cemeteries were permanent sites "well laid out and planted with shrubs, trees, ornamental plants or flowers" like the Colonial Cemetery in Happy Valley.[12]

In July 1912 Lugard's successor, Francis May, happily approved the request. As May explained to the Colonial Office, Lugard had supported the proposal because "it would tend to create a colonial feeling and to specialize a class who desire to identify themselves with the Colony." May proposed that approximately two acres be granted at a 999-year lease, with Crown Rent at a nominal one Hong Kong dollar per annum. The land would be used solely as a cemetery for "persons of Chinese nationality permanently resident in the Colony," and the Chinese would contribute to the management and upkeep of the cemetery.[13] When in 1927 a group of Chinese requested an extension to the permanent cemetery, Registrar General E. R. Hallifax explained to the colonial secretary that "the Cemetery has had an effect in the direction of making for H. K. Chinese a closer bond with the colony: a matter of no small importance." In June 1928 Acting Governor W. T. Southorn approved the extension, noting that "Hong Kong Chinese have throughout shewn a very keen interest in the Institution, which has been entirely successful in attaining its primary object—the strengthening of the ties which bind true Hong Kong Chinese to the Colony."[14]

One of the true Hong Kong Chinese, Ho Kai embodied a nationalism that was inseparable from the colonial situation in which he lived. Ho was the son of Ho Fuk Tong, a Protestant minister, land speculator, and merchant. Like so many other members of the Chinese business elite, Ho Fuk Tong had identified his interests with Hong Kong soon after it became a British colony, despite repeated orders from Canton authorities to leave the island. Traveling with the missionary James Legge, Ho arrived at Hong Kong in 1843 after studying at the London Missionary Society's Anglo-Chinese College, in Malacca. Ordained in 1846 as the first Chinese pastor in Hong Kong, the elder Ho worked with the London Missionary Society until his death in 1871. His devotion to his religion was matched by his dedication to business, and Ho began investing in land soon after arriving in the colony. By the time of his death, Ho Fuk Tong had one of the largest estates in the colony.[15]

Ho Kai was educated entirely in British schools, both in Hong Kong and in Britain. He received his early education at the Central School, founded in 1862 to help train young Chinese as teachers, clerks, interpreters, and merchants for what colonial officials hoped would be a new China. As in other European colonies, the Hong Kong government itself encouraged the growth of Chinese nationalism by providing schools and selecting students for further training in Europe, and by generally encouraging the idea of citizenship. Ho went to Britain in 1873 for further schooling at Palmer House School in Margate, followed by training in medicine at St. Thomas's Medical and Surgical College at Aberdeen University, and in law at Lincoln's Inn. In 1881 Ho became a member of the Royal College of Surgeons and a Senior Equity Scholar at Lincoln's Inn. Ho Kai returned to Hong Kong and opened his own medical practice, which he quit in disgust after realizing that many Chinese residents would accept Western medicine only if it were provided free of charge. Ho began his career as barrister-at-law in 1882 and, like his father, invested in real estate and local businesses.[16]

Ho Kai soon developed a distinguished career in public service. In 1890, when he replaced the first Chinese member of the Legislative Council, Wong Shing, the *Hong Kong Telegraph* reported that "great things" were expected from him and that Ho was was "essentially the man to represent his Hong Kong fellow countrymen in our local Parliament." A "sworn enemy of the Chinese mandarins," he was a "well read man of the world, and a deservedly popular citizen."[17] Ho was the main founder of the Alice Memorial Hospital (named after his deceased wife, Alice Walkden, whom he had married while in England) in 1887, and of the College of Medicine for Chinese, where he taught physiology and medical jurisprudence. He was instrumental in the development of a Chinese medical profession in Hong Kong. He also helped establish the Faculty of Arts at the University of Hong Kong. Ho was on every major board in Hong Kong during the last twenty-five years of his life. He was a Justice of the Peace for twenty-six years and served three terms on the Legislative Council, more than ten years on the Sanitary Committee, and five years on the Public Works Committee. He was also a committee member of the Po Leung Kuk, the Tung Wah Hospital, and the District Watch Committee. For his services to the colony, Ho was awarded the Companion of the Order of St. Michael and St. George in 1892, and was knighted in

1912. In honor of his knighthood, the members of the Chinese Club held a celebratory dinner.[18]

Ho was proud of Hong Kong, which he considered more prosperous and politically stable than any Chinese city, its government less corrupt and repressive, and its education and civil service systems better than anything China had to offer. Hong Kong represented the best of two worlds: British free trade and liberal government with the enterprise of Chinese merchants, free of the restrictions and prohibitions they faced on the mainland. Ho showed this pride in 1898 when he and his friend Hu Liyuan refuted Kang Youwei's criticism of Hong Kong Chinese as little more than British lackeys. Unlike the Chinese government, Hong Kong's colonial system appointed and promoted officials for their talent and merit, not on their knowledge of the Chinese classics. It provided schools that trained students in science and technology, schools at which more than 90 percent of the students were Chinese. Colonial Hong Kong offered many ways for Chinese to rise in both government and business. Refuting Kang's charge that the highest position a Chinese in Hong Kong could ever obtain was that of comprador, Ho offered himself as a living example. He held concurrently some eight political posts, one being member of the Legislative Council. At the time, Ho argued, there were two Chinese in the Legislative Council and eleven Justices of the Peace, while Chinese could also serve on juries. Nor was the position of comprador to be taken lightly. Compradors held most of the Chinese political positions in the colony, improved the colony's social welfare through organizations such as the Tung Wah Hospital, and provided important relief services in Hong Kong and in China.[19]

Hong Kong and China

It is tempting to dismiss Ho's defense of Hong Kong as an example of what Partha Chatterjee calls the "colonized mind" trapped in its "middleness." But Ho's pride in Hong Kong and his commitment to the colony's welfare did not conflict with his concern for his ancestral homeland. Nor did he make any attempt to hide this concern. In a letter to the editor of the Hong Kong *China Mail* in February 1887, Ho declared: "I deeply sympathize with China in every wrong which she has suffered, and I long with every true-hearted Chinaman for the time to come when China shall take her place among the foremost nations and her people be welcomed and esteemed everywhere."[20]

Rather than let his commitment to Hong Kong conflict with his commitment to China, Ho realized that his position enabled him to take an active interest in Chinese affairs. As the only Chinese faculty member at the Hong Kong College of Medicine for Chinese, of which he was also the main founder, Ho was in an ideal position to share his liberal ideas with young Chinese students from Hong Kong and the mainland. One such student was the young Sun Yatsen, who had previously studied in Hawaii. Not all graduates of the college went on to become revolutionaries, but many left the school with at least a trace of revolutionary thought. One of these was Kwan Sun Yin, Sun's roommate during their five years at the college and a member of the colony's new medical elite. In 1909 Kwan formed a club called the "Cut Queues but Unchanged Clothing Association" at the exclusive Chinese Club. As a symbol of their opposition to the Qing, the members cut their queues but continued to wear traditional Chinese robes.[21] Ho himself was involved with the revolutionary movement at the turn of the century and played an important role in the history of the Revive China Society (Xing-Zhonghui). Along with several other local Chinese merchants, Ho helped finance the society's revolutionary newspaper, the *China Daily* (*Zhongguo ribao*). He also helped organize the aborted 1895 uprising in Canton. During the planning of the Huizhou uprising in 1900, Ho tried to use his connections with the Hong Kong English press on behalf of Sun Yatsen's rebels to obtain British aid or at least to ensure a friendly Hong Kong government.[22]

Some have seen Ho's attempt to remain committed to both Hong Kong and China as a struggle in which his commitment to Hong Kong, particularly its capitalist economic system, eventually won. Jung-fang Tsai has explained this as the "predicament of the comprador ideologist": as a Westernized intellectual alienated from the Chinese peasantry and gentry, Ho could call for using foreigners to help reform China, even at the risk of compromising China's sovereign rights. But although Ho's involvement with the revolutionary movement ended after the 1900 uprising, as did his attempts to act as middleman between the Chinese revolutionaries and the Hong Kong government, his concern for Chinese affairs was not diminished. Rather, Ho, who believed China should be a constitutional monarchy like

England rather than a republic, had come to believe that the republican ideas of Sun and his revolutionaries were too radical. As his longtime friend and fellow Legislative Councillor Wei Yuk once explained, "in all his life," Ho was "in favour of Reformation and not Revolution." Over the next fourteen years of his life, Ho would remain committed to the welfare of China. In July 1908, after disastrous floods in Guangdong and Guangxi, Ho and Wei encouraged the Legislative Council to approve a donation of thirty thousand Hong Kong dollars to the affected regions.[23]

Nor did Ho see any difference between what was good for Hong Kong and what was good for China. Just as commerce had made Hong Kong more prosperous and stable than China, the cure for China would also be commerce, supported by British liberalism and parliamentary government. With his friend Hu Liyuan, Ho expressed this belief in a series of political treatises that were later published in 1900 in a six-volume work called the *True Meaning of New Government*. For example, Ho and Hu were convinced that Hong Kong's role as an entrepot, rather than as a British military base, was the reason for its success. In one of their earliest essays, written in 1887, Ho and Hu refuted the writings of the reformer Zeng Jize, who had argued that military reforms must be China's first priority. Ho and Hu agreed that China must develop a strong military, but they argued that China's first priority must be civil, social, and economic reforms. Rather than trying to enrich and strengthen itself through colonization, as Zeng had suggested, China should instead put its own house in order.[24] In "Discourse on New Government," Ho and Hu stressed the role of private enterprise. Unfettered by government restrictions and interference, private capital would build a nationwide mining, railway, and shipping network that would fully exploit the potential of China's natural and agricultural resources.[25]

Ho and Hu were especially critical of Zhang Zhidong's famous formula of "Chinese learning for the essence, Western learning for the application," arguing that it was futile to borrow Western military technology to learn the secret of the West's strength. One of the key figures in the Self-Strengthening Movement, Zhang had established military academies, technical schools, foundries, and arsenals, promoted China's technological and industrial development, and sent students to Japan, all the time hoping to preserve China's Confucian essence. In their 1898 "Review of [Zhang's] 'Exhortation to Learning'," Ho and Hu argued that China's essence was what needed to be changed. China needed a constitutional monarchy with parliamentary rule and people's rights. China needed not just more schools, as Zhang had argued, but universal education to prepare the populace for official appointments and as parliamentary representatives.[26]

Because he did not see any difference in what was good for Hong Kong and for China, Ho was not critical of the Western presence in China. Ho did not dispute that many Chinese were oppressed and humiliated, both in China and across the globe. But, unlike revolutionaries such as Sun Yatsen, he did not blame the West for this. In "Review of 'Exhortation to Learning' " and "Flexibility in New Government," Ho and Hu blamed China's own weakness. In "Review of Kang's speech," Ho and Hu began by criticizing Kang Youwei for blaming the West for China's plight. They placed the blame on Chinese leaders for ignoring Western ideas. By stubbornly clinging to the idea of China as both the largest country in the world and its center, haughty Chinese officials such as Lin Zexu had been responsible for the Opium War and China's subsequent humiliation by the West. By focusing on military and technological reforms but refusing to forsake the superiority of Chinese culture, reformers such as Zhang Zhidong, Zeng Guofan, and his protégé Li Hongzhang had foolishly convinced themselves that China might eventually stand up to the West.[27] In "Foundations of New Government" and "Administration of New Government," both published in 1897, Ho and Hu blamed China for the Western domination of Chinese mining and railway rights. Because China had failed to develop its own economy and exploit its own natural resources, it was only natural that foreigners would obtain the upper hand.[28] Nor was the Western enterprise in China necessarily damaging to China. As Ho and Hu argued in "Review of 'Exhortation to Study'," the Western presence provided much-needed foreign capital and new, efficient business techniques to China. Foreign missionaries had opened free schools, orphanages, and hospitals; led campaigns against opium and footbinding; and organized efforts for flood and famine relief. Western educators had translated Western scientific, medical, and political texts. By introducing Western business techniques, foreign merchants had brought a new sense of fair play to the Chinese economy.[29]

Ho's support for the Western presence in China was not, however, a wholesale acceptance of this presence; it was Britain and not the other European nations on which countries like China should be modeled. But although Ho was especially impressed by Britain's government, jurisprudence, and education, he did not accept the British presence in China uncritically. In "Discourse on New Government," Ho and Hu condemned Britain for expelling Chinese from its Asian colonies. In his prefaces to "Practice of New Government" and "Foundations of New Government," Ho chastised Britain for its aggressive behavior in China and for taking Weihaiwei, on the Shandong Peninsula, and Zhoushan, the small island off the coast of Zhejiang Province.[30]

These treatises can be seen as evidence that Ho was interested only in the rights of merchants. Some scholars, for example, argue that Ho and Hu represented the demands of the newly emergent Chinese bourgeoisie.[31] Jung-fang Tsai has argued that the reason classical liberalism appealed to Ho and Hu was because it was "congenial to their bourgeois interests and aspirations." Like many members of the merchant-intelligentsia in late nineteenth-century China, Tsai argues, Hu and Ho asserted their own social and political demands in the name of patriotism. Chan Lau Kit-ching suggests that although the ultimate goal of Ho's reformist ideas was democracy in China, the main beneficiary of these reforms would be the bourgeoisie.[32]

It is true that merchants figure largely in the writings of Ho and Hu. In "Review of 'Exhortation to Study'" and "Discourse on New Government," they argued that commercialism was the way for China to achieve wealth and power, and that merchants should form the base of a new China. The government should form a ministry of commerce and make it the top position in government. It should make use of talented Chinese and overseas Chinese merchants and businessmen.[33] But what is even more significant is how Ho's Chinese nationalism and Hong Kong identity reinforced each other. Because of his conviction that Chinese merchants had helped make Hong Kong into a thriving entrepot, Ho was convinced that Chinese merchants could do the same for China. But in his call for economic, political and social reform in China—which he believed could be best implemented through commercialism—Ho, like other members of the Hong Kong Chinese bourgeoisie, indirectly reaffirmed his own status as a member of a special, privileged class.

Predicament of the Hong Kong Chinese Capitalist

Although Ho Kai did not see any difference between the welfare of Hong Kong and that of China, his own financial and political position frequently put him in an awkward position. As a locally born, English-educated, Chinese professional elite and colonial official, Ho was often torn by what was good for the stability and prosperity of the colony, what was good for the Chinese population of Hong Kong, and what was good for his own wallet.

In matters affecting the Chinese business elite, Ho generally acted consistently. For example, in the early 1890s Europeans accused the Po Leung Kuk of being corrupt, coercing subscriptions, and exercising police functions among the Chinese population. With its obscure proceedings, the organization seemed little more than a "secret society." But as someone "constantly in contact with the Chinese and especially those who are leading men in the community," Ho Kai helped Registrar General James Stewart Lockhart defend and obtain government legal status for the institution. Ho helped prove that the managers of the association had "not only acted with perfect bona fides but had taken the steps which were best calculated to secure the protection of the liberties and welfare of those concerned."[34] By defending the Po Leung Kuk, Ho succeeded in protecting local Chinese interests from a suspicious Western community and safeguarding an institution that served both as a charitable association and a mechanism for establishing Chinese elite status in Hong Kong. Similarly, when the Tung Wah Hospital was condemned by local Western residents and medical doctors during the plague of 1894, Ho and Lockhart came to the hospital's defense.[35]

On issues of interest to the larger Chinese community in Hong Kong, however, Ho Kai was less consistent. On the one hand, Ho could be a champion of the Chinese lower classes. During a popular strike by workers and boatmen in protest against the Sino-French War in 1884, Ho and several European lawyers agreed to defend the strikers. In 1901, as a member of the Legislative Council, Ho ensured that the new Tramways Bill, which allowed the Tramway Company to operate on Hong Kong Island, included lower prices for workers. In 1908 some three thousand rickshaw pullers went on strike when the rickshaw owners raised the daily rental rate by 4 cents. After Ho Kai and fellow Legislative Councillor Wei Yuk helped the government arrange a negotiation meeting, the owners agreed not to raise the rents.[36]

On the other hand, Ho Kai took great care to distance himself from the Chinese lower classes. In 1901 he led the group of wealthy Chinese merchants in a petition for a special school for their own children. In 1890 he had opposed the governor's penal reforms. Ho especially opposed the proposed extension of the colony's main prison to provide separate cells, arguing that this would only encourage poorer Chinese to commit crimes so that they might be sent to prison, "where they can have a lot of amusement and pay nothing."[37] In January 1893, Ho and sixteen other Chinese and Eurasians sent a memorial to Registrar General Lockhart explaining why they "and the overwhelming majority of the other members of the Chinese community" were "strongly opposed to the Gaol being extended in any way." Prisons in China were designed so that "bad characters [would be] afraid of committing crimes in case they may be lodged in them." The Victoria Gaol, however, "does not inspire much fear, and it would inspire still less if made more comfortable which would most certainly lead to an increase of crime, as criminals will have no dread of entering it." Thus, the memorialists argued, "the most efficacious way to prevent persons from committing crimes in the Colony is not to enlarge the Gaol but to use more freely the power of banishment and the rattan, and to make the prisoners' life not so much a life of ease as it is at present." Existing prison space was already sufficient, "so much so that the prisoners have more space allowed them than they have ever had when not in prison. In a word, they are far better off in gaol than out of it." The proposed separate-cell system would not deter crime: "such an opinion must be formed through ignorance of the habits of the Chinese criminals who will be in no way deterred by having to live in separate cells."[38]

On the one hand, Ho Kai was committed to improving the colony's health standards and was the major force behind the establishment of a hospital and a medical college. On the other hand, he opposed health measures that, as a physician, he must have known would benefit the colony and its inhabitants. In 1887 Ho opposed as "wholly unnecessary" a proposed bill to improve sanitation standards, but it was a bill that he had helped draft. Some years earlier, Colonial Secretary Lord Kimberly had appointed a British engineer to investigate the sanitary conditions of Hong Kong. The engineer's report calling for radical legislative changes in sanitation was published in 1882. When a bill was proposed in 1886 to improve sanitation standards in houses, Ho, a member of the committee that had drafted the bill and the first Chinese member of the Sanitary Board, opposed it. Ho now argued that the bill violated Chinese customs and that the Chinese should be left to live as they pleased, regardless of overcrowding and unsanitary conditions. In May 1887, Ho wrote the following complaint:

> Some Sanitarians are constantly making the mistake of treating Chinese as if they were Europeans. They appear to forget that there are wide constitutional differences between a native of China and one who hails from Europe. They do not allow for the differences of habits, usage, mode of living and a host of other things between the two. They insist upon the theory of treating all nationalities alike however much they may differ from one another physically, mentally, and constitutionally ... One might as well insist that all Chinese should eat bread and beefsteak instead of rice and pork, just because the two former articles agree better than the latter with an English stomach.[39]

"Just fancy the position of the poor tenant if this Bill becomes law," Ho continued. Such tenants "would be forced to pay enormous rent for space less than before, plus all sorts of Sanitary improvements which, however good in themselves from a European stand point, they do not care for, and which they think at least their constitutions do not require." They might insist that "they are habituated to such cities like Canton, Kowloon city&c., compared to which Hong Kong as it now stands is a paradise, a model of cleanliness, a perfect Sanitarium, and that if any more improvements are required, let those who advocate it pay for them and not they." Legislating changes in sanitation would be akin to claiming that local Chinese "are so ignorant of what is good for themselves that they must be taught, and forcibly too, by means of severe legislative measures." The proposal reminded Ho of "the Star Chamber and the Inquisition." If the colonial government were to interfere in its subjects' living conditions, why stop at sanitary standards? Why not prevent opium smoking altogether, force Chinese to convert to Christianity, or forbid Chinese doctors to practice in the colony? Although the proposed health bill would be based on the latest English laws, Ho argued that it made little sense for Hong Kong blindly to follow English laws. Rather, he offered his own list of possible alternative measures, which included renovating public drains and requiring efficient drains in every home, providing a plentiful water supply ("without which no cleanliness is possible"), filling in swampy areas, removing waste, and extending the town to the east and west.[40]

In 1901 Ho opposed another sanitary by-law on similar grounds. In his warnings against government interference in the daily lives of the Chinese population, Ho frequently referred to Captain Charles Elliot's proclamation in 1841 that all Chinese in the colony "shall be governed according to the laws and customs of China." When criticizing the 1886 sanitation bill, for example, he challenged the Sanitary Board: "As long as we govern the Chinese according to our promise given while this Colony was yet in its infancy, viz., to govern them as much as possible in accordance with their manners and customs, and to respect their religion and prejudices, we must of a necessity modify our laws in order to meet their peculiar requirements. Besides, does not common sense alone indicate to us the advisability of legislating especially in many cases to suit circumstances and surroundings?"[41]

In both cases, Ho Kai was perhaps placing his interests as a financier and landlord over his concerns as a physician. Carol Benedict has demonstrated that the European medical concepts introduced to China and Hong Kong in the late nineteenth century were social and cultural constructs. When Chinese residents in Hong Kong resisted the colonial government's health and sanitation measures, they were reacting to the intrusion of the colonial state. Thus we might argue that Ho Kai was protecting the Chinese of Hong Kong against an intrusive colonial state. But given Ho's training in Western medicine, it is doubtful that he would have seen these proposed health measures as merely social or cultural constructs. Similarly, during the anti-opium debate of 1908 Ho—along with other wealthy Chinese merchants—argued that although banning the sale of opium in Hong Kong would be good for the Chinese public, it would hurt both government and merchant revenues.[42]

Ho Kai was doing more than simply trying to protect his own class interests. He was trying to preserve Hong Kong as the kind of place that he and other Chinese believed they had helped create. Like many Hong Kong residents, Ho was convinced that Hong Kong's prosperity and order depended on admitting only the "right" type of Chinese from the mainland. Ho realized that, given Hong Kong's proximity to China, its economy would always depend on immigrants from China. In his opposition to the proposed health bill of 1886, Ho explained that "fortunately or unfortunately, we are close to the mainland, where thousands of poor Chinese are struggling for a bare subsistence. The labour market is always in excess of the demand, and there are many able bodies who are willing and even anxious to get their 10 or 20 cents a day. Those who stick out for higher wages on account of increased rent and less house accommodation will be supplanted by those who will be content with less."[43] In their opposition to the proposed reforms for the Victoria Gaol, Ho and the other petitioners explained that the reforms would adversely affect Hong Kong. "Because the Gaol is already looked upon as a paradise by many a rascal," they wrote, "and situated as we are within a stone's throw of the Chinese territory, any extension of the Gaol will certainly lead to an influx of bad characters from China."[44]

The petitioners reminded the registrar general that "being Chinese ourselves, it is not likely that we would discourage the Government from doing anything for the real benefit of our own countrymen, which would be of advantage to the Chinese community generally." But the extension "would bring harm to the community, and would lead to a large influx of criminals into the Colony, and a great increase in crime."[45] Hard as this may be to square with Ho's commitment to Chinese nationalism and his political liberalism, we should not forget that both nationalism and liberalism have been based as much on exclusion as they have been based on inclusion.[46]

Finally, Ho was also aware of the absurdity and hypocrisy of a colonial government trying to enforce legislation for the health of its Chinese subjects while these subjects—even the permanent residents—enjoyed no political representation. Regardless of how "sweeping a law is in England," he explained, "it is passed by the people through their representatives." Ho did not think it "a wise policy of any Government, especially when it is not of a representative character, to legislate arbitrarily concerning the property of its subjects, and particularly when such measures involve so large a sacrifice of property."

Such legislation would diminish public confidence and drive out capital. This might not "affect those who have no permanent interest in the Colony," but it could be "sufficient to excite alarm in the minds of those who are permanent residents and have the future welfare of the Colony at heart."[47] Again, Ho was distinguishing between "permanent" Hong Kong Chinese like himself and the sojourners who, although necessary for Hong Kong's economic progress, did not share the same commitment to Hong Kong.

The Tram Boycott of 1912–1913 and Ho Kai's Retirement

Ho Kai has often been seen as a "comprador reformer" or "collaborationist patriot" who, forced to choose between Hong Kong and China, chose the former. In the end, at least from the colonial government's perspective, Ho failed to make the proper choice. In 1912 rumors circulated that Ho was looking for a position in the new Chinese republican government.[48] The Tram Boycott of 1912–1913, which seemed to pit Ho's Chinese nationalism against his loyalty to the colonial government, finally ended his political career.

In April 1912 the Hong Kong government banned the circulation of Chinese coins. The economies of Canton and Hong Kong had been intertwined since the early days of the colony, with Chinese coins being used in Hong Kong since then. But as conditions in Canton deteriorated after the 1911 revolution, the colonial government worried about an influx of depreciated Chinese coins from Canton. Many Chinese in Hong Kong took the ban as an insult to the new Chinese republic. In November 1912 the new governor, Francis May, encouraged the Star Ferry Company and the colony's two tramway companies to refuse to accept Chinese coins. This caused even more resentment among the Chinese population because the shortage of Hong Kong coinage in comparison to Chinese meant less money for tram fares. When a colony-wide boycott broke out, its organizers used various means to intimidate those who violated the boycott.[49]

In late 1912 Governor May encouraged Chinese leaders to help end the boycott by traveling on the trams themselves. On 18 December at a meeting of about 150 leading members of the Chinese business community, May insisted that the boycott would hurt both Hong Kong and China because so much Chinese capital was invested in the tram companies. The tram companies' decision not to accept Chinese currency, May assured the meeting attendees, was purely an economic move and was not intended to insult China. He exhorted prominent Chinese to set an example by traveling on the tram themselves and asking their employees to do the same. After reiterating the need to end the boycott, several Chinese businessmen, including Ho Kai and Wei Yuk, rode the tram. On 20 December, during a meeting at the Chinese Commercial Union, Ho and Wei defended the tram companies and condemned the boycott for harming the economies of both Hong Kong and Canton.[50]

With help from local Chinese merchants, the boycott ended by early February 1913. To May, however, this help had been too little, too late. He was especially annoyed that Ho and Wei, both unofficial members of the Legislative Council, had waited until the meeting on 18 December to help end the boycott. Furthermore, the two had been absent from an important meeting at the Tung Wah Hospital that May had called to help end the boycott. May reported to Colonial Secretary Lewis Harcourt in August 1913 that "this Government, I regret to say, has lost confidence in Sir K'ai Ho K'ai." May began by accusing Ho of corruption and meddling in Chinese affairs. "For some time it has been common report among the Chinese that Sir K'ai Ho K'ai uses his position as a member of the Legislative Council to exact pecuniary contributions from many of the Guilds in the Colony." Although May admitted that he lacked concrete evidence for most of these charges, he insisted that "the rumour is not without foundation." Among these guilds was the "notorious" Sze Yap Association, which May believed had masterminded the tram boycott and which "was openly defiant of the Government and was so closely associated with the Government of Canton that it was practically managing that administration from the Colony." Ho himself had been "intimately connected" with the Guangdong uprising and with the Canton government "ever since." As evidence of this connection, May alleged that Ho had drafted an "elaborate Constitution" for the new Canton government. Furthermore, Ho "had sufficient interest in Canton to get his brother—a man of very poor character—appointed to an important post in Swatow." On top of all this, Ho was related by marriage to Ch'an Shui-pak (better known to students of Chinese history as Chen Shaobai), a newspaper editor, friend of Sun Yatsen, and first legal advisor to the Canton government, even "though he [Ch'an] possesses no legal knowledge or qualification."[51]

Most important, Ho Kai, who had been knighted two years earlier, was no longer useful to the colonial government. "Formerly," May wrote to Harcourt, "Sir K'ai could be relied on for information and advice when the Government wanted it. Now this is not so." During the tram boycott, Ho had given "practically no assistance to the Government." The Secretary for Chinese affairs, as the registrar general was now known, May reported, had also complained that Ho was no longer keeping him abreast of local Chinese affairs. In short: "Sir K'ai Ho K'ai no longer represents the Chinese community, whose confidence he has lost, as he has lost that of the Government. He is not in close touch with the Chinese mercantile community and his political bias has drawn him into close association with those whom the Chinese who have a real stake in the Colony recognize as the enemies of peace and good order, although they have not the moral courage openly to oppose their intrigues."[52]

But if Ho supposedly lacked moral courage, May had no more of it. May tried to avoid confronting Ho by suggesting to the Colonial Office that Ho not be given another term in the Legislative Council after his four six-year terms expired in 1914. He suggested that Sir John Jordan, senior British official in China, might persuade President Yuan Shikai to give Ho a position in the Chinese government where he could "utilise his knowledge of English and his undoubted ability" in the Chinese diplomatic service. Although Ho had "imbibed a certain respect for British institutions and no doubt some loyalty to the British empire" and was a British subject by birth, May did not think this would prevent the Chinese government from hiring him. If this plan failed, May would have to tell Ho himself that four terms was enough. "It will of course be a blow to Sir K'ai both financially and politically, for without the prestige of his seat on the Council he would sink to a position of insignificance in the Chinese community . . . but on the whole I am strongly of the opinion that this Government would gain by this change."[53]

In the end, the Colonial Office saved May from having to do the dirty work by passing a new rule limiting terms for colonial legislature members. In November 1913, Acting Governor Claude Severn recommended that Lau Chu Pak, comprador to A. S. Watson's, replace Ho Kai in the Legislative Council.[54] In January 1914, Severn, who had resumed his position as local colonial secretary, wrote Ho that "save in very exceptional circumstances," unofficial members of legislative councils in the colonies were not to be reappointed for more than one term. Aware of the situation and eager to avoid embarrassment, Ho replied that "the weak and unsatisfactory state of my health precludes any possibility of my acceptance of a further term on the Council were I to be re-appointed." Ho expressed his satisfaction at having been able to serve the "Colony in which I was born and bred."[55]

Ho ended his political career in early 1914 with a barrage of false praise from the governor. In a March 1914 letter to the Colonial Office, May wrote that "Sir Kai's loss will be felt in the Legislative Council where his acumen and knowledge were very useful factors in debate." May hoped that the government would "still have the benefit of his advice and co-operation."[56] In his address to the council on Ho's last day in office, 25 March 1914, May thanked Ho for his twenty-four years of service. The governor noted that Ho had "rendered extremely efficient service not only as a representative of the Chinese community, but as an independent member of the Council . . . Gifted with a thorough knowledge of the feelings of his fellow countrymen, with a clear intellect, sound judgment and fluent command of the English language, he has always been of the greatest assistance in the deliberations and debates held in this Chamber. Moreover, he has earned our admiration for the ungrudging manner in which, both inside and outside this Council, he has devoted his intellect and his energies to the advancement of the best interests of the Chinese community and for the good of the Colony as a whole."[57]

In his farewell speech to the Council, Ho insisted that he had always tried to do his best in the discharge of his public duties and had never allowed his "personal inclination or self-interest to interfere in the discharge" of his public duties both inside and outside the council. Ho promised to continue to do his best in "promoting any measure for the good of [the] Colony."[58] Ho Kai died four months later in July 1914, at the age of fifty-five, leaving so little money that the government had to agree to help educate his five sons.[59]

The Confines of Collaboration

By viewing Ho Kai's life and activities within the confines of collaboration, scholars have greatly simplified the richly complex situation in which Ho lived and operated. Ho's Hong Kong identity helped shape his views of Chinese nationalism. The lawyer Tso Seen Wan once explained that "it was Sir Kai Ho's sole aim in life to advance the interests of the Chinese and to induce them, both English speaking and Chinese speaking alike, to come forward and help the government and take an interest in public affairs."[60] As a Chinese nationalist, Ho was concerned about the fate of his ancestral homeland. He was proud of colonial Hong Kong, its prosperity and stability, and was committed to preserving these qualities. This pride and commitment, however, did not conflict with his concern for China; rather, Ho's financial and political position in Hong Kong enabled him to take an active interest in the Chinese reform movement. Because Ho saw commerce and liberalism as the reasons for Hong Kong's great success, he believed they could do the same for China, given the proper political environment.

Analogous to the British rulers' view of Hong Kong, Ho saw Hong Kong's historical mission as furthering the development of trade and commerce in China. When he eventually stopped supporting the Chinese revolutionary movement, Ho did so because he was convinced that constitutional reform, rather than radical revolution, was the key to China's salvation. Radical revolution would only lead China on the road to ruin, which might in turn jeopardize Hong Kong's own prosperity and stability. Ho's prediction almost came true during the great strike-boycott of 1925–1926. Fortunately for the colonial government, it had Chinese partners who chose to collaborate to preserve their Hong Kong.

~ 6

Preserving Hong Kong: The Strike-Boycott of 1925–1926

*T*HE TRAM BOYCOTT of 1912–1913 that triggered the collapse of Ho Kai's political career was a relatively minor incident in the history of Hong Kong. But it showed how dramatically the political changes in China could affect the colony. Most of the revolutionary and nationalist feeling in the new republic was directed toward Japan, which in the spring of 1915 forced the notorious Twenty-One Demands on the Beijing government, and toward Great Britain, which maintained the largest economic interests in China. The First World War and its aftermath brought new social and economic problems to China, the most serious of which was a strike in 1919 after rice prices had soared. Hong Kong saw its first general strike after a decade of relative calm when the Chinese Seamen's Union and twelve other trade unions went on strike in 1922.

The colony was hit hardest by the great strike-boycott of 1925–1926. Although the strike-boycott was sparked by events in China, it derived part of its local force from the popular feeling against the privileged status of foreigners. This was apparent from the demands of the strike commission, which—in addition to such standard reforms as an eight-hour workday, the abolition of contract and child labor, freedom of speech and press, and the right to organize—had a strong local component: permission for labor unions to vote for a Chinese member on the Legislative Council, and for Chinese to be treated as the equal of Europeans and to be able to live on the Peak.

For the leaders of the Chinese bourgeoisie, the strike-boycott was an ideological and economic war that threatened Hong Kong's very existence. One reason these men collaborated so actively with the colonial government to end the strike was to protect their own class interests. But fighting the strike also meant preserving the colony they had helped to build. It furthermore enabled the leaders of this bourgeoisie to prove themselves to the colonial government as loyal Hong Kong Chinese.

The May Thirtieth Incident and the Shajie Massacre

On 30 May 1925, Sikh police under British command opened fire on a crowd of Chinese demonstrators in the International Settlement of Shanghai. At least nine demonstrators were killed, with many others wounded. Word of this violence, which was soon known as the May Thirtieth Incident, spread like wildfire, prompting protests all across China but especially in the cities where British interests were most heavily concentrated: Shanghai and Canton. Although most Chinese in Hong Kong had not shown great interest in the nationalist revolution of the 1920s, the killings in Shanghai encouraged many to support their mainland compatriots. On 18 June most of the students at Queen's College heeded the call to strike. The next day cargo carriers walked out, followed by tram drivers and conductors, seamen, typesetters, and members of pro-communist unions.[1]

On 23 June during a particularly heated demonstration in Shamian—the British and French concession in Canton—troops under foreign command killed more than 50 Chinese protesters who were marching along Shajie, the embankment across from Shamian; almost 120 demonstrators were wounded. As news of the massacre spread, labor and union leaders in Canton called for a general strike in South China, especially in Hong Kong, which was the most visible example of British imperialism. Nationalist military leaders and their Soviet advisers even considered attacking the International Settlement in Shamian.[2] Anti-British pamphlets and placards in Hong Kong asked Chinese to rise up and drive out the British colonialists and their Chinese "hunting dogs." Strike leaders in Canton beckoned Chinese to leave Hong Kong, spreading rumors that the government planned to poison the colony's water supplies and offering free passage to Canton by train or steamer.[3]

The first to strike were those working for foreigners—the waiters and busboys at the Peak Hotel and the Peak Club, servants on the Peak, and hotel staffs. Governor Alexander Grantham, who arrived in Hong Kong as a cadet in 1922, recalled that the worst part of the strike was "trying to cope with my own cooking and other household chores, since all our servants had left." Students soon marched out of their classrooms in support. Next came laborers, shopkeepers, and tram employees. In the first two weeks, more than fifty thousand people left the colony. By late June, most Chinese staffs in restaurants, government agencies, and newspapers had left their jobs, as had bus drivers, ferry operators, and rickshaw pullers. Food prices soared, prompting a run on banks. Hong Kong's economy nearly came to a halt.[4]

On 22 June the colonial government declared a state of emergency. In a telegram to Colonial Secretary L. S. Amery on 26 June, Governor Reginald Stubbs asked the British Admiralty to dispatch a cruiser to "encourage local Chinese." Stubbs had already mobilized volunteers under the Peace Preservation Ordinance. Under the Emergency Ordinance, passed during the seamen's strike of 1922, he also prohibited the export of foodstuffs and money and granted Chinese bankers' request for a moratorium on Chinese banks. Chinese telegrams, mail, and newspapers were being censored.[5] The scope of Stubbs's emergency measures quickly widened. He limited the amount of currency that could be taken out of the colony, dispatched policemen to guard water supplies, sent troops to man the Star Ferry and patrol the streets, released schools early for summer vacation, and imposed a curfew. Stubbs also ordered the main Chinese and European department stores to remain open for at least four hours per day. Similar orders were issued for certain smaller shops.[6]

By early July, the colony was "like a ghost town." With pickets in Canton preventing strikers from returning to Hong Kong, the colony survived by relying on Chinese and European volunteers who kept the place running. Some delivered mail and ice, while others drove the trams. The navy ran the Star Ferry. On 10 July Stubbs wrote that "all regular trades are practically at a standstill." The police had been deporting vagabonds and other "undesirables." By the end of July, some 250,000 Chinese had left for Canton. On 18 September Stubbs described the colony's financial situation as "most serious." One prominent Chinese bank had already gone into liquidation, other firms were on the verge of bankruptcy, and Stubbs feared that more would follow suit. The Chinese Chamber of Commerce had asked for a trade loan from the British government. Although the worst was over by early October 1925, the strike devastated Hong Kong. It lasted over a year, and the British government had to provide a trade loan of three million British pounds to keep the colony's economy from collapsing.[7]

The Strike-Boycott in Hong Kong and Chinese History

Despite its importance in Hong Kong history, the strike-boycott has received rather uneven attention. In his general history, G. B. Endacott devoted only one paragraph to the strike, never mentioning the Chinese who helped Hong Kong survive the devastation. Scholars who have examined the strike more thoroughly have done so primarily from the perspective of the Chinese labor movement.[8] Those writers who have focused on the local implications of the strike have tended to see it as a sign of the growth of Chinese nationalism in Hong Kong. Chan Lau Kit-ching sets the strike in the middle of the often-turbulent relations among China, Britain, and Hong Kong. To Henry Lethbridge the strike "brought the leaders of the Chinese and European communities close together willing or not." Thus the strike represented an important coming of age for the colony: "it was no longer simply a congeries of various groups, composed of acquisitive, rootless, transient individuals, but was beginning to coalesce into a community and, if all racial divisions are included, into a plural society, its members bound together, as it were, in a network of contractual arrangements. It had begun to acquire an identity."[9]

From the perspective of the evolving relationship between the leaders of the Chinese bourgeoisie and the colonial government, the strike and its resolution were not isolated events. These leaders' support for the government was the culmination of decades of collaboration. They not only supported the government but even took an active role in combating the strike. Fighting the strike meant preserving the colony they had helped build. At the same time, by reinforcing the image of the strike as a communist, "Bolshevik" plot against Hong Kong, they used their relationship with the colonial government to protect their own class interests. By contrasting the chaotic conditions across the border in Canton with the situation in Hong Kong, they emphasized their own role in maintaining peace and order. Fighting the strike enabled the leaders of the Chinese bourgeoisie to present themselves as allies, to show their loyalty to the colonial government, and to prove themselves as Hong Kong Chinese.

The Colonial Government's View of the Strike

In their reports to London, colonial officials were adamant that the strike was directed by radical agitators in Canton and had nothing to do with economic or political conditions in the colony. In a confidential dispatch to Amery on 10 July Stubbs insisted that "there is still no anti-foreign feeling apparent in the Colony, and it is becoming increasingly clear that the whole affair is being engineered by the Russian Communists in Canton." Minimizing the anti-British aspect of the strike, Stubbs declared that "the attack which is being made upon the Colony is an attack upon all law and order, and it is aimed at the whole merchant class, both Chinese and foreign." In another confidential dispatch to Amery in late July, Stubbs reported that the strike was "paralysing" British trade in South China. When he later tried to convince London of a loan to anticommunist merchant groups in Canton to help end the strike, Stubbs warned that the "whole of the existence of the Colony is involved." In a telegraph in September, Stubbs predicted that "if the policy of inaction continues Hong Kong will probably be completely ruined and all British trade with South China probably lost." Just before he left Hong Kong in late October, Stubbs complained that although Chinese merchants in Canton had made "certain overtures" to help end the boycott, authorities there had no interest in negotiating.[10] Acting Governor W. T. Southorn, who temporarily replaced Stubbs, insisted that the strike was "political in origin, and neither provoked by any fault of omission or commission on the part of the local authorities, nor designed to remedy any economic grievance, real or imaginary." Secretary for Chinese Affairs D. W. Tratman stressed how the agitation in Hong Kong had been fanned by the "wilder elements" in labor and student circles, and how the Canton government was "working in the closest harmony with Moscow."[11]

Stubbs's successor, Cecil Clementi, was also convinced that the strike had been provoked by agitators in Canton and did not reflect local conditions. In a speech to the Legislative Council in early February 1926, Clementi accused the Canton government itself of organizing the strike, citing a communiqué from the Canton commissioner of foreign affairs claiming that the strike by Hong Kong workers was a patriotic protest against the British government. But why, then, Clementi asked, did the Canton Strike Committee have to post pickets in Canton to keep Hong Kong workers from returning to Canton? Why had almost all the Hong Kong workers since returned to work, despite intimidation from the Canton Strike Committee?[12]

Convinced that the strike was an attempt by the Canton government to ruin the colony, Clementi insisted that the colonial government would deal only with the Canton government, not the strike committee, and that it would "never agree in principle to strike pay or to compensation for non-reinstatement of labourers." Because the boycott was a violation of treaty rights and would mainly harm Chinese commerce, the Canton government should be responsible for ending the strike. "Only the unlawful activities of the Canton Strike Committee, instigated by the Bolshevik intrigue, prevent the resumption of normal relations between Canton and Hong Kong on the old, familiar footing."[13]

Only one month earlier, Clementi had been less opposed to negotiating with the strike commission. In late December 1925, he suggested that the Hong Kong government and local merchants offer "compensation" to the strikers in the form of a trade loan to Canton. Although "British habits of thought" might be offended by an arrangement, local Chinese would see nothing unusual or unsavory in it. "Unless a settlement of the boycott is made by an early date in January next, it is probable that there will be acute financial trouble among the Hong Kong Chinese." Clementi instructed representatives of the local Chinese business community to elect delegates to present the payment plan to Canton. On 24 December Chow Shouson and the Eurasian Robert Kotewall, the two "Chinese" unofficial members of the Legislative Council, met with the Chinese justices of peace, the executive committee of the Chinese Chamber of Commerce, representatives of the twenty-four merchant guilds, members of the District Watch Committee, senior Tung Wah Hospital Committee members, bankers, and "other responsible merchants." All agreed that the boycott should be ended as soon as possible and that they should elect representatives to go to Canton to negotiate.[14]

The "responsible" Chinese included Li Yau Tsun, who apart from having served on all the major Chinese committees was, as Clementi explained, a "very prominent Chinese business man—very sound and reliable and has long been of great assistance to Secretary for Chinese Affairs." Ma Tsui Chiu was director of the Tung Wah Hospital Committee. The Eurasian Lo Man Kam was head of Messrs. Lo and Lo, a prestigious solicitor firm. Kong E Suen, whose brother was on the Tung Wah, was a coal merchant. Tsoi Siu Woon, a "rich man with no particular business," was one of the directors of the Bank of Canton. Li Yiu Tong represented the twenty-four merchant guilds. A member of an earlier delegation sent by a Hong Kong commercial association, Tse Shu Tong was a salesman. Li Sing Kui was the manager of the Hong Nin Insurance Company and a former committee member of both the Tung Wah Hospital and the Po Leung Kuk.[15]

On 4 January 1926, Clementi reported to Amery that the mission to Canton had "completely failed," and that the Canton government was supporting the strikers.[16] The strikers would deal only with representatives of the Hong Kong government who had the authority to make a settlement. Clementi cited Lo Man Kam's report on the mission to show that the Canton government saw the boycott not as a struggle between capital and labor, but as a "political and patriotic contest with Great Britain and the Hong Kong government in particular." As long as this continued to be the case, no settlement would be possible.[17] On 25 January Clementi held a special Executive Council meeting to discuss ways to end the boycott. The consensus was that the boycott might end in one of only two ways. Hong Kong could hope for the overthrow of the Canton government by outside generals or through internal conflict; or it could simply wait out the boycott, hoping that the merchants would survive.[18]

In early February, Clementi reported that the strike pickets had intensified their aggression against Hong Kong. They were shooting at Indian troops on the Hong Kong side of the border and at police launches in the Shenzhen River between Hong Kong and China, blocking trains to and from China, and preventing villagers from crossing the border back into Hong Kong. A British military attack was out of the question, for although the Canton government was a "rebel government," military hostilities would hurt British trade with the rest of China. Better alternatives would be helping the Chinese navy defeat Canton or putting pressure on Moscow to end the boycott. Clementi rejected the idea of formal negotiations with the Canton strike committee, which included former workers from Hong Kong whom he did not want back in the colony. The last option was to try and persuade the Canton government to accept British rather than Russian assistance, though Clementi was not hopeful.[19]

When colonial officials attributed the strike to "Bolshevik" influence from Canton, they were not necessarily exaggerating this influence. Even before the strike, left-wing intellectuals and union organizers had tried to encourage nationalist sympathies in Hong Kong by distributing handbills urging workers to strike. Nor were they exaggerating the importance of funding from outside the colony. The bulk of the financial support came from the revolutionary Kuomintang government. The second-largest source came from overseas Chinese. Russian workers sent 10,000 rubles, while an anonymous British trade union sent 130 British pounds.[20] In 1928, A. G. M. Fletcher, the local colonial secretary, claimed that documents discovered at the Soviet military attaché in Beijing revealed the role that Russia had played in the boycott.[21]

But the extent of this Bolshevik influence is not the question here. The colonial government needed to convince the British government that the strike had nothing to with conditions in Hong Kong or with the Chinese business community. In England, most observers had little sympathy for the European expatriates in Hong Kong. As Robert Kotewall later put it, opinion in England had been "at best indifferent" and "at worst unfavourable" toward the plight of Hong Kong. The general impression was that the strike was a "just revolt of workers against conditions long since abolished in England." In London the Chinese Information Bureau, comprised of Chinese students, had been supplying the English press with information "calculated to present their case in a favourable light."[22] When trying, unsuccessfully, to justify to a skeptical Amery a regulation passed under the Emergency Regulations Ordinance to flog intimidators—not "ordinary Hong

Kong labourers" but "imported scoundrels"—Stubbs repeated emphatically that the strike was an attempt by "the Cantonese to ruin Hong Kong by terrorising [local workers] into desertion," not a strike for economic reasons.[23] Fletcher later insisted that "until June, 1925, there was no definitely anti-British movement in South China. . . . It is now admitted," he continued, that the boycott against Hong Kong "was instituted as a form of warfare against the British Government. As a boycott pure and simple, it would not have lasted long, for the Chinese merchants were never enthusiastic about it."[24]

"Loyal Chinese": Chow Shouson and Robert Kotewall

The Hong Kong government's response to the strike and denunciation of the agitators in Canton reveals how the colonial administration formulated its strategies with multiple sets of audiences in mind: the British Colonial Office, the strike organizers and government authorities in Canton, and the local communities. Clementi's strategies in particular—his insistence on dealing with the Canton government rather than with the strike commission, his declaration that the strike violated the treaty rights, and his decision to dispatch a delegation of "responsible" local Chinese—may have helped fashion a stronger sense of Hong Kong unity and identity by enlisting Chinese bourgeois support for the colonial administration. The leaders of the Chinese bourgeoisie may have even come to see the colony as *their* place partly as a result of such colonial strategies.

But just as it was important for the colonial government to present the strike as the product of Bolshevik agitation from Canton, so it was in the interest of the Chinese bourgeoisie to protect their own interests by convincing the government of the severity of the strike. Used to relying on servants, drivers, and cooks, many wealthy Chinese had to fend for themselves during the strike. They now found themselves cleaning streets, disposing rubbish and sewage, and helping to maintain cleanliness and order. It soon became clear that the businesses hurt most were Chinese firms, especially smaller and newer enterprises. Many pawnshops were looted and had to close down for the duration of the strike. Smaller Chinese banks never fully recovered from the blow. The Kwong Sang Hong, a cosmetics company that was founded in 1912 by local Chinese businessmen and established itself as a major competitor to foreign firms, never regained its prestrike strength.[25] The Chinese business community's inability to fund public welfare projects was a barometer of its financial condition. A proposed plan by Li Yau Tsun, chairman of the Chinese Chamber of Commerce, to build a Chinese library for chamber members and the public had to be postponed until late 1928.[26] Thus it is not surprising that much of the colonial government's view of the strike was informed by leaders of the Chinese business community, especially Chow Shouson and Robert Kotewall, both unofficial Legislative Council members, who advised the government and helped coordinate overall counterstrike efforts.

Can Robert Kotewall, a Eurasian who also went by his Chinese name, Lo Yuk Wo, truly be considered a representative of the Chinese bourgeoisie? Robert Ward, an American in Hong Kong during the Japanese occupation from 1942 to 1945, thought not. Men like Kotewall and Robert Ho Tung, who was also Eurasian, "were in fact little more than instruments of the British Colonial government, and whether as the result of deliberate selection or *faute de mieux*, they were men who were rarely highly regarded by the Chinese themselves, and often not actually Chinese." More recently, it has been argued that Eurasians like Ho Tung and Kotewall were never viewed by other Chinese, either in Hong Kong or on the mainland, as Chinese.[27]

To be sure, Eurasians in Hong Kong held a "precarious position between the foreign and native elements." Their status, as Lethbridge put it, was "ambiguous and uncertain." Governor Stubbs once reported that because "pure" Chinese disdained Eurasians as "the Bastards," the government had been reluctant to appoint them to official positions. As we saw in the attempts to exclude them from the Peak, Eurasians posed a threat to Europeans because of their slippery racial and class status. But Kotewall, although Eurasian, was always listed in directories of prominent local Chinese published by Chinese from Hong Kong or Canton. Hong Kong government officials often referred to him as an example of the "loyal Chinese" of the colony. Kotewall's daughter remembered him as a "very strong Confucian" who "worshipped his ancestors."[28] During the strike, Canton authorities singled out Kotewall and Chow, the two "Chinese" unofficial members of the Legislative Council, in their attempts to negotiate with the Hong Kong government. In his correspondence with government officials, Kotewall usually referred to himself as Chinese, or as a representative of the local Chinese population. In a 1926 letter urging the British government to build a Chinese Studies department at Hong Kong University as a way to counter the radical ideas emanating from China, Kotewall noted that he and Chow understood "the feelings and wishes not only of the Chinese community of the Colony but also of the more conservative elements of the Chinese people generally." After proposing that the local upper classes end their reliance on Cantonese servants by hiring outside of Guangdong or from the Philippines, Kotewall added, "I am sorry that as a representative of the Chinese I should have to make this suggestion, but my first consideration is the highest interests of the Colony."[29]

The strike-boycott showed that a major political crisis threatening the established political order might represent a major opportunity for men on the margin, like Kotewall, blurring lines between race, identity, and collective loyalty. Chow and Kotewall saw the strike as an ideological and economic war launched by Canton against Hong Kong, which they were careful to stress in their reports to the governor. As Kotewall reported in October 1925, "the strike was undoubtedly caused by Bolshevik intrigue in Canton, conducted with the avowed object of destroying the economic life of Hongkong." This was the view of the Chinese General Chamber of Commerce and the Association of the Twenty-Four Mercantile Guilds, expressed in a resolution passed in a meeting earlier in August. Kotewall insisted that the reason workers in Hong Kong had left both their jobs and the colony itself so spontaneously was due neither to "patriotic indignation" nor to "unbearable living conditions." Rather, it had been "an exhibition of pure terror, of panic fear, in all but a very few cases. One would imagine that only desperate danger could induce such extreme fright, but in point of fact, the very slightest causes—an unsigned scrawl on a slip of paper, a mere warning word or look, or a telephone message from an unknown person—were sufficient to send them hurrying and scurrying out of their jobs."[30]

The mastermind behind all of the unrest, Kotewall explained, had been the propaganda machine of the Canton government and the strike committee. Subsidized newspapers, such as the *China News (Chung Kwok San Man Po)*, had "preached Bolshevism, while from time to time attacks, most veiled, were made on the merchants and ruling

classes." The paper eventually "over-stepped the utmost limits of tol-
eration by ridiculing His Majesty [King George] on the eve of his
birthday." Only weeks earlier, the same paper had published a "scur-
rilous article" referring to the king as the "Big Devil" and to Governor
Stubbs as the "Little Devil."[31] Soon even members of the Chinese
middle class, especially women and children, were in a "veritable stam-
pede" to board steamers and trains for Canton and Macau "as a result
of the wild and lying rumours spread by our enemy." Those who later
tried to return were prevented from doing so by pickets hired by the
strike committee; others were flogged or forcibly exposed in the sun
for hours. Escaping sampans (small boats) were burned. One woman
was shot trying to cross the border at Shenzhen; several others
drowned in the river.[32]

Kotewall riddled his report with military metaphors. "In effect,
Canton is waging a war against us, only with means other than guns
and gas." Repeatedly referring to Canton as "our enemy," Kotewall
stressed the "necessity for preparedness" and that the colony needed
a Chinese volunteer organization to take over in "times of emergency,"
such as another strike. Although he and Chow rejected a proposal for
a curfew because it would only confirm rumors of arson and violence
and invoke even more panic, Kotewall recommended that "loyal" and
"law-abiding" Chinese be allowed to carry weapons, especially those
serving in the police reserve and on neighborhood and street committees. Recalling that he and Chow had asked the governor to order
routine military marches and demonstrations, Kotewall wrote: "[this]
had a most steadying effect on the populace, showing the enemy our
real strength, and convincing our friends that there was sufficient force
to protect them." When volunteers in the Chinese division of the St.
John Ambulance Association, led by the Eurasian Ho Kam Tong, requested that their uniforms resembling those of the Volunteer Defence
Corps be changed so that they would not be jeered by crowds, Kotewall and Chow disagreed. They hoped the confusion might make the
number of volunteers appear larger than it actually was, especially "at
a time when there was fear of an invasion."[33]

For Kotewall and Chow, the strike had provoked both the best and
the worst in Hong Kong Chinese society. They were especially dis-
turbed by the role high-school students had played. To Kotewall, the
"root of the evil" was clear: "Chinese education in Hongkong does

not seem to be all that it should be." Kotewall recommended that more emphasis be placed on "the ethics of Confucianism which is, in China, probably the best antidote to the pernicious doctrines of Bolshevism, and is certainly the most powerful conservative force, and the greatest influence for good." He called for more Confucian schools, observing that the colony only had one such school, founded two years earlier by Fung Ping Shan and other merchants. Any money spent on such schools would be "social insurance of the best kind . . . careful instruction in Confucianism and its application to the problems of modern civic conditions should be given in all the schools where there are Chinese students."[34]

Whereas for Kotewall the strike had brought out the worst in local Chinese students, he thought it had brought out the best in the older, more conservative Chinese. Some had proposed forming "Fascisti" organizations along the lines of the "Italian model." Kotewall discussed this with Chow, the secretary for Chinese affairs, and the assistant colonial secretary. They decided against the idea, however, because they were sure the British government would not approve, and because Kotewall knew "from the history of this organization in Italy, that if once it is allowed to get out of hand it becomes a danger to the community." Still, Kotewall was impressed and noted that "the men who advocated this belong mostly to the class of the old Chinese literati, and it is an interesting proof of the growth of a civic interest and self-reliance formerly lacking among the Chinese of this class."[35]

Counter-Propaganda

The strike prompted an intensive propaganda campaign orchestrated by "loyal Chinese," such as Chow and Kotewall, who soon advised the government to establish a Counter-Propaganda Bureau. Posters encouraging the population to resist the strikers were plastered along public thoroughfares, while leaflets were distributed among the Chinese community. Students at St. Paul's Girls' School and St. Stephen's Girls' School helped make posters. The propaganda was attributed to imaginary organizations, such as the "Peace and Order Preservation Society," or it was anonymous.[36]

The Counter-Propaganda Bureau also coordinated propaganda aimed at overseas Chinese. The May Thirtieth Incident had provoked patriotic feelings among overseas Chinese, who then sent money to support the strikers in Shanghai and Canton. To counter this, Kotewall and Chow had leaflets and copies of the *Commercial Press (Kung Sheung Yat Po)*, a counterpropaganda newspaper, sent to overseas communities in North America, Australia, and Southeast Asia. After the material "had time to work its influence," Kotewall and Chow had the Chinese Chamber of Commerce, the Association of the Twenty-Four Mercantile Guilds, and the Tung Wah Hospital Committee send a joint telegram to the overseas Chinese communities:

> The present commotions in Canton which are ruining trade and industries of Canton and Hongkong and bringing calamity to worker and merchant alike are beyond all doubt due to the Canton Government's outright adopting of Russian Bolshevik principles. The control of all the naval and military forces has passed entirely into the hands of Russians. It has been definitely decided to put Communism in force and impose a levy on all building construction and house property. A reign of unspeakable terror is being inaugurated throughout the Province to the unspeakable distress of its population. If assistance is not speedily given this poisonous tide of Bolshevism will steadily grow until it engulfs the whole of China beyond the hope of redemption. We on the spot see with our own eyes the appalling nature of the situation. But we fear that our friends in distant parts of the world may not realise the truth, and are therefore addressing you in order that you may know all the facts. We implore you not to be misled by lying propaganda. From the Chinese Chamber of Commerce, the Tung Wah Hospital and the Association of Twenty-Four Mercantile Guilds of Hongkong.[37]

Propaganda was also directed at European communities in Hong Kong, South China, and even in England. The South China Publicity Bureau revived the *Daily News*, a news sheet that was started during the First World War to spread news about the war. Kotewall and Chow proposed distributing propaganda in England to combat the image of the strike as a genuine workers' strike, an image Kotewall insisted "should never have been allowed to grow up." At the same time, Kotewall and Chow were careful not to implicate the Soviet

Union directly. Uneasy about the propaganda efforts from the start, the British government was concerned that any anti-Bolshevik propaganda might be seen as anti-Soviet propaganda, violating a treaty between the United Kingdom and the Soviet Union. In March 1926 Clementi, assuring Amery that the Hong Kong government was not doing anything that would violate the treaty, wrote: "[I am] firmly convinced of the importance of continuing these two undertakings [the *Daily News* and the *Commercial Press*] for the present, and that there is nothing contained in them which could be construed fairly as breaking the promise which has been given to Russia by His Majesty's Government."[38]

The Labour Protection Bureau

In early July 1925, at the recommendation of Kotewall and Chow, the colonial government also established a secret bureau to protect laborers from intimidators and to launch a counterattack against such intimidators. As Kotewall put it, such an organization was needed to counter the "absurd ease with which all classes of Chinese allowed themselves to be frightened by direct threats or general rumours." Since "the best defence is attack, such an organization should strike fear in the hearts of the intimidators who are no less subject to cowardice than their victims." But who would be in charge of this organization? The question was answered on 5 July, when Liang Weichen—a former pirate who had previously served as a general in Chen Jiongming's Guangdong Army—offered his services through Ma Tsui Chiu, chairman of the Tung Wah Hospital Committee. Kotewall, Chow, and Li Yau Tsun interviewed Liang and then introduced him to the governor, the colonial secretary, and the secretary for Chinese affairs. All approved, and the Labour Protection Bureau was formed. As Stubbs explained in a confidential dispatch to Amery on 10 July, "an attempt is being made to get together a small band of Chinese Special Police under the supervision of an ex-pirate and general in Chan Kwing-ming's [Chen Jiongming's] army, who undertakes that his men will be brave enough to arrest intimidators." Two weeks later, Stubbs reported that "this Government has been most fortunate in finding in General [Liang] a man with both the will and the power to organize counter-measures." Liang had formed from "his clansmen and former soldiers" 100 special police and 50 detectives "under his personal control" and "with orders that they are to concentrate upon the arrest of intimidators and persons engaged in political activities." As Stubbs explained further, the Labour Protection Bureau was successful. "It has become known," he wrote, "that this organization exists and means business, with the result that the intimidator, who has no more personal courage than the rest of his compatriots, has discontinued his activities."[39]

The organization, membership, and operation of the Labour Protection Bureau were kept secret, while the bureau itself was shrouded in mystery. Although it consisted of more than 150 men, the bureau was never mentioned in newspapers or government publications, and although the public never knew who or how many people were in the bureau, everyone knew of its existence. A favorite tactic was to place a Chinese lecturer in streets and other public places, with planted audiences made up of Liang's men disguised as workers. Officials in London expressed doubt about the bureau's "staff" members and their previous experience, but Kotewall and Chow were unconcerned. To intimidate the intimidators, Kotewall later insisted, the men had to be of "a bold type—a rare quality which was so very rare among Chinese at that time." Given the chaotic political conditions in China, the men were likely to have had a "somewhat adventurous existence, but this is no necessary disqualification for our purpose. Though it is necessary that our agents for this dangerous work should act for us in a clean way, they should not be required to furnish proof of having worn kid gloves from their youth up." The mysterious nature of the bureau was crucial. Since the public never knew exactly who or how many were in the bureau, they saw "spies everywhere." Kotewall explained that local Chinese, "so easily terrified, have proved equally easy to reassure. The lesson is that they must not be left without support in the face of an unknown terror." Both the Special Police Reserve and the Labour Protection Bureau had made the regular police and District Watchmen more vigilant. "In other words," Kotewall explained, "the regular police and watchmen were shamed into greater efforts by the example of these 'ex-pirates'." Stubbs shared Kotewall's enthusiasm for Liang and his bureau. In October he wrote that Liang and his men were continuing to do "excellent work," even though their services were required less frequently.[40]

The Commercial Press

The strike-boycott also ended up being a critical moment in the history of Hong Kong journalism. One of the most effective tools in the propaganda campaign was the counterpropaganda *Commercial Press* founded in mid-1925. Although it received a subsidy from the colonial government, the paper was the brainchild of Chow and Kotewall. The general manager was Hung Hing Kam, a local solicitor who hired other Chinese to write, edit, and proofread the paper and to monitor wire services from Canton and abroad.[41] The need for such a paper was clear. As Kotewall recalled, soon after the strike the majority of the local Chinese newspapers were either against the government or "at least afraid to publish what we wanted." Even as late as September 1926, as Clementi explained, some of the Canton papers printed in English continued to "teem with anti-British calumnies. The propaganda which I propose is aimed to set forward impartially and with strict regard for the truth the correct news, and fairly to represent British aims and actions."[42]

The *Commercial Press* was a propaganda instrument, designed to calm the populace, break up striker solidarity, and assure readers that the strike was on its last legs. Each day a column listed the number of people leaving Hong Kong and the number returning. The daily number of departees soon decreased, while the number of returnees increased. The paper painted a rosy picture of life in the colony during the strike. Copies were sent to overseas Chinese in North America and Australia who had been supporting the strikers in Canton.

The layout of the *Commercial Press* presented a chaos-ridden Canton, in contrast to a calm and peaceful Hong Kong. Canton news typically came before local news, the former highlighted by a larger typeface, with the title character exceptionally large and set off by circles or other markers. Section one of Canton news usually focused on political or military developments, section two on the strike. Articles in May 1926, for example, included coverage of the chaotic conditions in Canton caused by labor unrest and the strike, highlighting the conflicts in the labor movement there. The editorial for 7 May criticized Russian activities and influence in Canton. Other articles dealt with the struggles between the Kuomintang and the Chinese Communist Party (CCP), punctuated with reports of assassinations and other covert activities. The editorial for 10 May regretted that how, fifteen years after the revolution of 1911, China was still in a state of chaos. "Government," the editor lamented, "is not honest and enlightened; education is not universal; industry and commerce are not developed; and science is not prosperous . . . The nation is run by soldiers, the borders are ridden with bandits. Every year is filled with war, every moment with death and violence. The people suffer from one disaster after another."[43] The Hong Kong news usually came toward the end of the paper, after the women's section. The first section included the more important news: details of the strike and crimes such as looting and vandalism. The second section dealt mainly with less newsworthy affairs: boy-scout activities, a child who had been bitten by a dog, missing persons, and announcements by local societies. Still, even the first section was often devoted to minor events: why the trees on Nathan Road were being cut down, a pedestrian hit by falling bamboo from scaffolding at a construction site, or an automobile driver fined for reckless driving.

The editors of the *Commercial Press* were always careful to stress that opposition to the strike had nothing to do with Chinese patriotism or nationalism. They tried to show that the chaos in South China was due primarily to communist agitators. Articles in June 1926 exposed CCP exploitation of the workers in the Canton Machinists Union, whose members had been active in the strike. An article on 16 June reported that students in a high school in Xinhui County had become involved in a fight with communist students while resisting attempts by the communists to pressure other students into joining the CCP. More than thirty students had been injured in the melee. Another article the same day explained how the striking workers who had left for Canton had since become involved in myriad illegal activities, mainly looting and robbing stores, but that since the strike organizers, supported by the Canton government, were so powerful, the Canton press dared not even mention these activities. Other articles reported that the Canton authorities were implicitly involved in the strike: the police there had even been helping the striking workers in their looting. In addition to advertisements from local Chinese and foreign businesses, the paper carried advertisements from Chinese firms across the border. The Great South Tobacco Company urged all "patriots" to try its Sih Zung Kwei brand cigarette, "the patriotic, cigarette king of all Chinese-made goods." An advertisement for vegetarian products from the Ningbo-based Tian Yi Company declared how buying its products would help Chinese in China and abroad.[44]

The establishment of the *Commercial Press* shows how the reading public in Hong Kong was getting its news, and how public speech and opinion were formed in Hong Kong during the strike-boycott. It also represented a structural transformation of the Hong Kong bourgeois public sphere under the joint coordination of the colonial administration and its "loyal Chinese" subjects. Although it was plagued by a slow start and a lack of resources, the *Commercial Press* proved to be, in Kotewall's words, "the best medium of propaganda" and to have "done good from the very day of its issue." Despite anonymous death threats against its editors, the paper soon succeeded in encouraging other Chinese newspapers in the colony to resume publishing. By October 1926, the recently founded *Wah Kiu Yat Po* was back in business. Soon almost all the other Chinese newspapers followed suit and, as Kotewall put it, were "anti-Red." Concerned that two of the Chinese papers might be "converted by Russian money," however, Kotewall insisted on the need for continued propaganda: "Our enemy has been, and will be, unceasing in his attacks upon us, and his attempts to buy over some of our Chinese newspapers." The *Commercial Press* was so successful that Clementi proposed propaganda efforts be limited mainly to this newspaper and the South China Publicity Bureau's *Daily News*. After the boycott ended, Kotewall, Chow, and other merchants made the *Commercial Press* into a permanent newspaper.[45]

Middlemen and Advisers

Not only did Chow and Kotewall coordinate the government's anti-strike activities, they also served as middlemen between the Canton and Hong Kong governments. In early March 1926, when relations between Chiang Kai-shek and Wang Jingwei's left wing of the Kuomintang began to sour, Wang requested that Chow Shouson and Robert Kotewall meet in Macau with Fu Bingchang, Canton commissioner for foreign affairs. As this was the first move by Canton to open negotiations since the boycott began, Clementi was only too willing to agree. On 2 and 3 March, Fu relayed Wang's interest in ending the boycott, which was costing Canton dearly and causing problems be-

cause some forty thousand unemployed workers and their families had
come from Hong Kong. The three even discussed the idea of "paying
off" the strikers.[46]

At the meeting in Macau, Chow, Kotewall, and Fu discussed the
strike committee's demands, one by one, clause by clause. Some of the
questions Chow and Kotewall could not answer. Fu wondered why
the Kuomintang and other Chinese political organizations were illegal
in Hong Kong when the Kuomintang had branches in London, Liv-
erpool, Paris, and New York. Nor could they answer Fu's query about
the colonial government's ban on political propaganda (the strikers'
demand for "freedom in publication"). But for most of the other demands, Chow and Kotewall defended the policies of the colonial government. In response to Fu's questions about school books printed in
China (the demand for "freedom in education"), they explained that
all textbooks, regardless of origin, had to be approved by the Education Department. When Fu asked about the Peak Reservation Ordinance (the strike committee's demand for "freedom in residence"),
Chow and Kotewall defended the ordinance: "we said that the law
made it necessary for all, irrespective of race or nationality, to apply
for permission to live on the Peak, and that the existing legislation
was one which we personally could not quarrel with, because it was
purely economic and not racial."

In reply to the strike committee's demand for "freedom in patriotic
movements," Chow and Kotewall argued that in Canton parades and
processions also required police permission. When Fu asked why unions in the colony had been closed, Chow and Kotewall replied that
they did not know of any such happenings but that many unions had
to close because they could no longer afford to pay their rent. Dis-
agreeing with Fu's allegation that Hong Kong law treated Chinese
unfairly, Chow and Kotewall insisted that the law applied "equally to
all residents, irrespective of race or nationality." The reason why so
many more Chinese were deported than non-Chinese, they added, was
simply because 95 percent of the population was Chinese. When
pushed on the question of Chinese representation in the Legislative
Council, the two replied that "while the Hong Kong Government
would always be prepared to consider representations from its own
inhabitants, it manifestly could not permit interference with its own
internal affairs or internal constitution by outside people."

Chow and Kotewall agreed that child labor and working conditions in Hong Kong remained a problem. But they cited the 1922 Child Labour Ordinance, offering to match any program proposed by the Canton government. In response to the committee's concerns about the victimization of reinstated workers, Chow and Kotewall assured Fu that former strikers would not be dismissed "on flimsy grounds" after being reinstated. Jailed intimidators could not simply be released, but those strikers arrested as vagabonds might be freed. Regarding discrimination in employment, Chow and Kotewall claimed that Chinese of British nationality were treated the same as non-Chinese (Fu had asked about Germans and Portuguese) of British nationality. As for the strike committee's demand that Chinese currency be accepted in Hong Kong, Chow and Kotewall would not budge, insisting that this was purely an economic matter.[47]

Although no plans for future negotiations were made, Chow and Kotewall concluded that their mission had not been a failure. Fu was "friendly to Hong Kong," and Wang Jingwei—"if not also the Canton Government"—now seemed "genuinely desirous of a settlement." The Canton government did not appear to be "on its last legs, or to be in fear of imminent internal danger." But the two called for continued vigilance: "While we should carefully uphold our dignity and prestige, we ought not to repeat the mistake, committed by some English leading residents at the beginning of the strike, of belittling the strength of our enemy or placing too much hope on possible internal dissensions in the near future to solve our difficulty ... we need not thereby sacrifice either our dignity or our material interests."[48]

Chow and Kotewall also actively advised the government on how to prevent the strike from worsening. In response to their suggestion, on 22 June 1925 the government offered compensation of $2,000 (Hong Kong) to the families of returned laborers injured or killed on the job or by intimidators. The same day the government announced rewards of $250 for information leading to the arrest of agitators and intimidators. As we saw earlier, Chow and Kotewall persuaded the government to order routine military marches and demonstrations as a show of force. They also called for other security measures, including searching pedestrians and motorists for arms and bombs, police raids, and protecting reservoirs and other water supplies. Chow and Kotewall advised the government to help keep the colony running as close to normal as possible. They insisted on the importance of keeping open "pleasure resorts," such as teahouses and Chinese theaters. The government should encourage theatrical troupes to stay in Hong Kong, "even though we may have to resort to informal governmental intervention." Though they did not specify exactly what they meant by this government intervention, Chow and Kotewall stressed that "in times of panic and intensity anything which will provide relaxation on accustomed lines should be maintained, for they would have a great quietening influence on the minds of the public."[49]

At times, Chow and Kotewall even directly criticized government policy. When factional struggles within the Canton government forced Chinese politicians and their relatives to seek sanctuary in Hong Kong, Chow and Kotewall argued forcefully that they be turned away: "It is the opinion of the loyal Chinese that the traditional liberal policy of England which has made Hongkong a city of refuge for Chinese politicians ought now be modified." Giving asylum to political dissidents, as Hong Kong had done for Kang Youwei and Sun Yatsen several decades earlier, was one thing. "But when a whole party has been openly hostile to us, and has attempted to ruin us, it is foolish to give shelter to one faction of that party just because another faction has thrust it off the spoils of office. Such kindness earns not gratitude but contempt, and we should make it clear that we will not in future give asylum to those who have been our enemies."[50]

Chinese Help

As unofficial members of the Legislative Council, Chow and Kotewall were in a special position to help Hong Kong endure the strike. Their efforts to maintain order were paralleled at various levels by other leaders of the Chinese business community. Kotewall noted in his report that prominent Chinese had helped out during the strike. When the strike sent food prices soaring, Tung Wah Hospital committee members ran food stalls and sold food at low prices. The director of the committee, Ma Tsui Chiu, personally helped manage the stalls. From his office in City Hall, Dr. Tso Seen Wan coordinated the Chinese side of the new Labour Protection Bureau, the Chinese Labour Office, recruiting volunteers to fill the empty jobs. Only three days after the strike broke out, Tso had assembled more than 500 Chinese volunteers; twenty days later, he had 3000, much to the European community's surprise. Tso also organized a special company of Chinese constables and guards to counter intimidation. When the inspector general of police suggested establishing a police reserve force, Tso was asked to organize a Chinese company and was made honorary commissioner of the Police Reserve Force. Other "loyal Chinese" helped the government censor cables, mail, and newspapers. Still others joined the newly established Hong Kong Volunteer Defence Corps. This, reported Kotewall, showed the enemy "a spirit totally unexpected by him, and it had a tremendous moral effect on the whole Chinese community." The only reason even more Chinese had not joined the Corps, Kotewall explained, was because they had already formed their own Special Police Reserve under the supervision of B. Wong Tape, the overseas Chinese insurance magnate. Kwok Chan, comprador of the local branch of the Banque de l'Indochine, was an example of these reservists. Many Chinese joined the volunteer fire brigade. Ho Kam Tong was in charge of volunteers for the Chinese division of the St. John Ambulance Association.[51] Other Chinese formed street committees and street guards to patrol their neighborhoods. The District Watch Force helped maintain order, mediate, and prevent intimidation. Indeed, the colonial government hardly had reason to worry about mutiny or subversion among its Chinese employees. In September 1925 Captain Superintendent of Police P. P. J. Wodehouse praised the strong performance and loyalty of the Chinese members of the police force. Of the 105 Chinese clerks, telephone operators, and interpreters, only one had left his post. Out of 335 policemen, only 7 had deserted. Wodehouse reported similar performances among the Water Police and the Chinese detectives stationed along the border in the New Territories.[52]

Government Recognition

The Chinese bourgeoisie's role in helping the colony survive the strike brought its leaders special recognition from the colonial government. In a telegram to Amery in late June 1925, Stubbs noted that the "responsible Chinese" had been of "great assistance." In a confidential dispatch to Amery in September, Stubbs reported with pleasure a "growing antagonism among the Cantonese to the Bolshevist rule in

Canton, an antagonism which the Chinese merchants in Hongkong have been doing their utmost to foster."[53] Later in October, Stubbs stressed to Amery the important role of local Chinese businessmen, especially Chow and Kotewall: "In the first panic, when the Chinese might have been likened to a herd of frightened sheep, they immediately came forward and shamed and compelled their fellow-countrymen into at least a semblance of courage. Anonymous letters threatening violence and murder were received by them daily, a reward for their heads was posted in Canton, and still they worked incessantly, gathering at first a few of the more venturesome spirits, who in their turn brought in others, till in a short time the whole Chinese Community had forgotten its fears."[54] When Chinese generals and politicians came to Hong Kong for help and money, Kotewall and Chow explained Hong Kong's policy of nonintervention, even though they personally thought that supplying guns and money was the best way to help end the strike.

Explaining this "fanatical outburst" in his 1925 report to London, Secretary for Chinese Affairs D. W. Tratman wrote that it would "not be fitting to let the year pass without special record of the wonderful spirit of loyalty and solidarity shewn by the Chinese intelligentsia of the Colony in face of this great crisis." Offers of assistance had come in well before the government asked for help, and the government never had any trouble locating volunteers to censor the mails, press, and cables, and to help maintain security—even though these volunteers had been "instantly pilloried" in Canton as "hunting dogs" of British imperialism and despite numerous death threats. Tratman praised the "loyal advice and assistance" of the District Watch Committee, which had continued to be "of the greatest value to the Government." Thanks to the loyal Chinese of the colony, the "Moscow-Canton attack" had been repulsed. This had been the "turning point of the campaign."[55]

In his own report Kotewall, who represented both the Hong Kong government and the Chinese bourgeoisie, explained how peace and order had been maintained: through the collaboration of "almost the entire foreign community and the Chinese of the upper and middle class with the Government" and the "close co-operation between the Government and the Chinese representatives." Approximately ten days before the strike, the Chinese unofficial members of the Legislative Council met regularly with Tratman and Fletcher, hoping to prevent the strike. Although unsuccessful, they were at least able to prepare the government for the strike. The Chinese Chamber of Commerce and the Hongkong General Chamber of Commerce met to "exchange ideas and information." Most important had been the Chinese merchants' efforts and ability to serve as "emissaries of the truth to their fellow Chinese," who although "reasonable and shrewd," had been "bewildered, and did not know what to think." These men had prevented the confusion from turning into an "anti-British feeling." They had also kept in contact with Chinese from other groups. "In this way, while a sense of civic pride and civic responsibility was instilled in these men, contact was kept with Chinese public opinion at all times." Kotewall included a list of the "loyal Chinese" businessmen who had helped, some of whom received awards and honors from the British government for their service.

Chow Shouson's appointment in 1926 as the first Chinese member of the Executive Council shows just how well he had proved his loyalty to the government. A strategic move designed to show strikers in Hong Kong and Canton that the colonial government was willing to yield, this also represented a major shift in local policy. Some fifty years earlier, Colonial Secretary Lord Ripon had explained to Governor William Robinson why such a move was inevitable: "it would be invidious to and inequitable to lay down that Chinese subjects of the Queen shall be debarred from appointment to the Executive Council, and therefore the possibility of the appointment being hereafter filled by a Chinese gentleman must be reckoned with."[56] But in August 1895 Robinson explained to Colonial Secretary Joseph Chamberlain that "it would be extremely difficult, if not impossible to find a Chinese gentleman fit to sit in the Executive Council. A Chinaman pure and simple would not and could not be an independent member, and I do not think he would be an acquisition." An "Anglo-Chinese Representative" like Ho Kai would not "on the other hand have the confidence of the Chinese . . . The Chinese have no idea of Representative Government; they do not and cannot understand it."[57] Although Chamberlain ordered that Robinson add two unofficial members, with "no reference to the particular class or race to which the persons chosen belong," a Chinese was not appointed to the Executive Council until 1926.[58] And this time Clementi had some trouble convincing certain officials in the Colonial Office of the wisdom of his recommendation.

By 1926, then, the colonial government had concluded that some Chinese were capable of participating at the higher levels of government. When Clementi explained the disadvantages of appointing a Chinese, he was careful to explain that none of these applied to Chow. A Chinese member might have "a greater tendency to leakage of information." There would also be "perhaps greater danger of personal motives influencing the advice given," for "the Chinese character displays a different attitude to such matters." Clementi conceded, however, that such problems had also happened before, even without the Chinese. Having a Chinese would mean "greater risk that member may use for his own ends information obtained in Executive Council." Finally, "racial matters would be discussed with less freedom." Clementi explained, however, that "free discussion of racial questions" would in his opinion always be possible with "the best Chinese." The advantages outweighed the disadvantages: "there will always be loyal Chinese of high standing in Hong Kong for many years to come, and to show confidence is one obvious way of encouraging loyalty." Such an appointment "would afford clear proof of the intentions of this Government to frame its policy in close co-operation with leading Chinese of Hong Kong and might also have the result of staving off a demand (which cannot possibly be granted) for Chinese electoral representation on Legislative Council."[59] Chow served on the Executive Council until he was replaced in 1936 by Robert Kotewall, who served until the Japanese invasion in 1941.

Continued Threats

By October 1926, after a series of negotiations and a seemingly endless tide of political swings in Canton, the strike was over. As Clementi explained in his annual report, "there was a feeling of calm optimism; the Colony had not gone through the wood yet, but our enemies, though they had, under Bolshevik influence, striven their utmost, had failed to ruin the trade of Hong Kong."[60] Although Hong Kong's economy eventually recovered, relations with Canton remained tense. In the confusion leading up to Chiang Kai-shek's Northern Expedition, Hong Kong found itself again the target of anti-British attacks.

In late March 1927, Clementi reported that four gunmen from Canton had been sent to assassinate him and Registrar General E. R. Hallifax, Chow, Kotewall, and other "loyal Chinese" and to blow up the Labour Maintenance Bureau.[61] At a secret meeting in Canton "at the instigation of the Labour extremists," the would-be assassins had drawn by lot photographs of their intended victims. The explosives had been sent to Hong Kong in sections. An exhaustive police search of boarding houses produced nothing, and although the Labour Maintenance Bureau reported on 22 March that an assassin had arrived in Hong Kong, the assassin was not found. "The Chinese members of Council," wrote Clementi, "are inclined to treat this report with considerable respect." Reports of political assassinations in Shanghai and attacks on British, American, and Japanese consuls in Nanjing were "indications of how far fanaticism will go in China at the present time."[62]

Clementi's reports throughout this period reflect a fear that the violence and chaos in China would spread to Hong Kong. On 27 March, in a message published in the colony's leading English and Chinese newspapers, the British government thanked the leaders of the Chinese community and the "whole community of Hongkong" for their resolve during the "great difficulties" that had plagued the colony. It had to assure that "His Majesty's Government" would give the "fullest protection" to Hong Kong during "the civil war now unhappily raging in China," and that it had "no intention whatever of surrendering" Hong Kong, for which it held "the highest importance."[63] And throughout this period, Chow, Kotewall, and other members of the Chinese bourgeoisie continued to help defend their Hong Kong against what they considered the Bolshevik threat.

The May Thirtieth Movement that provoked the strike-boycott was the beginning of the end of the British imperialist enterprise in China.[64] But the revolutionary agenda of the Chinese nationalist and socialist movements of the 1920s forced important changes in colonial political strategies in Hong Kong, witnessed by Chow Shouson's appointment to the Executive Council. Viewed from the perspective of the relationship between the colonial government and the leaders of the Chinese bourgeoisie, the latter's support for the government during the strike was the culmination of decades of collaboration. But rather than simply supporting the government, these Chinese leaders

took a considerably more active role—helping the government negotiate with Canton authorities, advising the government, coordi-
nating propaganda activities, and reinforcing the image of the strike
as a Bolshevik plot against Hong Kong, with little support in the
colony. For the leaders of the bourgeoisie, fighting the strike meant
protecting the colony they had helped fashion from the fabled barren
island, and preserving a new way of life that they had helped shape.
At the same time, the strike enabled these men to present themselves
as allies, to prove their loyalty to the Hong Kong government, and to
prove themselves as Hong Kong Chinese. The colonial government's
old view of Chinese in Hong Kong as the scum of Canton was no
longer any more applicable than the image of Hong Kong as a barren
island.

Transforming the Barren Island: The 1941 Centenary

$\mathcal{I}$N 1941, HONG KONG observed its centenary as a British colony. But this was hardly a year for celebrating. The Japanese occupied the key cities of China; Britain and Germany were engaged in a bitter conflict; and war between Britain and Japan loomed on the horizon. Since the outbreak of war between China and Japan in 1937, refugees had been flooding into the colony—some five hundred thousand in 1938 alone—exacerbating already crowded housing conditions. Robert Kotewall, the Eurasian businessman who represented the Chinese population as an unofficial member of the Executive Council, understood the situation as well as anyone: the colony could hardly afford to celebrate or rejoice, especially while "half of the world is being battered by guns and bombs and the other half is living under the shadow of the sword."[1]

Compared with the 1891 jubilee commemorating Hong Kong's fifty years as a British colony, the 1941 celebration was subdued and almost nonexistent. The 1891 celebration had all the signs of a proper jubilee: ships decorated with lights, church services at the Anglican and Catholic cathedrals, a royal salute fired from ships in the harbor, a review of military forces at Happy Valley, an athletics contest, a public ball at City Hall, a cricket match and shooting contest, topped off with a concert at the Club Germania. A. S. Watson's, one of the oldest and largest companies in Hong Kong, had put on its own show because it too was celebrating its first fifty years in the colony. The *Daily Press* reported that Queen's Road was inaccessible for hours because of a "throng of Chinese who assembled to enjoy the sight." But the celebrations for the 1941 centenary were limited mainly to several newspaper supplements and commemorative volumes. Published in English, *Hong Kong Centenary Commemorative Talks* was a compilation of radio addresses. *A Century of Commerce (Bainian shangye)* was published by a local Chinese publisher. Originally prepared in 1941, *Centenary History of Hong Kong (Xianggang bainianshi)* was revised to include the Japanese occupation during the Second World War and published in 1948. All three volumes depict a Hong Kong magically transformed from a "barren island" or "barren rock" to a thriving metropolis in just one hundred years.[2]

Earlier chapters have demonstrated how spaces in colonial rule left room for upper-class Chinese to maneuver. This chapter examines how these Chinese also used *history* to distinguish themselves as Hong Kong Chinese. Although the 1941 centenary was free of the elaborate rituals generally associated with such occasions, it too was more than a way of observing the past.[3] It was an attempt to articulate a collective identity based on Hong Kong's economic success, its position within the British Empire, and its role in building a modern China—all rooted in a century of cooperation among the Chinese, British, and other communities. The centenary was also an occasion for Chinese in Hong Kong to appropriate the official, colonial account of Hong Kong's history to emphasize their own identity. By dating the "real" history of Hong Kong to its founding as a British colony in 1841, they launched the colony's historical development on a trajectory with which they were inextricably linked. By stressing the colony's commercial growth, they stressed their own role in this process. By contrasting its development and progress with that of the mainland, they highlighted their own uniqueness. At the same time, the centenary was a way to challenge a colonial history that marginalized the contributions of Chinese to Hong Kong's historical development and economic success.

One Centenary, Many Actors and Purposes

Hong Kong in 1941 was a very different place than in 1891. The colony now sat precariously at the edge of three empires: the British,

Chinese, and Japanese. After Taiwan became a Japanese colony in 1895, the local Chinese business community had been supplemented by Chinese businessmen from Taiwan with Japanese passports, while from the early 1930s Japanese merchants had a significant impact on Hong Kong's economy. But it was an ominous sign in 1941 when the Japanese government warned its citizens in Hong Kong to return to Japan unless they had important business in the colony.[4]

The colonial government had been in a bind since the Japanese invaded China. It sympathized with Nationalist China and was reluctant to alienate its Chinese subjects by clamping down on activities for aiding China. Yet it could not afford to alienate the Japanese or the British government since Hong Kong had been declared a neutral zone in September 1938 after the invasion of Canton. Like all British colonies, Hong Kong became part of the British war effort. But it was also part of the Chinese war effort as local organizations raised money for the Chinese resistance. At the same time, the colonial government invoked certain regulations to keep the colony neutral—prohibiting public meetings and censoring Chinese newspapers, pamphlets, and placards.[5] The British government had long realized that Hong Kong could not be defended against a Japanese invasion. But it also stressed the need to hold on to the colony to maintain face and morale, and to prevent the harbor from falling into enemy hands. Yet the Hong Kong government was in a weak position to prepare for an invasion: the huge number of refugees from China drained resources, while the colony's status as a free port, coupled with the open border with China, made controlling the movement of Japanese and their sympathizers practically impossible.[6]

This precarious position caught the attention of the British government, the local colonial authorities, and their Chinese and foreign subjects. These commemorative volumes together illustrate how the 1941 centenary, charged as it was in an era of wartime propaganda, could be used by different parts of the Hong Kong population for numerous purposes. For government officials and British residents, the centenary was an occasion for self-congratulation. As the colony's postmaster and chairman of broadcasting put it, this was "the opportunity of commemorating that day 100 years ago when the Union Jack was first run up to the masthead at Possession Point."[7] A newspaper article declared Hong Kong "a monument of British foresight, enterprise, and stamina . . . a haven of refuge, a symbol of democratic freedom, and a beacon for many who falter in these troubled and uncertain times."[8]

The anniversary also served as a propaganda campaign to raise money and morale for the British war effort. By stressing the chaos in Europe and China, the government underscored Hong Kong's role as a fortress at the edge of the British Empire. Acting Governor E. F. Norton urged the colony to contribute "100 percent of [Hong Kong's] resources of men, money and industry into the battle." Hong Kong's next century of "prosperity and greatness" depended, he said, on Britain winning the war in Europe.[9] A director of the Hong Kong Shanghai Bank reminded residents that the colony's low wartime tax rate meant it could provide even more for the war effort. The violence and destruction in China was frequently contrasted with the peace and order in Hong Kong. Small as it was, wrote Robert Kotewall, Hong Kong was playing an "important role in the Anglo-Chinese war against the invaders, and as a preserver of freedom and justice." Lo Man Kam, the Eurasian solicitor and "Chinese" unofficial representative on the Legislative Council, asked, "are we quite satisfied that we have each of us made our maximum contribution to the cause of Britain and China?" In sum, continued cooperation between British and Chinese was seen to be crucial, not just for Hong Kong's future but for both Britain's and China's.[10]

For the Chinese community, the centenary was an occasion to highlight its role in the development of both Hong Kong and China, and to drum up support for the war against Japan. After lamenting the violence and barbarity of the first half of the twentieth century, Guang Zhanming, publisher of *A Century of Commerce*, reminded readers that, "history is a sparkling clear lens. Always fair and righteous, it never lies or deceives . . . Never forget that you are the descendants of the Yellow Emperor." Hong Kong was seen as an important bridge for cooperation between China and Britain, its commercial success the foundation of this bridge. "Although we were born, and live, in Hong Kong, we gaze at our homeland from afar, as victory beckons us. Leaders of the commercial and industrial sectors, the Motherland awaits you—build and revive our new China!" The centenary was also a chance to pledge to the government, as Robert Kotewall did, "on behalf of the Chinese community . . . assurance of loyalty and continued co-operation in all activities conducing to its well-being."

Other members of the colony's foreign population used the occasion to highlight their own communities' contributions to Hong Kong's success. J. P. Braga, who in 1927 became the first Portuguese appointed to the Legislative Council, discussed the "Portuguese pioneers" who had been in the colony since its founding. Portuguese residents proved their loyalty through their active service in the Police Reserve during the First World War, while some later served in the St. John Ambulance Brigade and participated in preparations for air-raid defense.[11] An anonymous "Old Parsi Resident," one of the few left in the colony by this time, introduced some of the more prominent Parsi merchants in the colony. Hormasjee Mavrojee Mody, for example, a financier, landowner, real estate developer, and broker, had "whole heartedly devoted his energies and offered his best services for the welfare and prosperity of this Colony." Among Mody's many gifts to the colony were a bronze statue of Queen Mary in Statue Square ("a genuine token of the loyalty and esteem of the Parsis for their King and Queen") and the main building for the University of Hong Kong, which had "provided many brilliant Chinese scholars who are now giving their valuable service in the regeneration of China." Not to be left out were Hong Kong's "Indian pioneers"—the "peace-loving and law-abiding citizens engaged mainly in trade, commerce and industry, co-operating with the government of the Colony and other communities for making the Colony's life fuller and richer."[12]

Finally, European and Chinese companies used the centenary to advertise their goods by linking their own history with that of the colony. Watson's, which like the colony itself was "born at Possession Point in 1841," had also seen "one hundred years of progress." Originally founded as the modest Hong Kong Dispensary, the firm had since expanded into the largest chemists, druggists, dealers in wines and spirits, and manufacturer of aerated waters in Asia.[13] Lane, Crawford, Ltd. ("Now, as then, the Colony's Leading British Store") contrasted its birth in 1850 as a small matshed shop at the harbor's edge with its 1941 reincarnation, a multistoried department store in Central District. The Sincere Co., Ltd., the first Chinese department store, had "assiduously and sincerely served the Colony and helped to make its trade progress." Other local Chinese companies stressed their commitment to China's nation building and the war against Japan. An advertisement for the Hong Kong Mosquito Stick Manufacturing

Company promised only Chinese-made goods, even though its factory was at Ap Lei Chau, on the south shore of Hong Kong Island. Another local firm advertised air-raid defense equipment, such as gas masks, helmets, shovels and picks, canteens, lanterns, and mess kits.[14]

Identity and memory are not simply matters of being or not being, remembering or not remembering; they are having a way to communicate and maintain an articulate history of being and remembering.[15] Together, these commemorative volumes try to explain "who we are" and "who we should be." But commemorations can be intended for both internal and external use. They may show not only how people within a community think of themselves but also how they want others to think of them. Although we have no way of gauging the actual size of the readership of these three volumes, we can assume that, collectively, the publishers aimed to reach readers in Hong Kong, in China, in overseas Chinese communities, and in Britain.

Hong Kong: Past, Present, and Future

Commemorations are about using time for various purposes. A prominent theme in these pieces is Hong Kong's dramatic break with its precolonial past. Hong Kong's "real" history begins with its occupation by the British in 1839, before the island became a colony. Until the mid-1800s, a special newspaper supplement explained, "Hong Kong had no history in the accepted sense of the term." Hong Kong's history thus began only "when trade and commerce between China and Europe really attained dimensions of any importance." In the collection of radio talks, Acting Governor Norton began by noting the spectacular contrast between Hong Kong and 1841 and in 1941.[16] Li Shu-fan, a Chinese unofficial member of the Legislative Council and a distinguished doctor who had once been Sun Yatsen's personal physician, claimed that one reason the Empress Dowager Cixi agreed to cede the island to Britain was that she considered it "an insignificant island, no bigger than a fly's head in the vast map of China."[17] (Cixi, the so-called Old Buddha was only six years old at the time, but it makes for a good story. And contrasting the old, decrepit Empress Dowager with young, vibrant Hong Kong only accentuates the uniqueness of Hong Kong.) This tendency to trivialize Hong Kong's precolonial past is even more obvious in the Chinese sources, not because they overlooked Hong Kong's earlier history as did most English sources, but because they discussed it at some length yet minimized its importance. After examining the colony's pre-British history, one article noted that before the British took over Hong Kong, it was nothing but a tiny, almost uninhabited island with a few small fishing communities. The real past became Hong Kong's early colonial past, in which Hong Kong's future was solidly grounded.[18]

It was equally important to demonstrate that Hong Kong's history was a vibrant, ongoing process, in contrast to the chaos and destruction in Europe and China. The colony was often compared to a living person: constantly growing. "By the vigour and determination of its earliest settlers and their descendants," J. P. Braga marveled, Hong Kong had "overcome the difficulties of its birth, its adolescence and early manhood."[19] To Norton, it was especially impressive that even in a "stricken world," the colony was still a "live, vigorous and growing organization." That Hong Kong was becoming more prosperous "even in the chaotic state of the world to-day" suggested even faster growth "when the present troubles of the British Empire and of China are satisfactorily settled." Chow Shouson, one of the colony's oldest residents and the first Chinese member of the Executive Council, maintained that "Hong Kong has a bright future before her, and it is our duty to strive for her further development and prosperity."[20]

Using the past, present, and future to emphasize each other is common in commemorations. Legitimization of the present depends greatly upon knowledge of the past, and both new nations and old states often require old pasts. Even before the age of nation-states, governments used what today would be considered "national memory" for political, religious, and cultural objectives.[21] In the American and French revolutions, commemoration meant breaking with the past, creating the old, and separating the old from the new. The French invented their "Old Regime," with its exaggerated backwardness and injustice, to prove that 1789 meant a genuine move forward in time.[22] Similarly, the reconstruction of China's so-called feudal past accentuated the newness of post-1949 China. Emphasizing, even manufacturing, a common past is a vital part of a unified, collective history and identity.[23]

Stressing the break with the precolonial past was also a strategic move in 1941 Hong Kong. Not only did it make the colony's progress

seem more striking, it enabled the colonial government and local residents to showcase their own role in this history. But establishing a
collective memory and history for colonial Hong Kong was also a
problematic task. It was after all a rather brief history, pale in comparison with that of China or even Britain. The colony's various communities were split among residents and sojourners. As one newspaper
supplement explained, few people in Hong Kong "have more than a
vague idea of how Hong Kong came to be, for most of its population,
Chinese and foreign, has been a 'floating one', and it is only in very
recent years that there has been any considerable number to whom
Hong Kong was 'home'."[24] Because Hong Kong was taken from China
in a humiliating war and the overwhelming majority of its population
was Chinese, it would hardly be appropriate to celebrate the British
triumph in the Opium War. Apart from a handful of British officials
and opium traders, and Chinese merchants and compradors, the
colony lacked any "founding fathers."

But having such a short, rather dull history also has its advantages.
The lack of any other founding myth means that no one can seriously
dispute one of the main themes in the official, colonial version of
Hong Kong's history: it is foremost a history of *commerce*. More than
any other, this theme pervades all three volumes. Not only is one
Chinese volume entitled *A Century of Commerce*, its cover is illustrated
with a photograph of the Hong Kong and Shanghai Bank building
rather than, say, the colony's famous harbor or picturesque night skyline.[25] The collection of radio addresses includes not only photographs
of the bank's different buildings since its founding but also portraits
of its directors who, along with the early governors, become founding
fathers by default. That so many of the colony's residents are sojourners sets apart those who consider themselves permanent residents.

Having a reasonably short history also means having people who
have lived long enough to remember much of this history, especially
important since identity and memory depend so much on each other.
These three volumes use the same means to link Hong Kong's early
colonial past with its present and its future: wealthy, elderly residents
who personally recalled and contrasted Hong Kong's past with its
present. Robert Ho Tung, the Eurasian comprador was "proud to have
lived in the pioneering days when Hong Kong was still a barren rock

and to have the satisfaction of sharing in its progress and prosperity."[26] The "Grand Old Man of Hong Kong," Ho Tung had risen from a junior position with Jardine, Matheson to become the firm's chief comprador. A millionaire by age 30, he was probably the richest man in the colony in 1941. In another article, Ho Tung recalled how the past 79 years had passed by "almost imperceptibly," even while bringing remarkable physical, economic, social, and cultural changes.[27] Similar sentiments about Hong Kong's transformation from a "barren little island" came from Chow Shouson, born in Hong Kong 81 years earlier in the small fishing village of Aberdeen. Chow's ancestors had lived on the island before the British arrived; one had even helped the British post Charles Elliot's famous proclamation on 2 February 1841 that Hong Kong would be a free port.[28] These "living relics" do more than add color and character to Hong Kong's history; they personally vouch for its authenticity. By communicating Hong Kong's "real" past to a younger generation, they also prevent this past from fragmenting or splintering, which often occurs when communication across generations is hindered by alternate groups of memories.[29]

While many of the articles by British officials and residents focus on Hong Kong's heroic early history, those by Chinese or Eurasians generally emphasize the colony's remarkable progress, to which they had contributed. An anonymous writer explained how in one short century this "barren island" had become a modern, prosperous metropolis. And it was still changing fast: more area was being developed, and the city's appearance was becoming more attractive.[30] A brief history pointed out how in the early years after Hong Kong became a British colony, the life of British settlers was a hard one. But after a hundred years of progress, Hong Kong had become a "lovable" free port, and people in Britain were all envious of living there.[31] Chen Datong, editor of *A Century of Commerce*, briefly recounted the colony's history in terms of its progress. Chinese were now involved in passing legislation, even while the Chinese population was able to keep some of the same customs enjoyed in China. After a century of construction and development, the city's landscape had changed completely. Much progress had been made in sanitation, industry had developed to the point where opium was no longer the most important commodity, and all the major world banks had offices here. Hong Kong had an educated populace, with extensive commercial skills.

Hong Kong was now not just a different place than it was in 1841; it was a better, more prosperous, and more appealing place.[32]

Anglo-Chinese Cooperation

How did Hong Kong become such a different, better place? The commemorative volumes consistently downplay the historical conflict that led to the colonization of Hong Kong in 1841. The hostilities between Britain and China culminating first in the Opium War and the establishment of the colony, and again in the Second Opium War, are generally referred to as "the troubles" or "the friction at Canton," while Britain's acquisition of the colony is described in the Chinese sources simply as "the opening." When the Anglo-Chinese conflicts are discussed, they are generally done so in two main ways. One approach portrays them as inevitable conflicts based on "differences of opinion" between "two proud states," each "proudly scornful of the other."[33] The other approach abbreviates the conflicts, as if to get them out of the way as quickly as possible. The racial discrimination that had plagued Hong Kong society since its inception is discussed in only one article. Instead, Hong Kong's historical development and economic growth is repeatedly based on "fair play," "mutual respect," "integrity," and, above all, Anglo-Chinese "cooperation" and "co-partnership."[34]

Although it might seem logical to downplay the conflict between Britain and China while emphasizing Anglo-Chinese cooperation in a territory so close to China and so heavily populated by Chinese, this approach was relatively new in British sources on Hong Kong. In the 1891 jubilee, an article in the *Daily Press* explained: "The attitude of the Chinese Government towards Europeans has been the outcome of centuries of isolation from types of civilization superior to its own, and every step towards bringing into line the ordinary intercourse of people between people has been harassed and thwarted by the exalted attitude which the Chinese Government assumes."[35] Another article described that the events leading to Britain's acquisition of the island "arose out of the arrogance of the Chinese authorities at Canton."[36] If the British ever questioned the legitimacy of the Opium War and the cession of Hong Kong, they invariably justified it with what the British had done for Hong Kong. The Right Rev. Bishop Burdon's address at the 1891 jubilee church service at St. John's Cathedral was a typical example of how many Britons saw their role in Hong Kong:

> It is too late now even to ask the question whether England was right or wrong in taking possession of this island fifty years ago. Whatever may be said of the morality of those old wars, we have a right to claim that we have more than justified the act by returning to China something more vastly valuable than we took. We took a treeless, barren rock, the abode of a few hundreds, or at most of a few thousands of Chinese fishermen, ready on occasion to exchange their peaceable occupation for piracy, and we have long since made it a security of peace with China and a profitable home for tens of thousands—at the present moment two hundred thousand—of Chinese who have been attracted hither by the abundant means of obtaining a livelihood and even wealth under the security of a just and stable Government . . . We have thus awoke something like new hopes in the heart of this old country while we have at the same time been a means of physical benefit to vast members of its population.[37]

But in 1941 Acting Governor Norton attributed Hong Kong's success to "a happy combination between the peoples of these two great nations." The Chinese may be racially different from the British, but in certain ways they are closer to the British than are even other "members of the same Aryan-speaking stock." Both loathe war and are "traders by instinct." R. A. C. North, secretary for Chinese affairs, explained that for a century Hong Kong had been "a meeting place for two great and ancient civilisations."[38]

The emphasis on cooperation, rather than conflict, between British and Chinese is even more prominent in the articles by Chinese and Eurasians. Lo Man Kam remarked on the incredibly large amount of government revenue that had resulted from a century of Anglo-Chinese cooperation.[39] To Chau Tsun-nin, lawyer and former unofficial member of the Legislative Council, Hong Kong's "phenomenal rise" from a "sparsely-inhabited island to a world port of the first importance with a huge population, is a striking monument to the close co-operation between the British and Chinese peoples." Robert Kotewall credited Hong Kong's "remarkable progress" to the "combined enterprise and the genius of the British and Chinese."[40] The colony's "magical transformation" was due to British "enterprise, fore-sight and initiative" and Chinese "hard work, patience and adapta-bility." Even while displaying a "spirit of healthy and friendly rivalry," Britons and Chinese had cooperated in business, industry, and in public and social affairs. Both peoples had learned that Hong Kong was a place where they could prosper and live in justice, peace, and harmony. The concerted efforts to combat the strike-boycott of 1925–1926 were only one example of how they have cooperated to ensure this. "Above all," concluded Kotewall, "these two peoples display in common the qualities of integrity and fair dealing."[41]

One of the most remarkable ways this Anglo-Chinese cooperation is expressed is through sports. All three commemorative volumes con-tain articles on the importance of sports in the colony. This focus on sports, which might be dismissed as coincidence were sports not so central to the histories of both British colonialism and modern China, serves five functions. Above all it is a metaphor for cooperation, not just between British and Chinese in Hong Kong, but between the two nations. Representing "all Chinese in Hong Kong," Lo Man Kam hoped that "such Sino-British co-operation in the Colony, which has so happily existed in the past—not only in sport, but in business, com-merce and social affairs—will continue and increase to the benefit and happiness of both great Democracies."[42] Second, even though Hong Kong in 1941 was still a place where Europeans and Chinese often had little contact with each other, the image of the two races meeting on the playing field suggests narrowing racial gaps. As Kotewall put it, British sports had "promoted physical fitness and the spirit of team-work and fair play ... [and] done much to bring the two races to-gether."[43] But emphasizing sport also enabled the Chinese to be good sports about living in a British colony. "That the striking progress which Chinese in Hong Kong have made in the realm of sport is in a large measure due to the encouragement, friendly rivalry, co-operation and example of British sportsmen in the Colony," wrote Lo Man Kam, "is a fact which all Chinese sportsmen would wish grate-fully to acknowledge." Furthermore, it let the British take credit for selflessly introducing modern civilization to the rest of the world. Thus Acting Governor Norton could describe Hong Kong as a place with "all the facilities for these games and sports with which the young Chinese of Hong Kong to-day take on us British who have taught them to beat us at our own games."[44] Finally, it proved that the Chinese could successfully embrace modernity and progress. In an article entitled "Progress of Sport in Hong Kong," Lo Man Kam explained that the "Chinese conception of sport and sportsmanship" was so "modern" and "current" that the terms still were not included in some dictionaries. When Lo left for school in England in 1906, few Chinese children in Hong Kong played any sports. Since then, Chinese had founded swimming clubs, the Chinese Recreation Club, and the South China Athletic Association. In the 1936 Olympic Games in Berlin, 17 of the 22 athletes on the Chinese team were from Hong Kong.[45]

Given the timing of the centenary, many of the articles called attention to the need for continued Anglo-Chinese teamwork. An article in the *Daily Press* reminded readers that the "future of China as a free and independent nation is contingent on the issue of the present war which Britain is fighting on behalf of the free nations throughout the world."[46] "This co-operative spirit, so evident in the past," declared Chau Tsun-nin was, "doubly necessary at present when both these peoples, believing in orderly progress and freedom to fulfil their destinies, are each engaged in a grim struggle against ruthless aggression."[47] Robert Kotewall, speaking both "to and for the Chinese community," pled:

> Let us, the Chinese residents in Hong Kong, ask ourselves whether, in this hour of their dire need, we have done all we could for our country, and for the country which has given us here one hundred years of security and peace. Let us also ask ourselves whether we have done enough to relieve or minimise the sufferings of our compatriots in China and of our friends in England, who daily, and every hour of the day, are facing unprecedented perils with such heroic fortitude. I fear that our conscience will tell us that we have fallen short of what is an imperative duty. Let us, then, hearken to this call of duty, and discharge it, to the limit of our capacity, to Hong Kong, to China and to Britain.[48]

Kotewall's call gives urgency to a common theme in almost all of these articles: just as Hong Kong's past depended on Anglo-Chinese cooperation, so did its future.

Hong Kong Chinese and the Secrets of Hong Kong's Success

One of the main goals of the commemoration was to demonstrate a collective Hong Kong memory and identity. Colonial officials had for decades stressed the need to cultivate a "colonial feeling" among the Chinese population (see Chapter 5). But the commemoration was not simply a top-down effort to create a collective memory, for even some Chinese who had no ties to the colonial government participated. Nor was it just an occasion to praise the colonial government or the Anglo-Chinese cooperation that had built Hong Kong. Some local residents used the centenary both to praise the colony's past and to draw attention to its problems. In *Commemorative Talks*, Robert Kotewall lamented that "there is still much to be done in the clearing of slums, in the improvement of the health and fitness of the community, and in the betterment of the conditions of life of the people." Li Jowson, a prominent Chinese businessman, listed the many problems that had accompanied Hong Kong's economic success: inflation, crime, poverty, and suicide. Lo Man Kam cautioned against being too complacent with Hong Kong's past achievements. "Can we be content with the prevalence of squalor and abject poverty of the masses; of slums; of lack, or inadequacy, of social services, such as hospitals, sanatoriums, workmen compensation, industrial insurance; etc.?"[50]

The centenary was also a chance to criticize the colonial government. Lo Man Kam used the occasion to chide the colonial government, albeit obliquely, for imposing censorship during times of strife. Arguing that one of Hong Kong's most impressive features over the past century had been its freedoms of thought and expression, Lo reminded his audience of the power of a free, informed press in shaping public opinion and nurturing public consciousness.[51] But what might appear to be effusive praise came from one of the most vocal critics of the government, the only unofficial member of the Legislative Council to protest the government's lavish executive power. In 1920 Lo had advised a local mechanics' union in a labor strike. Shortly before the centenary he had tried unsuccessfully to end the censorship of the Chinese press that had been in place since the strike-boycott of 1925–1926. In June 1939 he criticized the Telecommunications Bill, which empowered the postmaster general to authorize searches and arrests.[52]

Nor was everyone impressed by the image, conjured up by the rhetoric of Anglo-Chinese cooperation, of Hong Kong as a cheerful meeting place of East and West. Su Fuxiang, a local journalist, wrote that although Hong Kong had truly become the meeting point of East and West, it was an uneven meeting. Chinese were more willing to accept Western culture than Westerners were to accept Chinese culture. Su saw the mix of East and West as uneven, hilarious, and often pathetic. Many Chinese had adopted British habits. "If it were possible to change the color of one's hair or eyes, they would have already done so."[53] Although the centenary was not as contested as national commemorations were in Europe and North America, for example, it was nonetheless an occasion to highlight the difference between what Hong Kong was and what it should or could be.

The centenary was thus more than an attempt to glorify British colonialism. And within the discourse of Anglo-Chinese cooperation was a vigorous effort by prominent Chinese and Eurasians to emphasize their own role in Hong Kong's growth. That the Chinese were largely responsible for Hong Kong's development might seem obvious, but it was often mentioned only in passing, if at all, in the British accounts. For example, a brief commercial history of Hong Kong assigned the colony's early economic success to the Taiping Rebellion, which drove Chinese laborers and merchants to Hong Kong; Chinese emigration to Australia, Southeast Asia, and the United States; and remittances from overseas Chinese back to China via Hong Kong ("an invisible export").[54] But it said nothing about the role of local Chinese in building Hong Kong.

This tendency to de-emphasize the role of Chinese while stressing the role of the British had been quite common in English-language sources. Quoting Governor William Des Voeux, an article commemorating the 1891 jubilee doubted "whether the evidences of material and moral achievement . . . make anywhere a more forcible appeal to eye and imagination, and whether any other spot on the earth is thus more likely to excite, or much more fully justifies, pride in the name of Englishman [*sic*]."[55] Chinese could sometimes even be an obstacle to Hong Kong's progress: another article argued that "Hongkong is also interesting as a test of the adaptability of British institutions to a very abnormal state of things. The British flag shelters under it in this Colony a population drawn almost exclusively from the confines of the enormous empire of China."[56]

In these earlier accounts, the colony's commercial history was mainly a history of *British* commerce. When Chinese contributions were mentioned, it was mainly through their connections to British business. Chinese were important in the growth of the entrepot trade during the late nineteenth and early twentieth centuries, but mainly as consumers who, "under the influence of a Western standard of living," were now demanding more Western goods. When Chinese industry was mentioned at all, it was often financed by British capital. One account ended by listing the three people who had "loomed large in the business life of the Colony": William Keswick, taipan of Jardine, Matheson; Thomas Jackson, chief manager of the Hong Kong and Shanghai Bank and "foremost in guiding the destiny not only of the Bank but of the Colony"; and Paul Chater, a renowned businessman and philanthropist of Armenian descent. "These three men," readers were told, "deserve our gratitude for what Hong Kong is to-day." Not one Chinese was mentioned by name.[57]

Although they did not try to diminish the contributions of the British, Chinese and Eurasians showed their own role in Hong Kong's development in several subtle ways. Octogenarian Chow Shouson diplomatically insisted that Hong Kong's prosperity had been both created and shared by the Chinese community. Chinese controlled much of the colony's trade, while Chinese were involved in industry, shipping, real estate, and banking. "We therefore must agree," Chow concluded, "that the Chinese have contributed to and received a fair share from Hong Kong's prosperity." But they stressed repeatedly that Hong Kong was still very much a Chinese city. Robert Ho Tung admitted that much of Hong Kong's growth had been the result of the work of Western merchants and their business and management techniques. Still, he reminded readers that Chinese formed 97 percent of the colony's population.[58] Ip Lan Chuen, one of the colony's older Chinese business leaders, pointed out that all aspects of life in the colony had connections to the Chinese.[59] Another common method was to list some of Hong Kong's more famous Chinese residents. Although Ho Tung credited Hong Kong's success partly to its "brilliant cadets and Governors," he singled out some of the more important Chinese for their contributions: Ng Choy, Wong Shing, Ho Kai, and Wei Yuk— all once leaders of the local Chinese community and members of the Legislative Council.[60] The active role of local Chinese in Hong Kong's younger industries was often highlighted, a point we shall return to later. After noting that the Chinese had set up their own Western-style banks, Robert Kotewall argued that it was the Chinese who had been "principally responsible" for the "striking development" in some of Hong Kong's newer industries, such as rubber shoes, flashlights, and batteries.[61]

All three volumes dwell on the secrets of Hong Kong's success: its geographical location, free trade, and political stability. Chow Shouson attributed Hong Kong's prosperity partly to the colony's location but cautioned that "a favourable geographical position alone does not alone make for prosperity." Hong Kong's growth was due "in a large measure to her sound and just administration and to the peace and stability which she offers to trade, investment and industry."[62] L. Kadoorie, a prominent Jewish businessman and philanthropist, described Hong Kong as "a conveniently situated 'clearing house' at the Gateway of China" where "all nationalities have and can benefit equally from the facilities and amenities offered . . . The past policy of tolerance, unrestricted freedom, co-operation and mutual understanding, laid down in the historical proclamations of 1841, is the basis upon which the Colony's development has been built."[63] After listing some of Hong Kong's many advantages for someday becoming a major industrial center—accessibility to markets, strong banks, and a large supply of cheap labor—Robert Kotewall listed the colony's most important blessing: "Hong Kong is free from recurrent political and consequential economic disturbances, and enjoys the benefits of a stable government which affords to all peace and security."[64]

The Chinese and Eurasians, however, often took this one step further. Hong Kong's legendary political stability depended not only on the colonial government but also on the Chinese community. After reminding readers how long he had lived in Hong Kong, Ip Lan Chuen explained that the stability (compared with China) that the colonial authorities had provided over the past one hundred years had allowed Chinese in Hong Kong to prosper. But the many strong qualities that Hong Kong Chinese exhibited, such as good manners, public spirit, and generosity, had also contributed immensely to Hong Kong's prosperity and stability.[65] For Robert Kotewall, the "one all-important factor" that explained Hong Kong's stability was giving the Chinese community a voice in the Legislative, Executive, and Urban councils.

The Hong Kong Chinese "have consistently displayed their understanding of what is involved in good citizenship." They always abided
by the law, fulfilled their civic obligations, and gave when needed.
During the First World War, some served as constables, guards, and
mail censors. They also donated money to the British war funds. In
the present war, they were helping in the planning of local defense.
Thus Hong Kong's success became inextricably linked with the Chinese population of the colony.[66]

Exhibiting Hong Kong Chinese Commerce, Industry, and Society

Not only did the centenary let local Chinese demonstrate their contributions to Hong Kong and China, it enabled them to publicize a
realm deliberately left out of the English accounts of Hong Kong's
historical development. The Chinese commemorative volumes became exhibitions of Hong Kong's Chinese-led commerce, which was
generally minimized, if not ignored entirely, in the colonial accounts.
Although both Chinese volumes mention briefly the colony's leading
foreign firms, especially the old trading hongs, the emphasis is
squarely on Chinese companies. Both contain histories of the five big
Chinese department stores in Hong Kong: Wing On, Sincere, Sun,
and two mainland-Chinese emporiums that sold only Chinese-made
goods.[67] A brief review in *A Century of Commerce* of the most important
trades in Hong Kong focused mainly on Chinese commerce. It showed
how Hong Kong's economy had been built on the work of local Chinese and on the growth of Chinese communities overseas. The expanding Chinese population had contributed to vigorous paper,
printing, and publishing industries. Chinese were now even competing
successfully with foreigners. In sugar refining, for example, although
the foreign-owned Taikoo plant was the largest, there were also 5 or
6 large local Chinese companies, and some 30 smaller ones.[68]

The centenary also enabled the Chinese business community to
challenge the official, colonial account of Hong Kong's history. The
colonial version of Hong Kong's economic history—British liberal
government and laissez-faire economic policies—is echoed in most of
the English sources on the centenary, although some articles occasionally mention the recent ventures by Chinese "small capitalists" in

sugar, rope-making, spinning, and weaving. An article on shipping explained that "Hong Kong is almost entirely a shipping and trading entrepot," and that no "primary products are produced on the Island." The colony's "premier industry" was almost always cited as European-run shipbuilding and repairing, especially the Hong Kong & Whampoa Dock Co., Ltd. If Chinese small industries were discussed, they were generally mentioned in negative terms: "lack of capital, proper supervision, technical guidance, and skilled labour were largely responsible for these small and promising industries not improving as they should have done."[69]

Control of a society's collective memory supports the hierarchy of power. But by showing a thriving Chinese-run industry, the two Chinese volumes challenged the colonial government's official version of Hong Kong's economic growth. A short history of Chinese-capitalized industry in Hong Kong listed all the important industries. Chinese industry in Hong Kong had been flourishing over the past twenty years, making Hong Kong the industrial center of South China. Hong Kong's convenient location, its status as a tax-free port, the colonial government's effective rule, and the resulting stability and order had all encouraged Chinese to invest in Hong Kong industry. Locally manufactured products had even become good enough in quality to compete worldwide. Wares of all kinds—from automobile parts, to salt, hemp, and burlap—were now exported to China and all over Southeast Asia.[70] Before Chinese opened local canning companies, Hong Kong had to rely on imports from the United States, but now it even exported its own canned goods. Pharmaceutical and mosquito-coil factories founded in the late 1910s and early 1920s were exporting to China and all over the world. Whereas Hong Kong imported fireworks from the United States, one firework factory founded in 1912 had become so big that it also had plants in China. A flashlight-battery factory founded in 1913, before any such plant existed in China, immediately began researching and testing batteries designed especially for tropical climates. By the 1930s there were 20 to 30 such factories in the colony.[71] In these articles, Chinese were the leaders of the industries that would launch Hong Kong into its next century.

The Chinese sources do more than exhibit Chinese industry in Hong Kong. They acknowledge the people and society that made all this possible—people whom the English sources treat primarily as colonial subjects and the fortunate beneficiaries of enlightened colonial rule, free trade, and British impartial justice; and a society that most English sources usually describe as a community of transients interested only in making a quick fortune before returning to their native homes in China. Apart from listing the primary Chinese industries, both Chinese volumes portray a vibrant and cohesive Chinese community with a plethora of recreation facilities, such as teahouses, roller-skating rinks, theaters, dance halls, and swimming pools. Although this community had its share of problems, including triad societies, prostitution, and gambling, it was also a community that took care of its own, witnessed by the growth of an extensive network of charitable and philanthropic associations, mutual assistance leagues, native-place associations, religious organizations, and various trade and professional clubs. The Chinese of Hong Kong were not simply colonial subjects. They had become *citizens*.

Hong Kong's Relationship to Modern China

Remembering that commemorations are for both insiders and outsiders helps explain why so many of the news commemorative articles, especially those by Chinese and Eurasian residents, emphasize Hong Kong's role in the development of modern China. Li Shu-fan, physician and member of the Legislative Council, argued that in the "Asian Enlightenment" Hong Kong had been "the great beacon of Western learning and British culture . . . From this acorn in the vast map of China has sprung up a sturdy oak, a stronghold of goodwill, a haven in many a blinding storm. After a century of its edifying presence, China has progressed a thousand years."[72] Robert Kotewall noted that students from Hong Kong schools were serving in the Chinese government and all over the world. Hong Kong also served as a haven for Chinese refugees, giving Chinese the freedom to come and go. This had greatly helped maintain good relations between China and Hong Kong.[73]

A common example of Hong Kong's contributions to modern Chinese history is the colony's role in the republican revolution of 1911. Li Shu-fan proudly noted that Hong Kong had produced "two of the world's greatest men": the father of tropical medicine, Patrick Manson, and his pupil, the "emancipator of one-fifth of mankind, one of the greatest champions for the cause of Democracy, and Founder of the Chinese Republic, the deathless Dr. Sun Yat-sen."[74] In *Centenary History of Hong Kong*, several articles cover the full spectrum of Sun's experiences in Hong Kong: his early days at the Hong Kong College of Medicine for Chinese; his use of the colony as a base to preach revolution; and his famous speech at Hong Kong University in 1923, when he claimed that all his revolutionary ideas had been formed entirely in Hong Kong, and that the extreme contrast between the peace and order in Hong Kong, and the disorder and corruption in China, had made him a revolutionary. Another article recalls the local celebrations after the 1911 revolution.[75]

Stressing the role of Hong Kong in the development of modern China enabled local Chinese to accomplish three main goals. First, it de-emphasized the historical tensions between Britain and China. It also highlighted the role of Hong Kong Chinese in rebuilding China. One article, for example, described how the Hong Kong Chinese community had developed an extensive network of charitable services, enabling local Chinese to donate money to both local and mainland causes. This network had become even more important in recent years as hostilities between China and Japan worsened.[76] Another article explained that although in the early years of Hong Kong's history only a few traditional guild-like organizations existed in Hong Kong, the Chinese community now boasted a group representing almost every possible interest, commercial or otherwise. These groups all raised money for relief in China and for assisting needy local people.[77] Finally, showing how Hong Kong's role in China's development depended on the colony not being part of China justified their living in a British colony. As Ip Lan Chuen explained, the colony's political stability helped Chinese in Hong Kong prosper, thereby allowing them to contribute more fully to rebuilding China.[78]

Ip's comment highlights another prominent theme in the Chinese sources: Hong Kong was very much a Chinese city and had played an important role in modern Chinese history, but it was also significantly different from any city or region in China. Hong Kong was often compared favorably with Mainland China, especially for its political stability and economic success. An article on the importance of commerce and industry, for example, lamented how backward China was in this respect.[79] But Hong Kong was also simply a different kind of place. One article addressed the complexities of the Hong Kong dialect (not the Cantonese dialect). Others explained the Legislative Council, wedding registration laws, and local press regulations. A brief review of the legal system mentioned that Hong Kong law required severe penalties for crimes that in China were treated more leniently, then listed twenty-six such crimes. Yet another discussed laws against animal abuse and the various regulations for dogs.[80]

The emphasis on Hong Kong's difference from China is particularly important considering the timing of the commemoration. Refugees from China had been entering the colony in huge numbers since 1937. The Chinese commemorative volumes were intended also as guidebooks to help refugees navigate and avoid running afoul of the law in a new city and a new culture. Yet guidebooks are often intended as much for "locals" as for tourists and newcomers. Apart from showing outsiders how to find their way in a new city, they illustrate how people should think of themselves in this city.[81] These articles are thus not merely about ways in which Hong Kong is different; they are about how to behave in a place that was different.

Commemorations and Implications

The commemoration of the 1941 centenary has implications for the histories of both Hong Kong and China. Although the centenary demonstrates that commemorations can be appropriated, it also illustrates that they can both support and challenge official versions of historical reality. Hong Kong's dominant narrative of economic progress and political stability was constructed not only by the colonial government but also by the Chinese and foreign residents of the colony. Yet the centenary was an opportunity for the Chinese business community to display its contributions to Hong Kong's industry—contributions that the colonial government had consistently downplayed because they challenged the hegemonic version of Hong Kong's reason for being.

Nor were such ceremonies and rituals confined to colonies such as Hong Kong. In her study of the commemoration of the Shanghai Jubilee in 1893, Bryna Goodman demonstrates how the jubilee could serve various interests. Juxtaposing Chinese and Western records and representations of the 1893 jubilee, Goodman shows that the ceremony and the appropriation of its meaning by the Anglo-American

"Shanghailanders" and Chinese residents of the International Settlement could be used to serve various interests. For the foreigners, Chinese participation in the celebration proved the success of the cosmopolitan settlement, of course under Western leadership and
guidance. But for the dominant Chinese merchants of the city, it was
a way to flaunt their wealth and influence to both Chinese and foreigners and to link themselves to the Manchu court (the jubilee coincided with the fifty-ninth birthday of the Empress Dowager).[82]

In Shanghai, Goodman argues, the "contact zone" of the International Settlement helped shape the course of Chinese nationalism in
the late Qing. As nation took precedence over native-place, it became
too embarrassing to identify with treaty ports like Shanghai. Thus the
invented traditions of the Shanghai Jubilee did not survive the chaos
of the late 1890s.[83] In Hong Kong, however, Chinese defined (and
continue to define) themselves both within and against the Chinese
nation. The political and territorial disintegration after the fall of the
Qing dynasty in 1911 highlighted and reinforced the differences between China and Hong Kong, as would the 1949 revolution, the Cultural Revolution, the Tiananmen Massacre, and the increased per-
meability of the border between Hong Kong and China in the 1980s.

Conclusion

O_N 8 DECEMBER 1941, Hong Kong time, Japanese bombers attacked Hong Kong, Malaya, Pearl Harbor, and the Philippines. As Japanese troops moved south across the New Territories and into Kowloon, propaganda leaflets called on Chinese and Indians in the colony to rise up and drive out their British overlords. With their outdated and insufficient artillery and ammunition, poor planning, and persistently weak intelligence, the British defenses crumbled quickly. On Christmas Day, one week after the Japanese launched a three-pronged attack on Hong Kong Island, Governor Mark Young, in the colony only since September, surrendered unconditionally to Japanese commander Lieutenant General Sakai Takashi. By February 1942, after the fall of Singapore (declared a holiday in Hong Kong and commemorated with lion dances, processions, and extra rations of rice), the sun had set on Britain's empire in East Asia.[1]

Thus began the three-and-a-half-year history of "The Captured Territory of Hong Kong," which although touted as part of Japan's "Great East Asia Co-Prosperity Sphere" was little more than Japanese colonialism. As elsewhere in their new empire, the Japanese in Hong Kong quickly showed that they could be far more brutal than the British had ever been. Systematic rape, mutilation, and executions, compounded by starvation and efforts to repatriate refugees who had come from China in the years leading up to war, reduced the population from over 1.5 million to about 500,000. Free to do as it pleased, the Kempeitai, the notorious military police, created an "empire unmatched by the Kempeitai branches in any other Japanese-occupied zone."[2]

The new rulers also tried to de-Anglicize Hong Kong as quickly as possible. Statues of British royalty and colonial officials were removed, while street and place names were replaced with Japanese names; even the racehorses at Happy Valley received Japanese names. The Gregorian calendar was replaced by the Japanese calendar based on the contemporary emperor's reign. The Japanese also introduced their own holidays, including the Yasukuni Festival for Japanese war dead, Empire Day, and the emperor's birthday—though they let the Chinese celebrate the Double Tenth holiday, commemorating the republican revolution of 1911, to show they were anti-British but not anti-Chinese.

As the Japanese consolidated their rule, they recruited many of the same local leaders who had worked with the British. Two councils consisting of leading Chinese and Eurasian businessmen were established for disseminating policy and managing the Chinese population. On the Chinese Representative Council were Robert Kotewall, the chair; Lau Tit-shing, manager of the Communications Bank and chairman of the Chinese Bankers' Association; Li Tse-fong, manager of the Bank of East Asia and former unofficial member of the Legislative Council; and Chan Lim-pak, who had once been comprador to the Hong Kong Shanghai Bank in Canton. The Chinese Cooperative Council, whose 22 members were selected by the Chinese Representative Council from the leading professionals, was chaired by Chow Shouson; other members included Lo Man Kam and Ip Lan Chuen.

Why did these Chinese and Eurasians collaborate with the Japanese? Were they happy to be rid of their British overlords and to be working with fellow Asians? On 10 January 1942, Lieutenant General Sakai invited some 130 of the leading Chinese and Eurasians to lunch at the Peninsula Hotel; Robert Kotewall (now referred to by his Chinese name) and Chow Shouson were the main guests of honor. After thanking the Japanese for not "harming the people of Hong Kong or destroying the city"—and declaring that because the goal of the Japanese was to "release the races of East Asia," he and other leaders would cooperate with them—Kotewall wished the emperor "banzai";

Chow agreed "heartily." Kotewall, Chow, and Li Tse-fong all expressed hope that China and Japan would soon end their war, which to Kotewall was "more like a family quarrel between two brothers due to a momentary loss of temper."[3]

Impressed by Japan's rhetoric of "Asia for Asians," some Chinese were more enthusiastic than others about working with the Japanese. Lau Tit-shing was president of the Chinese-Japanese Returned-Students Association and, according to Henry Lethbridge, "very pro-Japanese" having been "thoroughly brainwashed by his early education in Japan."[4] When Lau died in April 1945 he was honored by the Japanese governor. Chan Lim-pak had been arrested by the British during the Japanese invasion on charges of aiding the enemy. He was killed in 1944 by an American bomber while en route to Japan. Others perhaps had their own grudges against the British: Ho Kam Tong, the affable comprador and philanthropist who now became the first Chinese chairman of the Jockey Club, was said to have sworn that because he had been unable to serve on the committee under the British he would ensure that no Briton was ever admitted to the club.

Although life under the Japanese could be excruciatingly harsh, we should beware of portraying the occupation as little more than a tragic farce rather than considering what it offered to Chinese collaborators. Philip Snow argues that the Japanese brought more Chinese into the "central administration of the colony than the British had ever done."[5] The practice of delegating tasks gave Chinese a larger role than under the British, while the Japanese also created a network of district bureaus—another step the British had never taken. Unlike the British, the Japanese went to great lengths to publicize and explain their policies to the Chinese. The Japanese also made some positive changes in public health, education, and agriculture. With "something close to a mania" for preserving public health, they kept outbreaks of smallpox and cholera minor compared with the prewar years.[6]

But most Chinese and Eurasian leaders probably collaborated with the Japanese in the same way the majority of Hong Kong's population did: "with reluctance and misgiving, and as a matter of physical survival."[7] No one knew how the war would turn out, especially with the Japanese successes in China and their spectacular early victories in Southeast Asia. Fear and pragmatism were no doubt strong reasons for collaborating, as were preserving one's own class interests. Many people collaborated with the Japanese to help the local community. Several colonial officials, including former acting governor R. A. C. North, later testified that they had asked Chow and Kotewall to co-operate with the Japanese to protect the interests of the Chinese community.[8] Finally, some Britons also worked with the Japanese—for example, high-level bankers, who could have refused and been interned along with their compatriots in Stanley, on the south side of Hong Kong Island; instead, they chose to collaborate to ensure some level of financial stability. P. S. Selwyn-Clarke, the former director of medical services, collaborated with the Japanese for the sake of the Chinese community and the interned Europeans and prisoners of war. That there was so little Chinese resentment toward the two Chinese councils during or after the occupation suggests that most Chinese understood that the Chinese and Eurasian leaders had to cooperate.

Nor did the Chinese and Eurasian leaders, with the exception of Chan Lim-pak and Lau Tit-shing, ever collaborate as actively with the Japanese as they had with the British. By mid-1943 many in Hong Kong realized that the war was no longer in Japan's favor. By then "it was clear that in many ways Japanese colonialism was far more despotic, bureaucratic and corrupt, and less rational and efficient than the British variety."[9] On Christmas day 1943, Kotewall gave the radio broadcast in honor of the second anniversary of the Japanese occupation. Although he praised the progress under the governorship of General Isogai Rensuke, Kotewall showed nothing of the enthusiasm that he had for the 1941 centenary. Instead, he compared 1942 to the first weeks of chaos after the invasion, rather than to the years of British rule.[10] By 1944 the local leaders began to avoid their duties on the two Chinese councils, while Kotewall and Li Tse-fong withdrew from public life for health reasons.

As British officials began to plan in late 1943 for recovering Hong Kong after the war, the problem arose of what to do with the old business and professional elite. The British needed a local support base, but some interned Europeans had criticized Kotewall and Chow for being too compliant with the Japanese. Where were Chinese helpers to be found if not among the old guard? Furthermore, there was the problem of convincing the local Chinese population that Britain, rather than Nationalist China, deserved to rule Hong Kong after the war. The British "needed Hong Kong Chinese, Chinese loyal to the concept of a separate status for Hong Kong, even if some among this group had worked seemingly for the establishment of a Japanese 'New Order' in Hong Kong."[11] By working with the Japanese instead of fleeing to "Free China," these "loyal Chinese" had "proved that their loyalty was, in the last resort, to Hong Kong exclusively. For the sake of Hong Kong they would strike an accommodation with whoever happened to rule it. They were thus, paradoxically, the segment of society on whom the returning British could now best rely in the face of the intensified threat from the mainland."[12] This rationale explains both why the British, who could not to afford to lose the people they had depended on for so long, decided to keep the old leaders, and why these leaders worked so hard to restore British rule. The Colonial Office eventually decided that Chow and Kotewall had been acting in the colony's best interest. Shortly after Japan surrendered to the United States in August 1945, Kotewall and Chow began to work with the Japanese, who now encouraged the local elite's pro-British attitude, for a smooth transition back to the British.

Thus when on 30 August 1945 British ships under Rear Admiral Cecil Harcourt entered the harbor to accept the Japanese surrender, the British again relied on their "loyal Chinese." But the situation was not as neat as it had been after the strike-boycott of 1925–1926, when the British lavished honors on their Chinese and Eurasian helpers. In October 1945, Kotewall was asked to withdraw from public life until his wartime record could be fully cleared. When the colonial civil government was restored the following May, Kotewall had to resign his seat on the Executive Council. Kotewall was never allowed to return to public life, Chow never completely returned, and Li Tse-fong did not win reappointment to the Legislative Council. But Lo Man Kam, the loudest critic of the colonial regime before the war, was able to return to public life because the British believed he had worked with the Japanese only with great reluctance. Lo was later appointed to the Legislative and Executive councils. Chau Tsun-nin, who had avoided collaborating by taking refuge in neutral Macau, was also appointed to the Legislative and Executive councils. Chau was later made Commander of the British Empire, while Lo was knighted for helping to rebuild Hong Kong.

Hong Kong, Colonialism, and Collaboration

What can Hong Kong's experience teach us about colonialism? Jürgen Osterhammel has noted that from 1500 to 1920 most of the world was, at least at some point, a colony of Europe. But this remarkable phenomenon must not, cautions Osterhammel, obscure the fact that colonial reality was "multifaceted and often failed to conform to arrogant imperial strategies. It was shaped by particular local features overseas, and by broader tendencies in the international system."[13]

Osterhammel notes that not "every domination by foreigners has been perceived by its subjects as *illegitimate* foreign domination."[14] This observation fits the case of Hong Kong. Although British military might was used to secure the island from China, colonial expansion in Hong Kong was made possible with Chinese cooperation throughout the early history of the colony. Many of the prominent Chinese businessmen in early Hong Kong came from a long tradition of cooperating with foreigners. Loo Aqui and Kwok Acheong had helped the British during the Opium War, while contractors such as Tam Achoy who were instrumental in the building of the infant colony had worked with the British in other colonies. For Ho Kai, British domination had made Hong Kong into a vibrant commercial center. During the strike-boycott of 1925–1926, both the colonial government and the Chinese bourgeoisie saw the strike as an illegitimate attack by authorities in Canton. And in the 1941 centenary of Hong Kong as a British colony, local Chinese supported the official, colonial history of Hong Kong that began with Britain's occupation.

Osterhammel wisely cautions that it is "problematic to interpret 'collaboration' and 'resistance' as positions that can be assessed *on principle,* or even morally. Conduct in a given set of circumstances arose from the type of contact situation and the way it was interpreted." Collaboration is thus an "unfortunate choice of term that inevitably recalls the treacherous cooperation of individuals and small cliques with a military occupation regime hated by the remainder of the subjugated population during World War II, causing untold damage to their compatriots."[15] Osterhammel's analysis is particularly appropriate for the case of Hong Kong. Collaboration between Chinese and the colonial government occurred from the earliest days of the colony. Indeed, all Chinese who came to British Hong Kong were collaborators of a sort, not the least because, apart from the small population on the island before the British occupation, most of these Chinese subjects were self-selected, having come to the island willingly. Such was the case with Loo Aqui, Kwok Acheong, and Tam Achoy. Later, in the nineteenth and twentieth centuries, Ho Kai genuinely felt that Hong Kong, because of its Britishness, had an important role to play in the development of a new, strong China. When Chow Shouson, Robert Kotewall, and other leaders of the Chinese bourgeoisie collaborated with the colonial government during the 1925–1926 strike, they were acting not simply out of economic interest but out of a need to preserve *their* Hong Kong in a turbulent era.

Nor did collaboration with the British in Hong Kong necessarily come at the expense of the local Chinese population or at the expense of China. Connections to the colonial government and to European commerce enabled Chinese merchants to amass large fortunes, which enabled them to establish charitable and philanthropic organizations. Although they served to preserve elite status, these organizations offered invaluable services to Chinese of lesser means. They also provided equally important services to China: funds for famine relief, the construction of hospitals, and informal diplomatic functions for the Qing government. Indeed, when the Qing government began to change its official image of overseas Chinese from that of "Chinese traitors" to "overseas Chinese," it did so not simply because it needed their help but because they had shown their commitment to helping China.

Not all the characteristics of Osterhammel's redefinition of colonialism, however, apply very well to the case of Hong Kong. Colonialism, according to Osterhammel, is "not just any relationship between masters and servants, but one in which an entire society is robbed of its historical line of development, *externally manipulated* and transformed according to the needs and interests of the colonial rulers."[16] Far from robbing Hong Kong of its historical line of development, colonialism gave Hong Kong a new historical line of development—but only with help from events in China and across the globe. Although colonialism in Hong Kong was built on cooperation, this was not sufficient to develop the island into anything more than a minor port and colonial outpost, and to create a group of small merchants, landowners, and compradors. The colonial government could not control piracy in the waters surrounding the colony, and it did little to control crime within Hong Kong itself. Nor was the government able to assure Chinese merchants that it was committed to keeping the island. It required the combination of Western capitalism and imperialism and Chinese domestic turmoil to attract enough men like Li Sing and his brothers, their wealth, and their business connections to make Hong Kong a great commercial center. These events saw the meeting of two world systems that were related but distinct, changing the island's basic reason for being and allowing the realization of this new historical line of development.

How did the leaders of the Chinese business community view their own position in colonial Hong Kong? In *Black Skin, White Masks* and *The Wretched of the Earth*, two works that once galvanized anticolonial sentiment across the globe, Frantz Fanon argued that colonialism dislocated and distorted the psyche of colonized peoples by reducing the non-white subject to nothingness.[17] But as Frederick Cooper has argued, Fanon was "denying colonized people any history but that of oppression, any ambiguity to the ways they might confront and appropriate the intrusions of colonizers."[18] Like Fanon, Osterhammel argues that a "feeling of inadequacy inheres in the basic mental outlook of every colonized people."[19] If this is true, then the Chinese bourgeoisie of Hong Kong did a remarkable job of either disguising or overcoming this feeling of inadequacy. Loo Aqui and Tam Achoy wasted no time in adapting to their new home. When Li Sing sent money for relief projects in China, was he doing so out of guilt for having left China for a British colony? Ho Kai was proud of being part of Hong Kong, and he was not afraid to express this pride. In Ho's own era, the founders of the Chinese Club and the Chinese Recreation Club did not simply accept their exclusion from the social world of the European bourgeoisie. They created a new, equally exclusive social world in which they were the undisputed masters. Nor did they try to overcompensate by trying to become more British than the British. Instead, they created a social world that was neither fully British nor Chinese, but Hong Kong Chinese. When the leaders of the Chinese bourgeoisie helped preserve order during the strike of 1925–1926, they showed no tolerance for the radical developments in China and urged the colonial government to take a tough stance against the strike. These do not seem like the actions of men suffering from feelings of inadequacy.

Was Hong Kong sui generis, a cultural, economic, and political anomaly? Although recent work on colonialism has opened up new horizons, it has led to generalized pronouncements about "the colonial project" and "the colonial encounter." But as Nicholas Thomas reminds us, "colonialism can only be traced through its plural and particularized expressions."[20] If Hong Kong was unique, its uniqueness lay not in the reasons the Hong Kong government traditionally enjoyed citing: British impartial justice, humane government, and free trade coupled with Chinese entrepreneurship. Rather, it lay more in Hong Kong's geographic position. A very small tail on a very large Chinese elephant, Hong Kong provided Chinese merchants a vantage point from which they could compare and contrast conditions there with those on the mainland.

Hong Kong and Chinese Outside of China

The prevailing view of Hong Kong's position in modern Chinese history stresses Hong Kong's contributions to nation building: the graduates of local schools who served in the Chinese Civil Service and the Imperial Chinese Maritime Customs during the Qing and in the various governments of the republican era; the part played by the colony in the 1911 revolution; its role as a haven for Chinese refugees; its philanthropic and relief works; and the commercial and industrial activities by Hong Kong entrepreneurs in South China.[21] These themes were strongly accentuated especially in Mainland Chinese scholarship during the decade leading up to Hong Kong's transfer to Chinese rule in 1997, one of many strategic moves designed to wean local Chinese away from Britain and back to the "motherland."[22] But this emphasis on contributions oversimplifies the picture. It overlooks how Hong Kong Chinese residents could use their role in modern Chinese history to emphasize their own distinctiveness. Similarly, scholarship on Chinese outside China overwhelmingly emphasizes the selfless patriotism of Chinese emigrants and their commitment to China's nation building. But the ability of these overseas Chinese to send remittances, provide relief funds, and open village schools and hospitals depended on their being *outside* China.

Finally, rather than focus on the "Chineseness" of Chinese society outside China, we might consider some of the similarities to non-Chinese colonial or settler societies.[23] The Chinese business community in Hong Kong greatly resembled the British business community in colonial Hong Kong, as well as that of the British "Shanghailanders" in semicolonial Shanghai.[24] Both British and Chinese were dedicated to opening markets in China, to the point where Hong Kong Chinese were in a sense both colonized and colonizers. Both benefited from their connections in the British Empire and both were dependent on the power wielded by that empire. Members of both societies saw themselves as either long-term or permanent residents, rather than as expatriates or sojourners. Yet they continued to send money home to support philanthropic causes and, when necessary, to assist the national war effort. Both British and Chinese could have a number of identities: British or Chinese, imperial or national, and local. Both communities based their local identities on self-images of industriousness, entrepreneurship, and public spirit. As the commemoration of the 1941 centenary shows, both saw themselves as having transformed *their* Hong Kong from a barren rock into a thriving metropolis.

Hong Kong and Chinese History

What can Hong Kong's experience teach us about Chinese history? Chinese business elites in Hong Kong played an active role in civic affairs—no doubt for their own purposes but nonetheless affecting the nature of the colony profoundly. Was this possible only under *British* auspices, and only through the participation of *Chinese* business elites? Or were these Chinese conditioned to collaboration by the nature of the Chinese political economy? In many ways, the secret to Hong Kong's success was China's failure: its inability to provide a secure business environment in the late nineteenth century, its failure to control factionalism and regionalism in the early twentieth century, and its unwillingness to grant merchants any more political power than they might achieve in European colonies. This made collaboration with the British an attractive option.

Yet Hong Kong was perhaps the most important place in China for more than 150 years, precisely because it was politically not part of China. And although Hong Kong was not part of China "proper," there were many cities like Hong Kong all along the Chinese coast: Canton and Shanghai, for example—treaty ports opened to foreign trade at gunpoint, both figuratively and literally. Although these "in-formal colonies," as they have often been called, were opened at gun-point, Chinese moved there in large numbers, not despite but because of this foreign domination. These treaty ports led to new, multiple, and often overlapping, communities, identities, and loyalties that have only recently begun to be studied.[25] The case of Hong Kong also suggests that we need to consider the types and shades of Chinese nationalism. Recent works have tended to focus on how and by whom Chinese nationalism was created, but we also need to look at how ideas of nationalism may have differed—among different classes, in different locations, and at different times.

Colonialism in Hong Kong: Past and Present

What does a new understanding of colonialism tell us about Hong Kong today, as its people enter a critical new phase in their history? No one knows for sure how Hong Kong will fare under its new rulers, but we might consider what Hong Kong's past has to say about its future. Although Hong Kong has returned to China, it has not been de-colonized. Rather, it has been re-colonized, with the metropole simply shifting from London to Beijing.[26] The new cadres coming down from Beijing are reminiscent of the early British administrators in the 1800s, with their own language, their own clubs, and their own condescending attitudes toward their new subjects. But Hong Kong also finds itself both colonial and colonized, once again complicating the notion of subaltern: although the former colony is politically sub-ordinate, it is economically and politically more advanced than Main-land China.

The impending transfer to Chinese rule added urgency to some of the issues we have seen. In June 1989, for example, hundreds of thousands of Chinese in Hong Kong took to the streets to protest the massacre at Tiananmen Square. Many observers saw this as the birth of a new Hong Kong identity. Lynn White and Li Cheng rightly argue that the Tiananmen tragedy forced many Hong Kong Chinese "con-sciously to reevaluate their identities and their options for the fu-ture."[27] But Tiananmen and its aftermath simply highlighted the com-plex relationships between Chinese nationalism and Hong Kong identity. When Hong Kong Chinese protested the killings at Tiananmen, they did so as Chinese nationalists and as Hong Kong Chinese. Tiananmen alienated many Hong Kong Chinese from the Chinese Communist Party, but it also "intensified their Chinese patriotism."[28] As White and Li put it, "Hong Kong people became more fully Chinese in that year, even while their disaffection with the Chinese government soared and while they looked for safe havens they might later need."[29] As in the periods of history examined in this book, the relationship between Chinese nationalism and Hong Kong identity was shaped by developments on both sides of the Hong Kong-Chinese border. Similarly, the recent Right of Abode case was ostensibly about the autonomy of the Hong Kong judicial system under a new government. But it was also about who qualified as Hong Kong Chinese.

For many Hong Kong Chinese, rule by China is far more repellent and worrisome than rule by Britain. Although it has promised the Hong Kong Special Administrative Region (SAR) a "high degree of autonomy" for fifty years, Beijing has interfered regularly in the SAR's political affairs from its inception, determining to prove that it, not Hong Kong people, will determine the SAR's future. It has, for example, already taken several measures to limit the growth of democracy in Hong Kong. Surveys regularly find that public dissatisfaction with the Hong Kong government's handling of relations with the central authorities in Beijing is very high, while public satisfaction with the SAR government is usually very low.

But rarely do we read or hear questions about how Hong Kong's colonial past has prepared its people to deal with their new colonial future. Academics and journalists frequently (and justifiably) lament the recent erosion of political liberties in Hong Kong. But less often do they pay attention to the new attempts in Hong Kong to make sure this former colony does not become just another part of China— from parents who fight the government's directives to emphasize Chinese rather than English in schools because they fear their children will be less competitive in the international market, to artists and journalists who encourage the use of more Cantonese in their work. Even the new government is trying to find ways to keep Hong Kong alive as a distinct entity, from a Disney theme park on one of the last undeveloped areas of the region, to failed proposals for a new "cyberport," to various names and symbols designed to give the place a new image: "City of Life" and "Asia's World City."

Finally, just as British colonization was made possible by help from local Chinese, so Chinese re-colonization is being made possible by local Hong Kong Chinese. Although the appointment of prominent local people to run the region since 1997 certainly does not mean that Beijing has yielded to local demands for representation, it is an admission that Hong Kong is so different from anywhere else in China that it cannot be run without local help. More than 150 years of colonial rule may have prepared Chinese in Hong Kong to cope with the changes they now face. Chinese in Hong Kong may not have seriously challenged colonialism and all its trappings, but neither did they simply accept it. They worked around it and borrowed what they wanted. They did so in the nineteenth century and the twentieth century, and I suspect they will do so in the twenty-first.

Notes

Bibliography

Index

Notes

Introduction

1. Marc Chadourne, *China*, trans. Harry Block (New York: Covici Friede, 1932), pp. 25–26.

2. Ibid., p. 36.

3. C. Mary Turnbull, "Hong Kong: Fragrant Harbour, City of Sin and Death," in Robin W. Winks and James R. Rush, eds., *Asia in Western Fiction* (Honolulu: University of Hawaii Press, 1990), pp. 117–118.

4. Su Fuxiang, " 'Zhongxi hebi' de xianggang wenhua" [Hong Kong culture: the "junction of East and West"], in Li Jinwei, ed., *Xianggang bainianshi* [Centenary history of Hong Kong] (Hong Kong: Nanzhong chubanshe, 1948), pp. 168–169; Su Fuxiang, "Mantan 'Xianggangren' " [A chat about 'Hong Kong people'], in Li, *Xianggang bainianshi*, p. 133.

5. For examples of British historiography, see G. B. Endacott, *A History of Hong Kong*, rev. ed. (Hong Kong: Oxford University Press, 1973) and *Government and People in Hong Kong, 1841–1962: A Constitutional History* (Hong Kong: Hong Kong University Press, 1964), Geoffrey R. Sayer, *Hong Kong: Birth, Adolescence, and Coming of Age, 1841–1862* (London: Oxford University Press, 1937) and *Hong Kong 1862–1919: Years of Discretion* (Hong Kong: Hong Kong University Press, 1975); for an example of the Chinese Marxist approach, see Ding You, *Xianggang chuqi shihua* [Early Hong Kong] (Beijing: Lianhe chubanshe, 1983).

6. Chan Wai Kwan, *The Making of Hong Kong Society: Three Studies of Class Formation in Early Hong Kong* (Oxford: Clarendon Press, 1991) and Elizabeth Sinn, *Power and Charity: The Early History of the Tung Wah Hospital, Hong Kong* (Hong Kong: Oxford University Press, 1989).

7. Jung-fang Tsai, *Hong Kong in Chinese History: Community and Social Unrest in the British Colony, 1842–1913* (New York: Columbia University Press, 1993) and

Cai Rongfang (Jung-fang Tsai), *Xianggang ren zhi Xianggangshi, 1841–1945* [The Hong Kong People's History of Hong Kong, 1841–1945] (Hong Kong: Oxford University Press, 2001); K. C. Fok, *Lectures on Hong Kong History: Hong Kong's Role in Modern Chinese History* (Hong Kong: Commercial Press, 1990) and Huo Qichang (K. C. Fok), *Xianggang yu jindai Zhongguo* [Hong Kong and modern China] (Taipei: Shangwu, 1993); Chan Lau Kit-ching, *China, Britain and Hong Kong, 1895–1945* (Hong Kong: Chinese University Press, 1990); Stephanie Po-yin Chung, *Chinese Business Groups in Hong Kong and Political Change in South China, 1900–25* (Basingstoke, Eng.: Macmillan, 1998); and Christopher Munn, *Anglo-China: Chinese People and British Rule in Hong Kong, 1841–1880* (Richmond, Surrey, Eng. Curzon Press, 2001).

8. Marie-Claire Bergère, *The Golden Age of the Chinese Bourgeoisie, 1911–1937* (Cambridge: Cambridge University Press, 1986); William T. Rowe, *Hankow: Commerce and Society in a Chinese City, 1796–1889* (Stanford: Stanford University Press, 1984) and *Hankow: Conflict and Community in a Chinese City, 1796–1895* (Stanford: Stanford University Press, 1989); and Mark Elvin and G. William Skinner, eds., *The Chinese City Between Two Worlds* (Stanford: Stanford University Press, 1974).

9. Richard Hughes, *Hong Kong: Borrowed Place, Borrowed Time* (London: André Deutsch, 1968).

10. Akbar Abbas, *Hong Kong: The Culture of Disappearance* (Minneapolis: University of Minnesota Press, 1997), p. 4.

11. Lau Siu-kai, *Utilitarianistic Familism: An Inquiry into the Basis of Political Stability in Hong Kong* (Hong Kong: Chinese University of Hong Kong Social Research Centre, 1977), pp. 21–24, and *Society and Politics in Hong Kong* (Hong Kong: Chinese University Press, 1982), pp. 7–9; for the quote on Britain's goals in Hong Kong, Steve Tsang, ed., *Government and Politics: A Documentary History of Hong Kong* (Hong Kong: Hong Kong University Press, 1995), p. 4.

12. Partha Chatterjee, *The Nation and Its Fragments: Colonial and Postcolonial Histories* (Princeton: Princeton University Press, 1993), p. 14.

13. Abbas, *Hong Kong*, p. 2.

14. Nonintervention myth: Ming K. Chan, "The Legacy of the British Administration of Hong Kong: A View from Hong Kong," *China Quarterly* 151 (September 1997): 574–575; modern medicine: Philippa Levine, "Modernity, Medicine, and Colonialism: The Contagious Diseases Ordinances in Hong Kong and the Straits Settlements," *positions* 6:3 (Winter 1998): 675–705 and Carol Benedict, "Framing Plague in China's Past," in Gail Hershatter et al., eds., *Remapping China: Fissures in Historical Terrain* (Stanford: Stanford University Press, 1996), pp. 27–41; rejuvenation: John L. Comaroff, "Images of Empire, Contests of Conscience," and Susan Thorne, " 'The Conversion of Englishmen and the Conversion of the World Inseparable': Missionary Imperialism and the Language of Class in Early Industrial Britain," both in Frederick Cooper and Ann Laura Stoler, eds., *Tensions of Empire: Colonial Cultures in a Bourgeois World* (Berkeley: University of California Press, 1997), pp. 163–197, 238–262, and John M. Mackenzie, *Propaganda and Empire: The Manipulation of British Public Opinion, 1880–1960* (Manchester: Manchester University Press, 1984), p. 2; and Adrian Hastings, *The Church in Africa, 1450–1950* (Oxford: Oxford University Press, 1994).

15. David Cannadine, *Ornamentalism: How the British Saw their Empire* (Oxford: Oxford University Press, 2001), pp. xvi–xvii.

16. Edward Said, *Orientalism: Western Conceptions of the Orient* (New York: Pantheon, 1978), pp. 1, 3; Said's critics, for example, C. A. Bayly, *Empire and Information: Intelligence Gathering and Social Communication in India, 1780–1870* (Cambridge: Cambridge University Press, 1996) and John M. MacKenzie, *Orientalism: History, Theory, and the Arts* (Manchester: Manchester University Press); and Sumit Sarkar, "Orientalism Revisited: Saidian Frameworks in the Writing of Modern Indian History," in Vinayak Chaturvedi, ed., *Mapping Subaltern Studies and the Postcolonial* (London: Verso, 2000), pp. 241, 249, 252.

17. Ranajit Guha, "On Some Aspects of the Historiography of Colonial India," in Ranajit Guha and Gayatri Chakravorty Spivak, eds., *Selected Subaltern Studies* (New York: Oxford University Press, 1988), p. 43. On lack of new theoretical insights, see, for example, the essays in Chaturvedi, *Mapping Subaltern Studies*. In his contribution to the volume, "Rallying Around the Subaltern," pp. 117–118, C. A. Bayly argues that "Subaltern authors generally use theory as the elite historians used it, as a piquant garnish for footnotes, though in the process, Foucault, Gramsci and Derrida have been stirred in with Weber, Marx or Pareto."

18. On the shift to textual analysis: Sumit Sarkar, "The Decline of the Subaltern in *Subaltern Studies*," in Chaturvedi, *Mapping Subaltern Studies*, pp. 300–323; Rajnarayan Chandavarkar, " 'The Making of the Working Class': E. P. Thompson and Indian History," in Chaturvedi, *Mapping Subaltern Studies*, p. 65.

19. Alijaz Ahmad, "The Politics of Literary Postcoloniality," in Padmini Mongia, ed., *Contemporary Postcolonial Theory* (London: Arnold, 1996), pp. 280–281; Anne McClintock, "The Angel of Progress: Pitfalls of the Term 'Postcolonialism'," in Patrick Williams and Laura Chrisman, eds., *Colonial Discourse and Post-Colonial Theory* (New York: Columbia University Press, 1994), p. 293; Ann Laura Stoler and Frederick Cooper, "Between Metropole and Colony: Rethinking a Research Agenda," in Cooper and Stoler, *Tensions of Empire*, p. 33.

20. Aihwa Ong, *Flexible Citizenship: The Cultural Logics of Transnationality* (Durham: Duke University Press, 1999), p. 34; McClintock, "Angel of Progress," pp. 292–294.

21. McClintock ("Angel of Progress," p. 293; original emphasis) notes how often the term "postcolonial" refers to singularity rather than to multiplicity and variance: terms such as "*the* post-colonial condition," "post-coloniality," and "*the* post-colonial Other" tend to reduce history to a "single issue." For other criticism of the ahistorical nature of Orientalism and postcolonialism, see MacKenzie, *Orientalism*, p. 11; Dennis Porter, "*Orientalism* and Its Problems," in Williams and Chrisman, *Colonial Discourse*, p. 152; Dane Kennedy, "Imperial History and Post-Colonial Theory," *Journal of Imperial and Commonwealth History* 24.3 (September 1996): 350–351; Ania Loomba, *Colonialism/Postcolonialism* (London: Routledge, 1998), p. 17.

22. Pier M. Larson, " 'Capacities and Modes of Thinking': Intellectual Engagements and Subaltern Hegemony in the Early History of Malagasy Christianity," *American Historical Review* 102.4 (October 1997): 1000.

23. "We should never forget that the British Empire was first and foremost a class act, where individual social ordering often took precedence over collective racial ordering" (Cannadine, *Ornamentalism*, p. 10); Gail Hershatter, "The Sub-

altern Talks Back: Reflections on Subaltern Theory and Chinese History," *positions* 1.1 (Spring 1993): 110–111.

24. This attitude persisted in both China and Taiwan after 1949: for example, a study of Chinese education in Hong Kong published in Taiwan in 1958 explained that "Hong Kong's Chinese society is purely a commercial one. These permanent residents are almost all merchants or the sons and grandsons of merchants. Their main goal is accumulating capital, generating commerce, and amassing personal or family fortunes—to the point where they usually do not have the time for scientific or cultural development." Ma Hongshu and Chen Zhenming, *Xianggang Huaqiao jiaoyu* [Chinese education in Hong Kong] (Taipei: Haiwai chubanshe, 1958), p. 5.

25. He Jian, "Huaqiao yu Xianggang jianshe" [Overseas Chinese and the building of Hong Kong], in Chen Datong, et al., *Xianggang Huaqiao tuanti zonglan* [Chinese organizations in Hong Kong] (Hong Kong: Guoji xinwenshe, 1947), p. 7.

26. On the problem of hybridity and authenticity, see Nicholas Thomas, *In Oceania: Visions, Artifacts, Histories* (Durham: Duke University Press, 1997), p. 11; Frederick Cooper, "Conflict and Connection: Rethinking Colonial African History," *American Historical Review* 99.5 (December 1994): 1532.

27. Arif Dirlik, "Chinese History and the Question of Orientalism," *History and Theory* 35.4 (December 1995): 96–120; MacKenzie, *Orientalism*, p. 11; Sarkar, "Orientalism Revisited," p. 242.

28. On the "vagueness" of colonialism, Jürgen Osterhammel, *Colonialism: A Theoretical Overview*, trans. Shelley L. Frisch (Princeton: Marcus Wiener, 1997), p. 4; Nicholas Thomas, *Colonialism's Culture: Anthropology, Travel and Government* (Princeton: Princeton University Press, 1994), p. 17.

29. For dialogue in the colonies, see, for example, the essays in Stuart B. Schwartz, ed., *Implicit Understandings: Observing, Reporting, and Reflecting on the Encounters Between Europeans and Other Peoples in the Early Modern Era* (Cambridge: Cambridge University Press, 1994); "traumatic relationships," Loomba, *Colonialism/Postcolonialism*, p. 2; and "unitary representation," Thomas, *Colonialism's Culture*, p. 60.

30. Great Britain, Colonial Office, Original Correspondence: Hong Kong, 1841–1951, Series 129 (CO129), Public Record Office, London, CO 129/23, Feb. 26, 1848, "Memorial from the European and Chinese Inhabitants in Hong Kong relative to the Payment of Ground Rents," pp. 222–226.

31. Bergère, p. 191.

32. David Blackbourn and Richard J. Evans, eds., *The German Bourgeoisie: Essays on the Social History of the German Middle Class from the Late Eighteenth to the Early Twentieth Century* (London: Routledge, 1991), p. xiv.

33. Laura Hostetler, *Qing Colonial Enterprise: Ethnography and Cartography in Early Modern China* (Chicago: University of Chicago Press, 2001).

34. James A. Millward, *Beyond the Pass: Economy, Ethnicity, and Empire in Qing Central Asia*, 1759–1864 (Stanford: Stanford University Press, 1998).

35. James L. Hevia, *Cherishing Men from Afar: Qing Guest Ritual and the Macartney Mission of 1793* (Durham: Duke University Press, 1995), p. 26.

36. James L. Hevia, *English Lessons: The Pedagogy of Imperialism in Nineteenth-Century China* (Durham: Duke University Press, 2003), p. 166.

1. Colonialism and Collaboration

1. Great Britain, Colonial Office, Original Correspondence: Hong Kong, 1841–1951, Series 129 (CO129), Public Record Office, London, CO129/73, March 29, 1859, Bowring to Lytton, pp. 296–297.

2. E. J. Eitel, *Europe in China: The History of Hong Kong from the Beginning to the Year 1882* (1895; repr., Hong Kong: Oxford University Press, 1983), pp. 569–570; on "policy of conciliation," Lennox A. Mills, *British Rule in Eastern Asia: A Study of Contemporary Government and Economic Development in British Malaya and Hong Kong* (London: Oxford University Press, 1942), p. 413; for an example of free-market economist view, see Alvin Rabushka, *Hong Kong: A Study in Economic Freedom* (Chicago: University of Chicago Press, 1979); on social noninterventionism, Lau Siu-kai and Kuan Hsin-chi, *The Ethos of the Hong Kong Chinese* (Hong Kong: Chinese University Press, 1988); on apathy, Norman Miners, *The Government and Politics of Hong Kong* (Hong Kong: Oxford University Press, 1975); on fair government, Steve Tsang, ed., *Government and Politics: A Documentary History of Hong Kong* (Hong Kong: Hong Kong University Press, 1995), p. 5. For critiques of the notion of political stability, see Stephen W. K. Chiu and Ho-fung Hung, "State Building and Rural Stability," and Tai-lok Lui and Stephen W. K. Chiu, "Social Movements and Public Discourse on Politics," both in Tak-Wing Ngo, ed., *Hong Kong's History: State and Society under Colonial Rule* (London: Routledge, 1999), pp. 74–100, 101–118; and Fred Y. L. Chiu, "Politics and the Body Social in Colonial Hong Kong," in Tani E. Barlow, ed., *Formation of Colonial Modernity in East Asia* (Durham: Duke University Press, 1997), pp. 295–322.

3. Ronald Robinson, "Non-European Foundations of European Imperialism: Sketch for a Theory of Collaboration," in Roger Owen and Bob Sutcliffe, eds., *Studies in the Theory of Imperialism* (London: Longman, 1972), pp. 117–142, and "European Imperialism and Indigenous Reactions in British West Africa," in H. L. Wesseling, ed., *Expansion and Reaction: Essays in European Expansion and Reactions in Asia and Africa* (Leiden: Leiden University Press, 1978), pp. 141–163 (Robinson's argument is applied to the case of Indonesian and Chinese collaborators in Leonard Blussé, *Strange Company: Chinese Settlers, Mestizo Women and the Dutch in VOC Batavia* [Dordrecht, The Netherlands: Foris, 1986], especially chapter 4); Frederick Cooper, "The Dialectics of Decolonization: Nationalism and Labor Movements in Postwar French Africa," in Frederick Cooper and Ann Laura Stoler, eds., *Tensions of Empire: Colonial Cultures in a Bourgeois World* (Berkeley: University of California Press, 1997), p. 409.

4. Carter J. Eckert, *Offspring of Empire: The Koch'ang Kims and the Colonial Origins of Korean Capitalism, 1876–1945* (Seattle: University of Washington Press, 1991), especially chapter 2.

5. Fearon's report on the first six months of the Census and Registration Office, CO 129/12, June 24, 1845, pp. 305–306; Cheng Zhi, "Xianggang jianshi" [Brief history of Hong Kong], and Yu Lou, "Xianggang chuqi haidaoshi [Piracy in early Hong Kong]," both in Li Jinwei, ed., *Xianggang bainianshi* [Centenary history of Hong Kong] (Hong Kong: Nanzhong chubanshe, 1948), pp. 7–14; Great Britain, Foreign Office, Records of Letters between the Plenipotentiary and the High Provincial Authorities, and Proclamations by H. E. the Governor and Chief Magistrate, 1844–1849, Series 233 (FO 233), Public Record Office,

London, FO 233/185, Jan. 6, 1845; Lu Yan, *Xianggang zhanggu* [Hong Kong stories], vol. 1 (Hong Kong: Guangjiaojing chubanshe, 1977), pp. 111–114; Zhang Yueai, "Xianggang, 1841–1980" [Hong Kong, 1841–1980], in Lu Yan et al., *Xianggang zhanggu* [Hong Kong stories], vol. 4 (Hong Kong: Guangjiaojing chubanshe, 1981), pp. 2–4.

6. On the region's tradition of trade, Luo Xianglin, *Yiba siyinian yiqian zhi Xianggang ji qi duiwai jiaotong* [Hong Kong's overseas relations before 1841] (Hong Kong: Zhongguo xueshe, 1963), chapter 1; Jiang Zulu and Fang Zhiqian, eds., *Jianming Guangdongshi* [Concise history of Guangdong] (Guangzhou: Guangdong renmin chubanshe, 1993), pp. 6–8; Macau as emporium: Jonathan Porter, *Macau: The Imaginary City* (Boulder: Westview Press, 1996), p. 3.

7. Peter Y. C. Ng and Hugh D. R. Baker, *New Peace County: A Chinese Gazetteer of Hong Kong Region* (Hong Kong: Hong Kong University Press, 1983), p. 77.

8. William C. Hunter, *The "Fan Kwae" at Canton before Treaty Days, 1825–1844* (London: Kegan Paul, Trench, 1882), p. 26; Colin Crisswell, *The Taipans: Hong Kong's Merchant Princes* (Hong Kong: Oxford University Press, 1981), pp. 4–5, 11, 27. On the early foreign trading houses, see Solomon Bard, *Traders of Hong Kong: Some Foreign Merchant Houses, 1841–1899* (Hong Kong: Urban Council, 1993), and Feng Bangyan, *Xianggang Yingzi caituan, 1841–1996* [British financial organizations in Hong Kong, 1841–1996] (Hong Kong: Sanlian, 1996), chapter 1. The Parsis were Zoroastrians who had left Persia for India to escape religious persecution. As in India, many Parsis in Hong Kong became successful merchants and prominent philanthropists.

9. Eitel, *Europe in China*, pp. 53–57; John King Fairbank, *Trade and Diplomacy on the China Coast: The Opening of the Treaty Ports, 1842–1854*, 2 vols. (1953; repr. 2 vols. in 1, Cambridge, Mass.: Harvard University Press, 1964), p. 123; quote from *Canton Register* cited in Eitel, *Europe in China*, p. 60.

10. For example, Frederic Wakeman, Jr., *Strangers at the Gate: Social Disorder in South China, 1839–1861* (Berkeley: University of California Press, 1966); Chang Hsin-pao, *Commissioner Lin and the Opium War* (Cambridge, Mass.: Harvard University Press, 1964); Michael Greenberg, *British Trade and the Opening of China, 1800–1842* (Cambridge: Cambridge University Press, 1951); Arthur Waley, *The Opium War through Chinese Eyes* (London: Allen and Unwin, 1958); Gregory Blue, "Opium for China: The British Connection," in Timothy Brook and Bob Tadashi Wakabayashi, eds., *Opium Regimes: China, Britain, and Japan, 1839–1952* (Berkeley: University of California Press, 2000), pp. 31–54.

11. Fairbank, *Trade and Diplomacy*, p. 123. Palmerston's successor, Lord Aberdeen, thought the island would be too costly to maintain and that acquisition would only cause further trouble with China.

12. Dafydd M. E. Evans, "The Foundation of Hong Kong: A Chapter of Accidents," in Marjorie Topley, ed., *Hong Kong: The Interaction of Traditions and Life in the Towns* (Hong Kong: Hong Kong Branch of the Royal Asiatic Society, 1975), p. 12–13.

13. Frederic Wakeman, Jr., "*Hanjian* (Traitor)!: Collaboration and Retribution in Wartime Shanghai," in Wen-hsin Yeh, ed., *Becoming Chinese: Passages to Modernity and Beyond* (Berkeley: University of California Press, 2000), p. 299; on Britain's "use of Chinese 'traitors,' " Ding Xinbao [Ting Sun Pao, Joseph], "Xiang-

gang zaoqi zhi Huaren shehui, 1841–1870" [Early Chinese Community in Hong Kong, 1841–1870] (Ph.D. diss., University of Hong Kong, 1989), pp. 146–148; Christopher Munn, "The Chusan Episode: Britain's Occupation of a Chinese Island, 1840–46," *Journal of Imperial and Commonwealth History* 25.1 (January 1997): 89; CO 129/1, June 21, 1841, Elliot to Auckland, p. 3.

14. Dian Murray, *Pirates of the South China Coast, 1790–1810* (Stanford: Stanford University Press, 1987), p. 16; Hunter, *Fan Kwae,* p. 84; CO 129/25, August 10, 1848, Inglis to Caine, pp. 144–146; Dafydd Emrys Evans, "Chinatown in Hong Kong: The Beginnings of Taipingshan," *Journal of the Hong Kong Branch of the Royal Asiatic Society* 10 (1970): 70; Carl T. Smith, *Chinese Christians: Elites, Middlemen, and the Church in Hong Kong* (Hong Kong: Oxford University Press, 1985), p. 110.

15. CO 129/12, June 24, 1845, p. 306; "Caine's Observations on the Replies of Witnesses Before the Select Committee of the House of Commons on Commercial Relations with China," CO 129/27, Feb. 25, 1848, pp. 286–287; *Canton Press,* March 19, 1842; *Friend of China,* May 6, 1846; *Qingdai chouban yiwu shimo, Daoguang* [Complete account of our management of barbarian affairs, Daoguang reign], vol. 58, pp. 39b–42b, cited in Fairbank, *Trade and Diplomacy,* p. 88; Carl Smith, *Chinese Christians,* p. 109; Rev. George Smith, *A Narrative of an Exploratory Visit to Each of the Consular Cities of China and to the Islands of Hong Kong and Chusan, In Behalf of the Church Missionary Society in the Years 1844, 1845, 1846* (London: Seely, Burnside and Seeley, 1847), p. 82; *Yingyi ru-Yue jilue* [The English barbarians' invasion of Guangdong], Yazheng [Opium War] section, vol. 3, pp. 25–26, cited in Ding, "Xianggang zaoqi zhi Huaren shehui," p. 204–209.

16. ". . . influx of natives," Edward H. Cree, *The Cree Journals: The Voyages of Edward H. Cree, Surgeon R. N., as Related in His Private Journals, 1837–1856,* ed. Michael Levien (Exeter, Eng.: Webb and Bower, 1981), p. 78; on makeshift godowns, William Fred Mayers, N. B. Dennys, and Charles King, *The Treaty Ports of China and Japan: A Complete Guide to the Open Ports of those Countries, Together with Peking, Yedo, Hongkong and Macao* (Hong Kong: A. Shortrede, 1867), p. 3, and George Smith, *Narrative,* p. 68; engineer's quote, John Ouchterlony, *The Chinese War: An Account of All the Operations of the British Forces from the Commencement to the Treaty of Nanking* (London: Saunders and Otley, 1844), pp. 216–217.

17. *The Hong Kong Almanack and Directory for 1846* (Hong Kong: China Mail, 1846).

18. French officer's observation, *Friend of China,* June 8, 1843; *Canton Press,* Dec. 4, 1841; Great Britain, Foreign Office, General Correspondence: China, 1815–1905, Series 17 (FO 17), Public Record Office, London, FO 17/56, Feb. 8, 1842, Pottinger to Aberdeen, pp. 111–112; *Canton Press,* Feb. 19, 1842.

19. Arthur Cunynghame, *The Opium War; Being Recollections of Service in China* (London: Saunders and Otely, 1844), p. 216.

20. Robert Fortune, *Three Years' Wanderings in the Northern Provinces of China, including a Visit to the Tea, Silk, and Cotton Countries: With an Account of Agriculture and Horticulture of the Chinese, New Plants, etc.* (London: J. Murray, 1847), p. 14, and, on a later visit to Hong Kong, Fortune, *Wanderings,* pp. 14–15. Not everyone shared Fortune's enthusiasm for these "noble buildings." A critical article in the *Canton Press* on Feb. 19, 1842, asked rhetorically, "How fitly express the utter disgust we feel at such monstrosities?"

21. Osmond Tiffany, Jr., *The Canton Chinese or The American's Sojourn in the Celestial Empire* (1849; repr. in Barbara-Sue White, ed., *Hong Kong: Somewhere Between Heaven and Earth* [Hong Kong: Oxford University Press, 1996]), p. 39.

22. *Canton Press,* July 24, 1841.

23. CO 129/16, April 15, 1846, Davis to Gladstone, p. 224.

24. On contractors fleeing the island, CO 129/2, July 6, 1843, Gordon to Malcolm, pp. 139–140; *Friend of China,* Jan. 18, 1845.

25. Timothy Mitchell, *Colonising Egypt* (Cambridge: Cambridge University Press, 1988; Berkeley: University of California, 1991), p. xii; Gwendolyn Wright, "Tradition in the Service of Modernity: Architecture and Urbanism in French Colonial Policy," in Cooper and Stoler, *Tensions of Empire* pp. 322–325, and *The Politics of Design in French Colonial Urbanism* (Chicago: University of Chicago Press, 1991); Brenda S. A. Yeoh, *Contesting Space: Power Relations and the Urban Built Environment in Colonial Singapore* (Kuala Lumpur: Oxford University Press, 1996), p. 243.

26. *China Mail,* Sept. 23, 1852; Eitel, *Europe in China,* p. 220; *Friend of China,* Jan. 5, 1856; Carl Smith, *Chinese Christians,* p. 114.

27. Cree, *Journals,* p. 30; *Canton Press,* Feb. 19, 1842.

28. *Friend of China,* June 8, 1843.

29. On the "vagabondage population," CO 129/20, July 1, 1847, Davis to Grey, p. 121; on Chinese initiative, CO 129/10, Oct. 30, 1843, Woosnam to Caine, p. 529.

30. *Friend of China,* Oct. 12, 1843.

31. Public Records Office of Hong Kong, Hong Kong Record Series (HKRS), HKRS 100, Williams to Tarrant, enclosed in Pope to Caine, Dec. 31, 1844, pp. 112–113; *Friend of China,* July 18, 1857.

32. *Friend of China,* July 22, 1846.

33. Great Britain, Colonial Office, Executive and Legislative Council Minutes: Hong Kong (from 1844), Series 131 (CO 131), Public Record Office, London, CO 131/2, Dec. 9, 1851, pp. 154, 170–171.

34. *Canton Press,* Feb. 19, 1842.

35. Robinson, "Foundations," pp. 120–121.

36. George Smith, *Narrative,* p. 82; Fearon's report, CO 129/11, June 24, 1845, p. 306.

37. *The China Directory for 1867* (Hong Kong: A. Shortrede, 1867), p. 39A.

38. Carl Smith, *Chinese Christians,* pp. 114–115, 123–124; William Tarrant, "History of Hong Kong," *Friend of China,* Nov. 23, 1860. Originally the term for an Indian governor under the Mughals, the term "nabob" later came to refer more generally to a man of great wealth and influence.

39. Cited in Carl T. Smith, "The Chinese Settlement of British Hong Kong," *Chung Chi Bulletin* 48 (May 1970): 29.

40. Christopher Munn, "The Hong Kong Opium Revenue, 1845–1885," in Timothy Brook and Bob Tadashi Wakabayashi, eds., *Opium Regimes: China, Britain, and Japan, 1839–1952* (Berkeley: University of California Press, 2000), pp. 111–112.

41. Munn, "Opium Revenue," p. 107; on Loo's opium acquisition, CO 129/11, June 13, 1845, Davis to Stanley, pp. 182–183 and *Hong Kong Register,* Jan. 27 and March 31, 1846; on sedar chairs and the ropewalk, FO 233/185, March 17 and June 16, 1845.

42. CO 129/2, July 6, 1843, Gordon to Malcolm, pp. 142–148.

43. When the government realized the temple was being used for purposes other than a Chinese school, it decided to charge rent on the land. HKRS 58.1.16–12, 1848 and 1900, correspondence regarding the Man Mo Temple.

44. "The Districts of Hong Kong and the Name Kwan Tai Lo," *China Review* 1 (1872): 333, cited in Smith, *Chinese Christians*, p. 109.

45. *Hong Kong Register,* July 27, 1847.

46. *China Mail*, Sept. 23, 1852.

47. London Missionary Society Archives, LMS/CWM, 1843–1872, South China and Ultra Ganges, School of Oriental and African Studies, London, box 5, folder 3, Sept. 5 1853, Hirschberg to Tidman. Thanks to Christopher Munn for sharing his notes on this document.

48. *Friend of China*, Feb. 27 and July 25, 1856, and April 8, 1857; *China Mail*, April 8, 1857; on harbormaster's retirement fund, from Carl T. Smith's unpublished list of philanthropy in Hong Kong.

49. Helping the distressed, "The Districts of Hong Kong and the Name Kwan Tai Lo," pp. 333–334, cited in Smith, *Chinese Christians*, p. 203; London Missionary Society Archives, Sept. 5, 1853, Hirschberg to Tidman; *China Mail*, Sept. 23, 1852.

50. Guang Shinan, "Xianggang de 'maiban' zhidu" [The comprador system in Hong Kong], in Li, *Xianggang bainianshi*, p. 130.

51. Yen-p'ing Hao, *The Comprador in Nineteenth Century China: Bridge between East and West* (Cambridge, Mass.: Harvard University Press, 1970); p. 1; Huang Yifeng, "Diguo zhuyi qinlue Zhongguo diyige zhongyao zhizhu: maiban jieji" [One important pillar of the imperialist invasion of China: the comprador class] *Lishi yanjiu* 91 (1965): 55–56 and "Guanyu jiu Zhongguo maiban jieji de yanjiu" [Research on the comprador class in old China] *Lishi yanjiu* 87 (1964): 89; Hunter, *Fan Kwae*, pp. 53–56; Ma Yinchu, "Zhongguo zhi maiban zhidu" [The comprador system in China], *Dongfang zazhi* 20.6 (March 1923): 129–132; Nie Baozhang, *Zhongguo maiban zichanjieji de fasheng* [The emergence of the Chinese comprador class] (Beijing: Zhongguo shehui kexue chubanshe, 1979), pp. 2–5; Sha Weikai, *Zhongguo zhi maiban zhidu* [The comprador system in China] (Shanghai: Shangwu yinshuguan, 1927), pp. 1–5; G. C. Allen and Audrey G. Donnithorne, *Western Enterprise in Far Eastern Economic Development: China and Japan* (New York: Macmillan, 1954), p. 47; Feng Bangyan, *Xianggang Huazi caituan, 1841–1997* [Chinese financial organizations in Hong Kong, 1841–1997] (Hong Kong: Sanlian, 1997), pp. 29–37; and Zhang Xiaohui, *Xianggang Huashangshi* [History of Hong Kong Chinese merchants] (Hong Kong: Mingbao, 1996), pp. 4–5.

52. Sherman Cochran, *Big Business in China: Sino-Foreign Rivalry in the Cigarette Industry, 1890–1930* (Cambridge, Mass.: Harvard University Press, 1980), pp. 28–30, 39.

53. Marie-Claire Bergère, *The Golden Age of the Chinese Bourgeoisie, 1911–1937*, trans. Janet Lloyd (Cambridge: Cambridge University Press, 1989), p. 39; Hao, *Comprador,* p. 99.

54. *China Mail*, April 22, 1880; *Hong Kong Daily Press*, April 23, 1880.

55. *Daily Press*, April 23, 1880.

56. Xu Ribiao, "Xianggang de shehui jiegou" [The structure of Hong Kong society], in Yu Shengwu and Liu Cunkuan, eds., *Shijiu shiji de Xianggang* [Nineteenth century Hong Kong] (Hong Kong: Qilin shuye, 1994), p. 339.

57. *Daily Press*, April 23, 1880.

58. Ming K. Chan, "All in the Family: The Hong Kong-Guangdong Link in Historical Perspective," in Reginald Yin-Wang Kwok and Alvin Y. So, eds., *The Hong Kong-Guangdong Link: Partnership in Flux* (Armonk, N.Y.: M. E. Sharpe, 1995), pp. 32–34, 42.

59. Munn, "Opium Revenue," p. 105.

60. Ibid., p. 106.

61. Nicholas B. Dirks, "Colonialism and Culture," in Nicholas B. Dirks, ed., *Colonialism and Culture* (Ann Arbor: University of Michigan Press, 1992), p. 7.

2. A Better Class of Chinese

1. *Canton Press*, July 2, 1842.

2. Alijaz Ahmad, "The Politics of Literary Postcoloniality," in Padmini Mongia, ed., *Contemporary Postcolonial Theory* (London: Arnold, 1996), pp. 280–281; Arif Dirlik, "The Postcolonial Aura: Third World Criticism in the Age of Global Capitalism," in Mongia, *Postcolonial Theory*, p. 95.

3. On colonialism as "midwife," Ania Loomba, *Colonialism/Postcolonialism* (London: Routledge, 1998), p. 4; on trial and error in colonialism and capitalism, Ann Laura Stoler and Frederick Cooper, "Between Metropole and Colony: Rethinking a Research Agenda," in Frederick Cooper and Ann Laura Stoler, eds., *Tensions of Empire: Colonial Cultures in a Bourgeois World* (Berkeley: University of California Press, 1997), p. 29 (original emphasis).

4. Robert Montgomery Martin's comments, "Report on the Island of Hong Kong," July 24, 1844, enclosed in Davis to Stanley, Aug. 20, 1844, Papers of the House of Commons, 1857, session 1, vol. 12, reprinted in R. L. Jarman, ed., *Hong Kong Annual Administration Reports, 1841–1941*, vol. 1: 1841–1886 (Oxford: Archive Editions, 1996), pp. 8–15.

5. Frank H. H. King, *Survey our Empire! Robert Montgomery Martin (1801?-1868): A Bio-Bibliography* (Hong Kong: Centre of Asian Studies, University of Hong Kong, 1979), pp. 233–256; Davis to Stanley, April 25, 1845, in "Copy of Correspondence of Mr. Montgomery Martin with the Secretary for the Colonies, relating to his resignation of the Office of Treasurer of Hong Kong," reprinted in Irish University Press Area Studies Series, *British Parliamentary Papers, China, 24: Correspondence, Dispatches, Reports, Ordinances, Memoranda and Other Papers Relating to the Affairs of Hong Kong, 1846–60* (Shannon: Irish University Press, 1971), p. 33; on the "finest harbour," Great Britain, Colonial Office, Original Correspondence: Hong Kong, 1841–1951, Series 129 (CO129), Public Record Office, London, CO 129/11, April 25, 1845, Davis to Stanley, p. 125; comparing Hong Kong and Singapore, CO 129/19, March 13, 1847, Davis to Grey, p. 221; Martin as "false prophet," Arnold Wright and H. A. Cartwright, eds., *Twentieth Century Impressions of Hongkong, Shanghai, and other Treaty Ports of China: Their History, People, Commerce, Industries, and Resources* (London: Lloyds, 1908), p. 149.

6. *China Mail*, Aug. 27, 1846; Robert Fortune, *Three Years' Wanderings in the Northern Provinces of China, Including a Visit to the Tea, Silk, and Cotton Countries: With an Account of Agriculture and Horticulture of the Chinese, New Plants, etc.* (London: J. Murray, 1847), p. 28; Rev. George Smith, *A Narrative of an Exploratory Visit to Each of the Consular Cities of China and to the Islands of Hong Kong and*

Chusan, In Behalf of the Church Missionary Society in the Years 1844, 1845, 1846 (London: Seeley, Burnside and Seeley, 1847), p. 513;

7. Lin Youlan, *Xianggang shihua, zengding ben* [Stories of Hong Kong, revised edition] (Hong Kong: Shanghai shudian, 1985), p. 24; P. S. Cassidy, "Commercial History of Hong Kong: A Century of Trade," in *Hong Kong Centenary Commemorative Talks, 1841–1941* (Hong Kong: World News Service, 1941), p. 39.

8. In 1857 Governor John Bowring wrote that there had never been any attempt by either the Chinese or the British to enforce the articles of the treaty. CO 129/63, May 15, 1857, Bowring to Labouchere, p. 118. Local European residents, however, were less convinced: the *Friend of China* (Nov. 16, 1844) once warned that colonial officials were "strangling the young commerce of Hongkong, by seizing any inoffensive junk that should enter the harbour without a pass and handing [it] over to the Mandarins at Cowloon, who if they could not purchase their acquittal, would torture them after the cruel custom of China."

9. On "celestial" influence, *Friend of China*, Oct. 12, 1843; Canton rather than Hong Kong, Julius Berncastle, *A Voyage to China: Including a Visit to the Bombay Presidency; the Mahratta Country; the Cave Temples of Western India, Singapore, the Straits of Malacca and Sunda, and the Cape of Good Hope* (London: William Shoberl, 1850), vol. 1, pp. 2–48; CO 129/11, April 25, 1845, Davis to Stanley, pp. 283–285; "Remarks upon the Native Trade of Hongkong from 1st April 1844–1st April 1845," enclosed in CO 129/11, May 3, 1845, Davis to Stanley, pp. 38–43; *Friend of China*, Nov. 16, 1844; George Smith, *Narrative*, p. 510.

10. "Remarks upon the Native Trade of Hongkong," p. 42. Karl Gützlaff was one of the many "old coasters" or "old Cantons"—European missionaries, traders, and adventurers who sailed the waters of South China in the early 1800s. He served as an interpreter for opium traders, in exchange for using their boats to spread the Christian scriptures and distribute religious tracts. See Jessie G. Lutz, "Karl F. A. Gützlaff: Missionary Entrepreneur," in Suzanne Wilson Barnett and John King Fairbank, eds., *Christianity in China: Early Protestant Missionary Writings* (Cambridge, Mass.: Harvard University, Council on East Asian Studies, 1985), pp. 61–87; and Arthur Waley, *The Opium War through Chinese Eyes* (London: Allen and Unwin, 1958), chapter 5. Gützlaff's memoirs are compiled in his *Journal of Three Voyages Along the Coast of China in 1831, 1832, and 1833, with Notices of Siam, Corea, and the Loo-choo Islands* (London: F. Westley and A. H. Davis, 1834).

11. "Remarks upon the present state of Native Trade with the Colony of Hong Kong," enclosed in CO 129/16, April 15, 1846, Davis to Gladstone, p. 151.

12. "Report on the Island of Hong Kong," p. 9.

13. "Remarks upon the present state of Native Trade with the Colony of Hong Kong," p. 151.

14. Negative comments by Martin and others, "Report on the Island of Hong Kong," pp. 8–9. Gützlaff appears to have had an amicable relationship with the Chinese mercantile community of the colony. When he left for England in October 1849, he received praise from 167 Chinese shopkeepers who offered the following address: "Since he came to this place his official character has been spotless as water, and not a cash even has he received as a bribe. We bear in grateful remembrance the influence he has exercised in turning men to virtue . . . he was truly 'a courteous, princelike man treating others as himself' " (*Hong Kong Register*, Oct. 2, 1849).

15. "Report on the Island of Hong Kong," p. 15.

16. George Smith, *Narrative*, p. 508; Fortune, *Wanderings*, p. 27.

17. Cited in E. J. Eitel, *Europe in China: The History of Hong Kong from the Beginning to the Year 1882* (1895; repr., Hong Kong: Oxford University Press, 1983), p. 242.

18. Fortune, *Wanderings*, p. 28; Osmond Tiffany, Jr., *The Canton Chinese or The American's Sojourn in the Celestial Empire* 1849; repr. in Barbara-Sue White, ed., *Hong Kong: Somewhere Between Heaven and Earth* (Hong Kong: Oxford University Press, 1996), pp. 38–39.

19. Population statistics, China Mail, *Hong Kong Almanack and Directory for 1846* (Hong Kong: China Mail, 1846); Tiffany, *Canton Chinese*, in White, *Hong Kong*, p. 39; lists of lots granted by Johnston and Pottinger, CO 129/2, 1843, pp. 152–175, and list of land sold by public auction on Jan. 22, 1844, CO 129/5, Feb. 13, 1844, pp. 148–151; CO 129/33, Aug. 1850, p. 424.

20. *Canton Press*, Dec. 4, 1841; Tiffany, *Canton Chinese*, in White, *Hong Kong*, p. 36.

21. On spies, "Remarks upon the Native Trade with the Colony of Hong Kong," p. 234; Berncastle, *Voyage*, p. 42; John M. Tronson, *Personal Narrative of a Voyage to Japan, Kamtschatka, Siberia, Tartary, and Various Parts of the Coast of China; in H. M. S. Barraracouta, 1854–1856* (London: Smith, Elder & Co., 1859), p. 55.

22. "Plundered" warehouse: J. Y. Wong, *Anglo-Chinese Relations, 1839–1860: A Calendar of Chinese Documents in the British Foreign Office Records* (Oxford: Oxford University Press, for the British Academy, 1983), p. 112; Great Britain, Foreign Office, General Correspondence: China, 1815–1905, Series 17 (FO 17), Public Record Office, London, FO 17/98, Jan. 25, 1845, Davis to Cochrane; pp. 64–65.

23. Combat piracy: CO 129/14, Sept. 1, 1845, Admiralty to Hope, pp. 11–12, and CO 129/16, June 5, 1846, Davis to Gladstone, pp. 398–400; auxiliary police force: *Hong Kong Register*, June 6, 1854.

24. Petition from Wong Aloong and other vessel masters, CO 129/47, Oct. 1854, pp. 212–213; petition from headman and shopkeepers of Lower Bazaar, CO 129/43, Oct. 1854, pp. 214–215.

25. Caine to Grey: CO 129/47, Oct. 17, 1854, pp. 197–199; Bowring to Russell: CO 129/51, April 9, 1855, p. 255.

26. For example, FO 17/98, Jan. 25, 1845, Davis to Cochrane.

27. CO 129/42, June 13, 1853, Bonham to Newcastle, p. 321; Martin's report, "Report on the Island of Hong Kong," p. 9; Tronson, *Personal Narrative*, p. 55.

28. *Friend of China*, May 4, 1843, May 9 and 16, Dec. 19, 1846, and Dec. 27, 1851; *Hong Kong Register*, Feb. 16, 1847; Arthur Cunynghame, *The Opium War; Being Recollections of Service in China* (London: Saunders and Otely, 1844), pp. 220–224; the "clique", *Friend of China*, Feb. 9, 1848.

29. George Smith, *Narrative*, p. 82; *Friend of China*, Nov. 9, 1861.

30. George Smith, *Narrative*, p. 513; *Canton Press*, March 19, 1842; *Friend of China*, May 6, 1846; "commerce of the colony", *Friend of China*, May 9, 1845.

31. Timothy Brook and Bob Tadashi Wakabayashi, "Opium's History in China," in Timothy Brook and Bob Tadashi Wakabayashi, eds., *Opium Regimes: China, Britain, and Japan, 1839–1952* (Berkeley: University of California Press, 2000), p. 5; Carl A. Trocki, "Drugs, Taxes, and Chinese Capitalism in Southeast Asia," in Brook and Wakabayashi, *Opium Regimes*, pp. 81–83.

32. George Smith, *Narrative*, p. 513; *Friend of China*, May 6, 1846; *Canton Press*, March 19, 1842.

33. *Friend of China*, July 28, 1842; CO 129/1, 1843, proclamation by Qiying on treaties and tariffs; *Canton Press*, July 24, 1844.

34. Anti-British placard: Great Britain, Foreign Office, Records of Letters between the Plenipotentiary and the High Provincial Authorities, and Proclamations by H. E. the Governor and Chief Magistrate, 1844–1849, Series 233 (FO 233), Public Record Office, London, FO 233/185, Nov. 3, 1844; Qiying forbids molesting foreigners, FO 233/185, April 23, 1845; additional placards, FO 233/185, Jan. 17, 1846; "English barbarians", Eitel, *Europe in China*, p. 310.

35. Ming K. Chan, "All in the Family: The Hong Kong-Guangdong Link in Historical Perspective," in Reginald Yin-Wang Kwok and Alvin Y. So, eds., *The Hong Kong-Guangdong Link: Partnership in Flux* (Armonk, New York: M. E. Sharpe, 1995), pp. 32–34; June Mei, "Socioeconomic Origins of Emigration: Guangdong to California, 1850–1882," *Modern China* 5.4 (October 1979): 470–471.

36. Mei, "Socioeconomic Origins," p. 493.

37. "Report on the Economic Prospects of Hongkong by W. H. Mitchell," enclosed in CO 129/34, Dec. 28, 1850, Bonham to Grey.

38. Bonham to Grey: CO 129/36, April 26, 1851, p. 161.

39. CO 129/42, June 13, 1853, Bonham to Newcastle, p. 321.

40. Geoffrey Robley Sayer, *Hong Kong: Birth, Adolescence, and Coming of Age* (London: Oxford University Press, 1937), p. 220.

41. Eitel, *Europe in China*, p. 149; Hosea Ballou Morse, *The International Relations of the Chinese Empire*, vol. 1, *The Period of Conflict, 1834–1860* (London: Longman's, Green, 1910), p. 171.

42. *Hong Kong Register*, June 6, 1854.

43. CO 129/52, Oct. 6, 1855, Bowring to Molesworth, pp. 108–109.

44. CO 129/73, March 29, 1859, Bowring to Lytton, pp. 309–311.

45. For example, Yu Shengwu, "Xianggang de jingji" [Economics of Hong Kong], in Yu Shengwu and Liu Cunkuan, eds., *Shijiu shiji de Xianggang* [Nineteenth century Hong Kong] (Hong Kong: Qilin shuye, 1994), pp. 232–238.

46. Mei, "Socioeconomic Origins," p. 490; Jung-fang Tsai, *Hong Kong in Chinese History: Community and Social Unrest in the British Colony, 1842–1913* (New York: Columbia University Press, 1993), pp. 25–26.

47. CO 129/50, June 5, 1855, Mercer to Caine, pp. 169–174.

48. Population and migration figures based on annual Blue Books and *Historical and Statistical Abstracts of the Colony of Hong Kong, 1841–1930* (Hong Kong: Noronha, 1932).

49. CO 129/51, July 4, 1855, May to Bowring, pp. 29–30.

50. James D. Johnson, *China and Japan: Being a Narrative of the Cruise of the U.S. Steam-Frigate Powhatan, in the Years 1857, '58, '59, and '60* (Philadelphia: Charles DeSilver, 1860), pp. 77–78.

51. CO 129/64, August 11, 1857, Bowring to Labouchere, p. 88.

52. CO 129/67, March 25, 1858, Bowring to Labouchere, pp. 332–334.

53. CO 129/73, March 29, 1859, Bowring to Lytton, pp. 293–294, 321–322.

54. Wang Tao, "My Sojourn in Hong Kong," trans. Yang Qinghua, *Renditions* (Hong Kong: Chinese University Press, 1988), repr. in White, *Hong Kong*, p. 64. On Wang's experiences in Hong Kong, see also Paul A. Cohen, *Between Tradition*

and Modernity: Wang Tao and Reform in Late Ch'ing China (Cambridge, Mass.: Harvard University Press), and Elizabeth Sinn, "Fugitive in Paradise: Wang Tao and Cultural Transformation in Late Nineteenth-Century Hong Kong," *Late Imperial China* 19.1 (1998): 56–81.

55. Carl T. Smith, *Chinese Christians: Elites, Middlemen, and the Church in Hong Kong* (Hong Kong: Oxford University Press, 1985), p. 117.

56. *China Directory for 1867* (Hong Kong: A. Shortrede, 1867).

57. Feng Bangyan *Xianggang Huazi caituan, 1841–1997* [Chinese financial organizations in Hong Kong, 1841–1997] (Hong Kong: Sanlian, 1997), pp. 14–24; James Hayes, "The Nam Pak Hong Commercial Association of Hong Kong," *Journal of the Hong Kong Branch of the Royal Asiatic Society* 19 (1979): 216–226; Zhang Xiaohui, *Xianggang Huashangshi* [History of Hong Kong Chinese merchants] (Hong Kong: Mingbao, 1996), pp. 11–12.

58. CO 129/73, March 29, 1859, Bowring to Lytton, pp. 293–294.

59. Yu, "Xianggang de jingji," pp. 237–238.

60. CO 129/51, Sept. 4, 1855, Bowring to Russell, p. 245.

61. *China Directory for 1867*, 33A; Hong Kong, *Administrative Report, 1880–1881* (Hong Kong: Government Printer, 1881); Carl Smith, *Chinese Christians*, pp. 117–118; Wright and Cartwright, *Impressions*, pp. 184–186; Feng, *Xianggang Huazi*, pp. 25–26.

62. Frederic Wakeman, Jr., and Wen-hsin Yeh, "Introduction," in Frederic J. Wakeman and Wen-hsin Yeh, eds., *Shanghai Sojourners* (Berkeley: Institute of East Asian Studies, 1992), pp. 1–2, 6; William T. Rowe, *Hankow: Commerce and Society in a Chinese City, 1796–1889* (Stanford: Stanford University Press, 1984), and *Hankow: Conflict and Community in a Chinese City, 1796–1895* (Stanford: Stanford University Press, 1989).

63. Fearon's report on the first six months of the Census and Registration Office, CO 129/12, June 24, 1845, pp. 308; "Remarks upon the present state of Native Trade with the Colony of Hong Kong," p. 225.

64. Robinson to Rogers, May 21, 1863, reprinted in Irish University Press Area Studies Series, *British Parliamentary Papers, China, 25: Correspondence, Dispatches, Reports, Returns, Memorials, and other Papers Respecting the Affairs of Hong Kong, 1862–81* (Shannon: Irish University Press, 1971), p. 62.

65. Johnson, *China and Japan*, p. 78.

66. Colin N. Crisswell, *The Taipans: Hong Kong's Merchant Princes* (Hong Kong: Oxford University Press, 1981), pp. 97–99.

67. Eitel, *Europe in China*, pp. 385–387; Yuan Bangjian, *Xianggang shilue* [History of Hong Kong] (Hong Kong: Zhongliu chubanshe, 1993), p. 124.

68. Buying American steamships: Eitel, *Europe in China*, p. 453; Hong Kong's successful shipping: Crisswell, *Taipans*, pp. 97–99; Eitel, *Europe in China*, pp. 385–387, and Yuan, *Xianggang shilue*, p. 115.

69. Yen-p'ing Hao, *The Commercial Revolution in Nineteenth-Century China: The Rise of Sino-Western Mercantile Capitalism* (Berkeley: University of California Press, 1986), p. 52.

70. Frank H. H. King, *The History of the Hongkong and Shanghai Banking Corporation*, vol. 1, *The Hongkong Bank in Late Imperial China, 1864–1902: On an Even Keel* (Cambridge: Cambridge University Press, 1987), pp. 47–49; Feng Bangyan, *Xianggang Yingzi caituan, 1841–1996* [British financial organizations in Hong Kong, 1841–1996] (Hong Kong: Sanlian, 1996), pp. 39–48.

71. Wang Jingyu, "Shijiu shiji waiguo qinHua qiyezhong de Huashang fugu yundong" [Investment by Chinese merchants in the foreign enterprises that invaded China in the nineteenth century], *Lishi yanjiu* 94 (1965): 51.

72. From Thomson's articles on photography in early colonial Hong Kong for *The British Journal of Photography*, reprinted in White, *Hong Kong*, p. 81; Sir G. William Des Voeux, *My Colonial Service in British Guiana, St. Lucia, Trinidad, Fiji, Australia, Newfoundland, and Hong Kong with Interludes*, vol. 2 (London: John Murray, 1903), p. 193; Eitel, *Europe in China*, p. 570 (born in Germany, Eitel eventually became a British citizen); G. B. Endacott, *An Eastern Entrepot: A Collection of Documents Illustrating the History of Hong Kong* (London: Her Majesty's Stationery Office, 1964), p. ix. Endacott's claim is especially unusual considering that his collection of documents on the history of Hong Kong includes reports and dispatches from colonial governors acknowledging the importance of Chinese merchants, conditions in China, and the emigrant trade in the growth of Hong Kong's economy.

73. Tak-Wing Ngo, "Industrial History and the Artifice of *Laissez-Faire* Colonialism," in Tak-Wing Ngo, ed., *Hong Kong's History: State and Society Under Colonial Rule* (London: Routledge, 1999), pp. 119–140. On Hong Kong's industrialization before 1949, see also Frank Leeming, "The Earlier Industrialization of Hong Kong," *Modern Asian Studies* 9.3 (1975): 337–342.

74. Alex H. Choi, "State-Business Relations and Industrial Restructuring," in Ngo, *Hong Kong's History*, p. 153; Kim-Ming Lee, "Flexible Manufacturing in a Colonial Economy," in Ngo, *Hong Kong's History*, pp. 162–179.

75. Carter J. Eckert, *Offspring of Empire: The Koch'ang Kims and the Colonial Origins of Korean Capitalism, 1876–1945* (Seattle: University of Washington Press, 1991), especially chapter 2.

76. The most persistent critic of this image has been Ming K. Chan [Chen Mingqiu]. See, for example, "Stability and Prosperity in Hong Kong: The Twilight of Laissez-faire Colonialism?" *Journal of Asian Studies* 42.3 (May 1983): 589–598; and "Gang-Ying huanghun jin, luori Xiangjiang hong: zhimindi buganyu zhuyi de moluo" [British Sunset in Hong Kong: The demise of colonial nonintervention], *Xinbao yuekan* [Hong Kong Economic Journal Monthly] 130 (January 1988): 36–42. On the long arm of the colonial state, see Carol Benedict, "Framing Plague in China's Past," in Gail Hershatter, et al., eds., *Remapping China: Fissures in Historical Terrain* (Stanford: Stanford University Press, 1996), pp. 27–41; Fred Y. L. Chiu, "Politics and the Body Social in Colonial Hong Kong," in Tani E. Barlow, ed., *Formation of Colonial Modernity in East Asia* (Durham: Duke University Press, 1997), pp. 295–322; and Philippa Levine, "Modernity, Medicine, and Colonialism: The Contagious Diseases Ordinances in Hong Kong and the Straits Settlements," *positions* 6:3 (Winter 1998): 675–705. See also the articles in Ngo, *Hong Kong's History*, especially Christopher Munn, "The Criminal Trial under Early Colonial Rule," pp. 46–73, and Stephen W. K. Chiu and Ho-fung Hung, "State Building and Rural Stability," pp. 74–100.

77. CO 129/51, Sept. 4, 1855, Bowring to Russell, p. 244.

78. Information on industry based on Chen Datong, comp., *Bainian shangye* [A century of commerce] (Hong Kong: N.p., 1941); Jingji ziliaoshi, *Xianggang gongshang shouce* [Hong Kong commercial and industrial guide] (Hong Kong: n.p. 1947); Wang Chuying, ed., *Xianggang gongchang diaocha* [Survey of Hong Kong factories] (Hong Kong: Nanqiao xinwen qiye gongsi, 1947); and *Xianggang Hua-*

qiao gongshangye nianjian [Hong Kong commercial and industrial yearbook] (Hong Kong: Xiequn, 1940).

79. G. B. Endacott, *A History of Hong Kong*, rev. ed. (Hong Kong: Oxford University Press, 1973), p. 289.

80. Wong Siu-lun, *Emigrant Entrepreneurs: Shanghai Industrialists in Hong Kong* (Hong Kong: Oxford University Press, 1988); Dick Wilson, *Hong Kong! Hong Kong!* (London: Unwin Hyman, 1990), chapter 2.

3. Strategic Balance

1. Lo Hsiang-lin, *The Role of Hong Kong in the Cultural Interchange between East and West* (Tokyo: Centre for East Asian Studies, 1963), p. i; E. J. Eitel, *Europe in China: The History of Hong Kong from the Beginning to the Year 1882* (1895; repr., Hong Kong: Oxford University Press, 1983), pp. 165, 569–570.

2. For example, Elizabeth Sinn, *Power and Charity: The Early History of the Tung Wah Hospital, Hong Kong* (Hong Kong: Oxford University Press, 1989); Jung-fang Tsai, *Hong Kong in Chinese History: Community and Social Unrest in the British Colony, 1842–1913* (New York: Columbia University Press, 1993); Christopher Munn, *Anglo-China: Chinese People and British Rule in Hong Kong, 1841–1880* (Richmond, Surrey Eng.: Curzon Press, 2001); Yu Shengwu and Liu Cunkuan, eds., *Shijiu shiji de Xianggang* [Nineteenth-century Hong Kong] (Hong Kong: Qilin shuye, 1994); and Yuan Bangjian, *Xianggang shilue* [History of Hong Kong] (Hong Kong: Zhongliu chubanshe, 1993).

3. Ming K. Chan, ed., *Precarious Balance: Hong Kong Between China and Britain, 1842–1992* (Armonk, New York: M. E. Sharpe, 1994).

4. Thomas Richards, *The Imperial Archive: Knowledge and the Fantasy of Empire* (London: Verso, 1993).

5. Bernard S. Cohn, *Colonialism and Its Forms of Knowledge: The British in India* (Princeton: Princeton University Press, 1996), p. 4. See also C. A. Bayly, *Empire and Information: Intelligence Gathering and Social Communication in India, 1780–1870* (Cambridge: Cambridge University Press, 1996).

6. Hong Kong in "imperial historiography": Robert Cottrell, *The End of Hong Kong: The Secret Diplomacy of Imperial Retreat* (London: John Murray, 1993), p. 16; Robinson's offer: G. B. Endacott, *A History of Hong Kong*, rev. ed. (Hong Kong: Oxford University Press, 1973), p. 108.

7. Christopher Munn, "The Criminal Trial under Early Colonial Rule," in Tak-Wing Ngo, ed., *Hong Kong's History: State and Society Under Colonial Rule* (London: Routledge, 1999), pp. 53, 67.

8. Steve Tsang, ed., *Government and Politics: A Documentary History of Hong Kong* (Hong Kong: Hong Kong University Press, 1995), p. 2.

9. "The Districts of Hong Kong and the name Kwan Tai Lo," *China Review* 1 (1872): 333, cited in Carl T. Smith, *Chinese Christians: Elites, Middlemen, and the Church in Hong Kong* (Hong Kong: Oxford University Press, 1985), p. 232. On the Man Mo Temple, see also Xian Yuyi [Elizabeth Sinn] "Shehui zuzhi yu shehui zhuanbian" [Social organization and social change], in Wang Gengwu [Wang Gungwu], ed., *Xianggangshi xinbian* [Hong Kong History: New Perspectives], vol. 1 (Hong Kong: Joint Publishing, 1997), pp. 165–166.

10. Zhou Hong, "Origins of Government Social Protection Policy in Hong Kong, 1842–1941" (Ph.d. diss. Brandeis University, 1991), p. 51.

11. Sinn, *Power and Charity*, pp. 33, 39; *Xianggang Donghua sanyuan bainian shilue* [One Hundred Years of the Tung Wah Group of Hospitals] (Hong Kong, 1971), vol. 1, p. 83.

12. Geoffrey Robley Sayer, *Hong Kong 1862–1919: Years of Discretion* (Hong Kong: Hong Kong University Press, 1975), p. 31; Xian, "Shehui zuzhi," pp. 167–170.

13. Sinn, *Power and Charity*, pp. 69–74, 89–96.

14. Ibid., p. 4.

15. *Hong Kong Government Gazette*, Feb. 16, 1878.

16. Great Britain, Colonial Office, Original Correspondence: Hong Kong, 1841–1951, Series 129 (CO129), Public Record Office, London, CO 129/43, Dec. 5, 1853, Bonham to Newcastle, pp. 289–292.

17. Sinn, *Power and Charity*, pp. 42–43.

18. *Donghua sanyuan bainian shilue*, p. 83.

19. *Government Gazette*, Feb. 16, 1878.

20. Li Minren, "Yiba basi nian Xianggang bagong yundong" [The 1884 Hong Kong strike movement], *Lishi yanjiu* 3 (March 1958): 89–90; Fang Hanqi, "Yiba basi nian Xianggang renmin fandi douzheng" [The 1884 Hong Kong popular anti-imperialist struggle], *Jindaishi ziliao* 6 (1957): 20–30.

21. *Hong Kong Register*, Sept. 17, 1850.

22. CO 129/51, Sept. 4, 1855, Bowring to Russell, pp. 243–244.

23. *Hong Kong Register*, Sept. 17, 1850.

24. "Scrapbook of Memories," in China Mail, *Hong Kong Centenary Number*, Jan. 20, 1941.

25. James William Norton-Kyshe, *The History of the Laws and Courts of Hong Kong* (Hong Kong: Noronha, 1898), vol. 2, p. 86; Henry J. Lethbridge, "The District Watch Committee: The Chinese Executive Council of Hong Kong?", in Henry J. Lethbridge, *Hong Kong: Stability and Change: A Collection of Essays* (Hong Kong: Oxford University Press, 1978), pp. 106–108.

26. "Registrar General's Report for 1868," in *Government Gazette, 1869*, pp. 128–129.

27. Hong Kong, *Report of the Special Committee Appointed by His Excellency Sir William Robinson, &c., to Investigate and Report on Certain Points Connected with the Bill for the Incorporation of the Po Leung Kuk, or Society for the Protection of Women and Girls, Together with the Evidence Taken before the Committee and an Appendix Containing Correspondence, Reports, Returns, &c.* (Hong Kong: Noronha, 1893); Xian, "Shehui zuzhi," pp. 171–173; Zeng Wu, "Xianggang Baoliangju shilue" [History of the Baoliangju (Po Leung Kuk)], *Guangdong wenshi ziliao* 61 (1990): 212–224.

28. Wu Xinglian (Woo Sing Lim), *Xianggang Huaren mingren shilue* [Prominent Chinese of Hong Kong] (Hong Kong: Wuzhou, 1937), pp. 3–4; Arnold Wright and H. A. Cartwright, eds., *Twentieth Century Impressions of Hongkong, Shanghai, and other Treaty Ports of China: Their History, People, Commerce, Industries, and Resources* (London: Lloyds, 1908), p. 109.

29. "Acting-Registrar General's Report for 1893, Laid before the Legislative Council by Command of His Excellency the Governor, on 7th March, 1894," in Hong Kong, *Hong Kong Legislative Council Sessional Papers, 1894*, p. 100.

30. "Registrar General's Report for the Year 1894," in *Sessional Papers, 1895*, p. 150.

31. "Registrar General's Report for 1895," in *Sessional Papers, 1896*, p. 392.

32. "Report of the Registrar General for the Year 1912," *Administrative Report for 1912*, reprinted in Tsang, *Government and Politics*, pp. 209–210.

33. "Report of the Secretary for Chinese Affairs for the Year 1916," *Administrative Report for 1916*, p. C5.

34. "Report of the Secretary for Chinese Affairs for the Year 1913," *Administrative Report for 1913*, p. C8.

35. "Report of the Secretary for Chinese Affairs for 1916," p. C6.

36. Lennox A. Mills, *British Rule in Eastern Asia: A Study of Contemporary Government and Economic Development in British Malaya and Hong Kong* (London: Oxford University Press, 1942), pp. 398.

37. For example, *Commercial and Industrial Hong Kong: A Record of 94 years Progress of the Colony in Commerce, Trade, Industry, & Shipping (1841–1935)* (Hong Kong: Bedikton, 1935), pp. 34–35.

38. Tak-Wing Ngo, "Industrial History and the Artifice of *Laissez-faire* Colonialism," in Ngo, *Hong Kong's History*, p. 119; on Hong Kong's industrialization before 1949, see also Frank Leeming, "The Earlier Industrialization of Hong Kong," *Modern Asian Studies* 9.3 (1975): 337–342. For directories and guides to local industries, see *Commercial and Industrial Hong Kong*; Great Britain, Office of the Commercial Attaché, Shanghai, *List of the Principal Foreign and Chinese Industrial Enterprises in China and Hong Kong* (Shanghai: Kelly and Walsh, 1918); Jingji ziliaoshi, comp., *Xianggang gongshang shouce* [Hong Kong commercial and industrial guide] (Hong Kong: n.p. 1947); Wang Chuying, ed., *Xianggang gongchang diaocha* [Survey of Hong Kong factories] (Hong Kong: Nanqiao xinwen qiye gongsi, 1947); and *Xianggang Huaqiao gongshangye nianjian* [Hong Kong commercial and industrial yearbook] (Hong Kong: Xiequn gongsi, 1940).

39. *Government Gazette, 1881*, pp. 274–275.

40. Sir G. William Des Voeux, *My Colonial Service in British Guiana, St. Lucia, Trinidad, Fiji, Australia, Newfoundland, and Hong Kong with Interludes* (London: John Murray, 1903), vol. 2, pp. 280–282.

41. Chen Yufan, "Nanbeihang gongsuo huishi" [History of the Nanbeihang (Nam Pak Hong)], in *Nanbeihang (Nam Pak Hong) gongsuo xinxia luocheng ji chengli bashiliu zhounian jinian tekan* [Commemorative edition in celebration of the completion of the new building and the eighty-sixth anniversary of the Nam Pak Hong] (Hong Kong: n.p., 1954), pp. 23–24; and *Nanbeihang (Nam Pak Hong) gongsuo chengli yibai zhounian jinian tekan* [Commemorative edition of the hundredth anniversary of the Nam Pak Hong] (Hong Kong: n.p., 1968), pp. 16–19; on Chinese Chamber of Commerce: Sinn, *Power and Charity*, pp. 28–29.

42. Hennessy's "glowing" report: "The Governor's Report on the Blue Book," in *Administrative Report, 1879–1880*; on "the great prosperity," *Government Gazette, 1881*, p. 276; on the "clear-headed" Chinese, *Government Gazette, 1881*, p. 430.

43. "Address of His Excellency Sir John Pope Hennessy, K. C. M. G., to the Legislative Council of Hongkong, 7th of February, 1882," in *Administrative Report, 1880–1881*; also in *Government Gazette*, March 4, 1882, p. 241.

44. Yen Ching-hwang, "Ch'ing's Sale of Honours and the Chinese Leadership in Singapore and Malaya (1877 1912)," *Journal of Southeast Asian Studies* 1.2 (September 1970): 20–32.

45. K. C. Fok, *Lectures on Hong Kong History: Hong Kong's Role in Modern Chinese History* (Hong Kong: Commercial Press, 1990), pp. 111–115; Huo Qichang [K. C. Fok], "Xianggang Huaren zai jindaishi dui Zhongguo de gongxian shixi" [The contributions of Hong Kong Chinese to modern China], *Haiwai Huaren yanjiu* 1 (1989): 81–88; Qu Shaoxuan, "Qiaotuan yu zuguo" [Overseas Chinese societies and the motherland], and He Jian, "Huaqiao yu Xianggang jianshe" [Overseas Chinese and the development of Hong Kong], both in Chen Datong, et al., *Xianggang Huaqiao tuanti zonglan* [Overseas Chinese organizations in Hong Kong] (Hong Kong: Guoji xinwenshe, 1947), pp. 1–2, 7–9; Wright and Cartwright, *Twentieth Century*, pp. 184–186.

46. Losing the "traitor" epithet: Yen Ching-hwang, "Ch'ing Changing Images of the Overseas Chinese (1644–1912)," *Modern Asian Studies* 15.2 (1981): 282; a scroll of thanks: Lethbridge, "Chinese Association," pp. 63–64; and Sinn, *Power and Charity*, pp. 98–100.

47. Eitel, *Europe in China*, p. 282.

48. The Tung Wah committee members as "gentry": Sinn, *Power and Charity*, p. 87; *Government Gazette*, Feb. 16, 1878; Wang Tao, "My Sojourn in Hong Kong," trans. Yang Qinghua, *Renditions* (Hong Kong: Chinese University Press, 1988), reprinted in Barbara-Sue White, ed., *Hong Kong: Somewhere Between Heaven and Earth* (Hong Kong: Oxford University Press, 1996), p. 64.

49. On the many meanings of dress, see Cohn, *Colonialism and Its Forms of Knowledge*, chapter 5; Joanne Finkelstein, *The Fashioned Self* (Philadelphia: Temple University Press, 1991); Philippe Perrot, *Fashioning the Bourgeoisie: A History of Clothing in the Nineteenth Century*, trans. Richard Bienvenu (Princeton: Princeton University Press, 1994); and Emma Tarlo, *Clothing Matters: Dress and Identity in India* (Chicago: University of Chicago Press, 1996).

50. Homi Bhabha, "Of Mimicry and Man: The Ambivalence of Colonial Discourse," in Frederick Cooper and Ann Laura Stoler, eds., *Tensions of Empire: Colonial Cultures in a Bourgeois World* (Berkeley: University of California Press, 1997), p. 153, and *The Location of Culture* (London: Routledge, 1994), pp. 86–87; Beth Fowkes Tobin, *Picturing Imperial Power: Colonial Subjects in Eighteenth-Century British Painting* (Durham: Duke University Press, 1999), p. 22.

51. "Notes by W. H. Adams, Chief Justice on the Tam Achoy filibuster case," enclosed in CO 129/78, Feb. 21, 1860, pp. 191–192.

52. Tam's testimony: "Affidavit by Tam Achoy, James Baker, and Thomas Brazil," enclosed in CO 129/78, Feb. 21, 1860, pp. 195–197; Tam's steamer: "Affidavit by Daniel Caldwell in the Tam Achoy filibuster case," enclosed in CO 129/78, Feb. 21, 1860, pp. 193–194; pleading guilty: W. H. Adams, Chief Justice, to Robinson, enclosed in CO 129/78, Aug. 24, 1860, pp. 187–190.

53. Cohn, *Colonialism*, p. 3.

54. Ibid., p. 125.

55. Liondance: Eitel, *Europe in China*, pp. 468–469; on Chinese donations: "The Governor's Report on the Blue Book," in *Administrative Report, 1879–80*; CO 129/189, July 9, 1880, Hennessy to Kimberly.

56. Des Voeux, *Colonial Service*, pp. 205–210.

57. Hong Kong, *Annual Report, 1889* (Hong Kong: Government Printer, 1889), p. 26.

58. Hong Kong Daily Press, *Fifty Years of Progress: The Jubilee of Hongkong as*

a British Crown Colony, Being an Historical Sketch to Which is Added an Account of the Celebrations of 21st to 24th January, 1891 (Hong Kong: Hong Kong Daily Press, 1891), p. 32.

59. Ho's banquets: Wright and Cartwright, *Twentieth Century*, p. 174, and Des Voeux, *Colonial Service*, p. 279; donating ambulances: Wright and Cartwright, *Twentieth Century*, p. 176, and Wu, *Xianggang huaren*, p. 1–3; on Chau Siu-ki: A. R. Burt, J. B. Powell, and C. Crow, eds., *Biographies of Prominent Chinese* (Shanghai: Biographical Publishing Co., 1925), p. 81; on Ip Lan Chuen: Burt, et al., *Biographies*, p. 129.

60. For example, Martin Carnoy, *Education as Cultural Imperialism* (New York: Longman, 1974).

61. Alastair Pennycook, *The Cultural Politics of English as an International Language* (London: Longman, 1994), p. 82.

62. Timothy Mitchell, *Colonising Egypt* (Cambridge: Cambridge University Press, 1988; Berkeley: University of California, 1991), pp. 75, 94; Gauri Viswanathan, *Masks of Conquest: Literary Study and British Rule in India* (London: Faber and Faber, 1990); on Indians demanding English education: Loomba, *Colonialism/Postcolonialism*, p. 86; attitudes toward education: Gail P. Kelly, "Colonialism, Indigenous Society, and School Practices: French West Africa and Indochina, 1918–1938," in Philip G. Altbach and Gail P. Kelly, eds., *Education and the Colonial Experience* (New Brunswick, New Jersey: Transaction, 1984), pp. 9–32; the Taiwanese elite: E. Patricia Tsurumi, "The Non-Western Colonizer in Asia: Japanese Educational Engineering in Taiwan," in Kelly and Altbach, *Education*, pp. 55–74.

63. Bernard Hung-kay Luk, "Chinese Culture in the Hong Kong Curriculum: Heritage and Colonialism," *Comparative Education Review* 35.4 (November 1991): 654, 658–660.

64. Alice Lun Ngai Ha Ng, *Interactions East and West: Development of Public Education in Early Hong Kong* (Hong Kong: Chinese University Press, 1984), p. viii.

65. Sinn, *Power and Charity*, pp. 120–122.

66. Bowring's successor, Hercules Robinson, however, favored the segregation. "My constant thought," he wrote in 1861, "has been how best to prevent a large Chinese population establishing themselves at Kowloon, and as some native population is indispensable, how best to keep them to themselves and preserve the European and American community from the injury and inconvenience of intermixture with them." Both quotes cited in Endacott, *History of Hong Kong*, p. 122.

67. "Inferior kind of animal": cited in James Pope-Hennessy, *Half-Crown Colony: A Hong Kong Notebook* (London: Jonathan Cape, 1969), p. 53; "pro-Chinese": Pope-Hennessy, *Half-Crown Colony*, pp. 78–79; and Eitel, *Europe in China*, p. 567.

68. Basis of prejudice: compare Henry J. Lethbridge, "Caste, Class, and Race in Hong Kong before the Japanese Occupation," in Lethbridge, *Hong Kong: Stability and Change*, p. 167, which argues that this prejudice was based on class rather than on ethnocentricity; Chinese as "superior": "The Straits Settlements and British Malaya," in Paul H. Kratoska, ed., *Honourable Intentions: Talks on the British Empire in South-East Asia Delivered at the Royal Colonial Institute, 1874–1928* (Singapore: Oxford University Press, 1983), p. 43; Lethbridge, "Caste, Class, and Race," p. 167; *China Mail*, March 4, 1847.

69. Bowring to Labouchere, March 26, 1856, in "Copies of Extracts of Correspondence between Governor Sir John Bowring and the Secretary of State for the Colonies relative to the Re-construction of the Legislative Council of the Colony of Hong Kong, in the years of 1855 and 1856," reprinted in Irish University Press Area Studies Series, *British Parliamentary Papers, China, 24: Correspondence, Dispatches, Reports, Ordinances, Memoranda and Other Papers Relating to the Affairs of Hong Kong, 1846–60* (Shannon: Irish University Press, 1971), p. 196.

70. Labouchere to Bowring, July 29, 1856, in "Copies of Extracts," p. 12.

71. CO 129/187, April 20, 1880, Hicks Beech to Pope, reprinted in Tsang, *Government and Politics*, p. 67.

72. On the planning and founding of the Central School, see Fong Mee-yin [Fang Meixian], *Xianggang zaoqi jiaoyu fazhanshi* [The First Hundred Years of Hong Kong Education] (Hong Kong: Zhongguo xueshe, 1975), pp. 23–30; Ruan Rou, *Xianggang jiaoyu: Xianggang jiaoyu zhidu zhi shi de yanjiu* [Historical Study of the Educational System of Hong Kong] (Hong Kong: Jinbu jiaoyu chubanshe, 1948), p. 40; Gwenneth G. Stokes, *Queen's College, 1862–1962* (Hong Kong: Queen's College, 1962), chapters 1 and 2; and Wong Chai-lok (Wang Qile), *Xianggang zhongwen jiaoyu fazhan shi* [History of the Development of Chinese Education in Hong Kong] (Hong Kong: Po Wen, 1982), pp. 144–149.

73. *Government Gazette, 1864,* p. 46; Stokes, *Queen's College,* pp. 22–23.

74. Wright and Cartwright, *Twentieth Century,* p. 178, 186–187.

75. Wright and Cartwright, *Twentieth Century,* p. 178; W. Feldwick, *Present Day Impressions of the Far East and Prominent Chinese at Home and Abroad: The History, People, Commerce, Industries and Resources of China, Hongkong, Indo-China, Malaya and Netherlands India* (London: Globe Encyclopaedia, 1917), p. 593.

76. Chau Siu-ki: Burt, et al., *Biographies,* p. 81; Wright and Cartwright, *Twentieth Century,* p. 176; Feldwick, *Present Day,* pp. 580–581. Lau Chu Pak: Chen Datong, ed., *Bainian shangye* [A century of commerce] (Hong Kong: Guangming wenhua shiye gongsi 1941), n.p.; Liu Fuzong, et al., *Liugong Zhubo xingshu* [Biography of the late Mr. Liu Zhubo (Lau Chu Pak)]; Wright and Cartwright, *Twentieth Century,* p. 174; Wu, *Xianggang Huaren,* pp. 5–6; Feldwick, *Present Day,* pp. 573–574. Ho Wing Tsun: Wright and Cartwright, *Twentieth Century,* p. 182. She Posham: Wright and Cartwright, *Twentieth Century,* p. 182. Ng Hon Tsz: Wright and Cartwright, *Twentieth Century,* p. 182; Feldwick, *Present Day,* pp. 591–592. Wong Lai-Sang: Wright and Cartwright, *Twentieth Century,* p. 187.

77. Howard L. Boorman, ed., *Biographical Dictionary of Republican China,* vol. 2 (New York: Columbia University Press, 1968), pp. 75–76; Burt, et al., *Biographies,* p. 14; Chen Datong, *Bainian shangye,* n.p.; China Mail, *Who's Who in the Far East, 1906–7* (Hong Kong: China Mail, 1906), p. 147; Feldwick, *Present Day,* pp. 582–583; Wright and Cartwright, *Twentieth Century,* p. 176; Wu, *Xianggang Huaren,* pp. 1–3; He Wenxiang, *Xianggang jiazu shi* [History of Hong Kong families] (Hong Kong: Mingbao, 1992), chapter 1.

78. Wright and Cartwright, *Twentieth Century,* p. 174; Wu, *Xianggang Huaren,* pp. 16–19.

79. Smith, *Chinese Christians,* p. 166; Wright and Cartwright, *Twentieth Century,* p. 178; *Who's Who,* p. 142.

80. Tobin, *Picturing Imperial Power,* p. 179.

81. The quotations, paraphrased factual material, and referenced photographs

cited through the end of this chapter can be found in pp. 174–178, 181–182, 186–188, 224–234 of Wright and Cartwright, *Twentieth Century* (page references reflect sequence of text citations).

4. A Place of Their Own

1. Gary Hamilton, "Hong Kong and the Rise of Capitalism in Asia," in Gary G. Hamilton, ed., *Cosmopolitan Capitalists: Hong Kong and the Chinese Diaspora at the End of the 20th Century* (Seattle: University of Washington Press, 1999), p. 23; non-European shareholder: Wang Jingyu, "Shijiu shiji waiguo qin-Hua qiyezhong de Huashang fugu yundong" [Investment by Chinese merchants in the foreign enterprises that invaded China in the nineteenth century] *Lishi yanjiu* 94 (1965): 55–56; more than 80 percent: pp. 68–69.

2. Blake to Chamberlain, in Hong Kong, *Annual Report, 1898* (Hong Kong: Government Printer, 1898), p. 13; on property: Wang, "Shijiu shiji," pp. 55–56; Blake to Chamberlain, in *Annual Report, 1899*, p. 44.

3. Feng Bangyan, *Xianggang Huazi caituan, 1841–1997* [Chinese financial organizations in Hong Kong, 1841–1997] (Hong Kong: Sanlian chubanshe, pp. 63–68; Zhang Xiaohui, *Xianggang Huashangshi* [History of Hong Kong Chinese merchants] (Hong Kong: Mingbao, 1996), pp. 76–80; Yang Guoxiong, "Xianggang zaoqi baihuo gongsi shi zenyang de?" [What were Hong Kong's early department stores like?], in Lu Yan, et al., *Xianggang zhanggu* [Hong Kong anecdotes], vol. 7 (Hong Kong: Guangjiaojing, 1984), p. 113.

4. *Xianggang Zhonghua zongshanghui chengli bashi zhounian jinian tekan* [Commemorative edition of the eightieth anniversary of the Hong Kong Chinese General Chamber of Commerce] (Hong Kong: Zhonghua zongshanghui, 1980); *Xianggang Zhonghua zongshanghui chengli liushi zhounian jinian tekan* [Special edition in commemoration of the sixtieth anniversary of the Hong Kong Chinese General Chamber of Commerce] (Hong Kong: Zhonghua zongshanghui, 1960); Chinese-capitalized bank: Elizabeth Sinn, *Growing with Hong Kong: The Bank of East Asia, 1919–1994* (Hong Kong: Bank of East Asia, 1994), pp. 4–7; Li Zhaohuan, "Huaqiao ziben de wujia yinhang" [Five overseas Chinese-capitalized banks] *Guangdong wenshi ziliao* 8 (1963): 135–136; Feng, *Xianggang Huazi*, pp. 79–82.

5. See, for example, Brian Willan's study of the black African bourgeoisie of Kimberly: *Sol Plaatje: South African Nationalist, 1876–1932* (Berkeley: University of California Press, 1984).

6. *Who's Who in the Far East, 1906–7* (Hong Kong: China Mail, 1906), p. 334; W. Feldwick, *Present Day Impressions of the Far East and Prominent Chinese at Home and Abroad: The History, People, Commerce, Industries and Resources of China, Hongkong, Indo-China, Malaya and Netherlands India* (London: Globe Encyclopaedia, 1917), pp. 575–576; Wu Xinglian (Woo Sing Lim), *Xianggang Huaren mingren shilue* [Prominent Chinese of Hong Kong] (Hong Kong: Wuzhou, 1937), pp. 3–4.

7. Fung Wa Chun: *Who's Who*, pp. 105–106; Hospital committee: Chan Wai Kwan, *The Making of Hong Kong Society: Three Studies of Class Formation in Early Hong Kong* (Oxford: Clarendon Press, 1991), p. 214; Tso Seen Wan: *Cao Shanyun boshi shizhui silu* [Biography of the late Dr. Cao Shanyun (Tso Seen Wan)] (Hong Kong: Qiaosheng chubanshe, 1956); Arnold Wright and H. A. Cartwright, eds., *Twentieth Century Impressions of Hongkong, Shanghai, and other Treaty Ports of China:*

Their History, People, Commerce, Industries, and Resources (London: Lloyds, 1908), p. 178, and Wu, *Xianggang Huaren*, pp. 8–11; Wei On: Carl T. Smith, *Chinese Christians: Elites, Middlemen, and the Church in Hong Kong* (Hong Kong: Oxford University Press, 1985), pp. 69, 159.

8. Great Britain, Colonial Office, Original Correspondence: Hong Kong, 1841–1951, Series 129 (CO129), Public Record Office, London, CO 129/306, Sept. 24, 1901, Blake to Chamberlain, pp. 672–673; also in Hong Kong, *Hong Kong Legislative Council Sessional Papers, 1902*, p. 14.

9. The "reformers": Blake to Chamberlain, p. 679; benefits of a "new school": pp. 673–674; also in *Sessional Papers, 1902*, pp. 14–15.

10. Blake to Chamberlain, pp. 677.

11. Ibid., Blake to Chamberlain, pp. 679.

12. CO 129/306, Sept. 27, 1901, Blake to Chamberlain, p. 671; also in *Sessional Papers, 1902*, p. 13.

13. Peter Wesley-Smith, "Anti-Chinese Legislation in Hong Kong," in Ming K. Chan, ed., *Precarious Balance: Hong Kong Between China and Britain* (Armonk, N.Y.: M. E. Sharpe, 1994), p. 98.

14. Indonesia: I. Schöffer, "Dutch 'Expansion' and Indonesian Reactions: Some Dilemmas of Modern Colonial Rule," in H. L. Wesseling, ed., *Expansion and Reaction: Essays in European Expansion and Reactions in Asia and Africa* (Leiden: Leiden University Press, 1978), p. 83; Kingston, Jamaica: Colin G. Clarke, "A Caribbean Creole Capital: Kingston, Jamaica (1692–1938)," in Robert Ross and Gerald J. Telkamp, eds., *Colonial Cities: Essays on Urbanism in a Colonial Context* (Leiden: Martinus Nijhoff, for Leiden University Press, 1985), p. 153–170.

15. *Hongkong Daily Press*, Jan. 31, 1901, p. 3; *China Mail*, Jan. 30, 1901, p. 2.

16. CO 129/306, Sept. 3, 1901, Blake to Chamberlain, pp. 309, 314, 319; also in *Sessional Papers, 1902*, p. 5, 8, 12. British parentage: CO 129/311, May 8, 1902, Blake to Chamberlain, p. 97. Ho Tung reluctantly agrees: cited in G. B. Endacott, *A History of Hong Kong*, rev. ed. (Hong Kong: Oxford University Press, 1973), p. 281.

17. Pan Kongyan, "Zhongzu qishi de bianlun [A debate about racial prejudice]," in Li Jinwei, ed., *Xianggang bainianshi* [Centenary history of Hong Kong] (Hong Kong: Nanzhong chubanshe, 1948), p. 53.

18. Frank H. H. King, *The Hongkong Bank Between the Wars and the Bank Interned, 1919–1945: Return from Grandeur* (*The History of the Hongkong and Shanghai Banking Corporation*, vol. 3) (Cambridge: Cambridge University Press, 1988), pp. 286–288.

19. CO 129/392, Sept. 14, 1912, May to Harcourt, p. 58.

20. Henry J. Lethbridge, "Caste, Class, and Race in Hong Kong before the Japanese Occupation," in his *Hong Kong: Stability and Change: A Collection of Essays* (Hong Kong: Oxford University Press, 1978), p. 173; R. C. Hurley, *Picturesque Hong Kong: A British-Crown-Colony and Dependencies* (Hong Kong: Commercial Press, 1925), pp. 83, 107–108; Geoffrey Robley Sayer, *Hong Kong 1862–1919: Years of Discretion* (Hong Kong: Hong Kong University Press, 1975), p. 66.

21. Dane Kennedy, *The Magic Mountains: Hill Stations and the British Raj* (Berkeley: University of California Press, 1996); Anthony D. King, "Culture, Social Power, and Environment: The Hill Station in Colonial Urban Development," *Social Action* 26.3 (July-September 1976): 195–213.

22. King, "Culture, Social Power, and Environment," p. 196.

23. Dane Kennedy, *Islands of White: Settler Society and Culture in Kenya and Southern Rhodesia, 1890–1939* (Durham: Duke University Press, 1987), p. 189.

24. Ann Laura Stoler, "Sexual Affronts and Racial Frontiers: European Identities and the Cultural Politics of Exclusion in Colonial Southeast Asia," in Frederick Cooper and Ann Laura Stoler, eds., *Tensions of Empire: Colonial Cultures in a Bourgeois World* (Berkeley: University of California Press, 1997), pp. 214, 222; Bernard S. Cohn, *Colonialism and Its Forms of Knowledge: The British in India* (Princeton: Princeton University Press, 1996), p. 155.

25. King, "Culture, Social Power, and Environment," p. 203.

26. Kennedy, *Magic Mountains,* p. 8.

27. Sir G. William Des Voeux, *My Colonial Service in British Guiana, St. Lucia, Trinidad, Fiji, Australia, Newfoundland, and Hong Kong with Interludes* (London: John Murray, 1903), vol. 2, pp. 222, 224.

28. Enclosed in CO 129/322, May 4, 1904, May to Lyttleton, p. 638.

29. *Hong Kong Hansard, 1904,* pp. 18–19, enclosed in May to Lyttleton, p. 639.

30. May to Lyttleton, pp. 633–636.

31. For "non-Chinese" only: CO 129/433, confidential, Sept. 5, 1917, May to Long, p. 384. Ho Tung's houses: Irene Cheng, *Clara Ho Tung: A Hong Kong Lady, Her Family and Her Times* (Hong Kong: Chinese University Press, 1976), p. 20.

32. Ho's house "Lysholt": May to Long, pp. 396–397, and planning to build: p. 385.

33. May to Long, pp. 386–390.

34. May to Long, p. 389.

35. CO 129/447, confidential, Jan. 24, 1918, May to Long, p. 70.

36. *Hansard,* 1918, p. 29.

37. Cheng, *Clara Ho Tung,* p. xiv.

38. *South China Morning Post,* Dec. 13, 1921.

39. "A Chinaman himself . . .": "Hong Kong Jubilee: 21st–24th January, 1891," in Hong Kong Daily Press, *Fifty Years of Progress: The Jubilee of Hongkong as a British Crown Colony, Being an Historical Sketch to Which is Added an Account of the Celebrations of 21st to 24th January, 1891* (Hong Kong: Hong Kong Daily Press, 1891), p. 4; E. J. Eitel, *Europe in China: The History of Hong Kong from the Beginning to the Year 1882* (1895; repr., Hong Kong: Oxford University Press, 1983), p. 575.

40. Lennox A. Mills, *British Rule in Eastern Asia: A Study of Contemporary Government and Economic Development in British Malaya and Hong Kong* (London: Oxford University Press, 1942), p. 410; "cheese-eating Westerners": Frank Welsh, *A Borrowed Place: The History of Hong Kong* (New York: Kodansha, 1993), p. 382.

41. For example, Yuan Bangjian, *Xianggang shilue* [History of Hong Kong] (Hong Kong: Zhongliu chubanshe, 1993); and Xu Ribiao, "Xianggang de shehui jiegou" [The structure of Hong Kong society], in Yu Shengwu and Liu Cunkuan, eds., *Shijiu shiji de Xianggang* [Nineteenth-century Hong Kong] (Hong Kong: Qilin shuye, 1994), pp. 299, 378.

42. Jan Morris, *The Spectacle of Empire: Style, Effect and the Pax Britannica* (London: Doubleday, 1982), p. 202; "amalgam of ideals": David W. Brown, "Social Darwinism, Private Schooling and Sport in Victorian and Edwardian Canada," in J. A. Mangan, ed., *Pleasure, Profit, Proselytism: British Culture and Sport at Home and Abroad, 1700–1914* (London: Frank Cass, 1988), p. 227; sports and character: James A. Mangan, *The Games Ethic: Aspects of the Diffusion of an Ideal* (New York: Viking, 1986).

43. On sport and social stratification, see M. A. Speak, "Social Stratification and Participation in Sport in Mid-Victorian England with Particular Reference to Lancaster, 1840–79"; John A. Daly, "A New Britannia in the Antipodes: Sport, Class and Community in Colonial South Australia"; and Brian Stoddard, "Cricket and Colonialism in the English-Speaking Caribbean to 1914: Towards a Cultural Analysis"; all in Mangan, *Pleasure, Profit, Proselytism*, pp. 42–66, 163–174, 231–257.

44. Jürgen Osterhammel, *Colonialism: A Theoretical Overview*, trans. Shelley L. Frisch (Princeton: Marcus Wiener, 1997), p. 87.

45. Morris, *Spectacle of Empire*, pp. 199–200.

46. Hong Kong Club, *Articles of Association of the Hongkong Club* (Hong Kong: Noronha, 1924).

47. Wu, "Xiangganghui," p. 54.

48. Cited in *The Ladies' Recreation Club, 1883–1983* (Hong Kong: Ladies' Recreation Club, 1983), pp. 1, 3.

49. *China Mail*, Feb. 1, 1884. On Western women in Hong Kong, see Susanna Hoe, *The Private Life of Old Hong Kong: Western Women in the British Colony* (Hong Kong: Oxford University Press, 1991).

50. C. Y. Choi, *Chinese Migration and Settlement in Australia* (Sydney: Sydney University Press, 1975), pp. 18–27; Arthur Huck, *The Chinese in Australia* (Croydon, Victoria, Australia: Longmans, 1967), pp. 1–5; Liu Daren and Tian Xinyuan, *Aozhou Huaqiao jingji* [Economic situation of the Overseas Chinese in Australia] (Taipei: Haiwai chubanshe, 1958), pp. 36–42; and Shen Yiyao (Shen I-yao), *Haiwai paihua bainianshi* [A Century of Chinese Exclusion Abroad] (Hong Kong: Wanyou tushu gongsi, 1970), pp. 78–86.

51. Tsai, *Hong Kong in Chinese History*, p. 97.

52. The Chinese Club: Chen Datong, ed., *Bainian shangye* [A Century of Commerce] (Hong Kong, 1941), p. 73; Wright and Cartwright, *Twentieth Century*, p. 172; Zhang Xiaohui, *Xianggang Huashangshi* [History of Hong Kong Chinese merchants] (Hong Kong: Mingbao, 1996), pp. 143; and Xian Yuyi (Elizabeth Sinn), "Shehui zuzhi yu shehui zhuanbian" [Social organization and social change], in Wang Gengwu (Wang Gungwu), ed., *Xianggangshi xinbian* [Hong Kong History: New Perspectives] (Hong Kong: Joint Publishing, 1997), vol. 1, p. 160. Founders of the club: Wright and Cartwright, *Twentieth Century*, p. 180; Wu, *Xianggang Huaren*, p. 97.

53. Wright and Cartwright, *Twentieth Century*, p. 184.

54. Ip Shu Kam: Feldwick, *Present Day*, pp. 585–586, and Wright and Cartwright, *Twentieth Century*, p. 184; Lau Pun Chiu: Carl T. Smith, "Compradores of The Hongkong Bank," in Frank H. H. King, ed., *Eastern Banking: Essays in the History of The Hongkong and Shanghai Banking Corporation* (London: Athlone Press, 1983), pp. 108–109, and Wright and Cartwright, *Twentieth Century*, p. 182; Sin Tak Fan: Wright and Cartwright, *Twentieth Century*, pp. 186–187; B. Wong Tape: Chen, *Bainian shangye*, n. p.; Wu, *Xianggang Huaren*, p. 32.

55. A former Hong Kong Bank employee recalled how in the 1930s and 1940s even his Eurasian squash partner could not join the Cricket Club. J. F. Marshall, *Whereon the Wild Thyme Flows: Some Memoirs of Service with the Hongkong Bank* (Surrey, England: Token, 1986), p. 29.

56. *Xianggang Zhonghua youlehui* [Chinese Recreation Club Hong Kong] (Hong Kong: Chinese Recreation Club, 1987), pp. 3–4; *Xianggang Zhonghua you-*

lehui qishinian jinian tekan [Hong Kong Chinese Recreation Club seventieth anniversary commemoration] (Hong Kong: Chinese Recreation Club, 1982), p. 42.

57. Cited in Daly, "New Britannia," p. 167.

58. "Moral fabric": J. Thomas Jable, "Latter-Day Cultural Imperialists: The British Influence on the Establishment of Cricket in Philadelphia, 1842–1872," in Mangan, *Pleasure, Profit, Proselytism*, pp. 175, 189; Lord Harris: Cited in Richard Cashman, "Cricket and Colonialism: Hegemony and Indigenous Subversion?," in Mangan, *Pleasure, Profit, Proselytism*, p. 258; batsman Ranjitsinhji: cited in Sadatru Sen, "Chameleon Games: Ranjitsinhji's Politics of Race and Gender," *Journal of Colonialism and Colonial History* 2.3 (2001): 75 (electronic journal); Mangan, *Games Ethic*, p. 153.

59. Pierre Bourdieu, "Sport and Social Class," in Chandra Mukerji and Michael Schudson, eds., *Rethinking Popular Culture: Contemporary Perspectives in Cultural Studies* (Berkeley: University of California Press, 1991), pp. 362–363; Richard Cashman, *Patrons, Players and the Crowd: The Phenomenon of Indian Cricket* (New Delhi: Longman Orient, 1980), p. 26; proper atmosphere: *Xianggang Zhonghua youlehui qishinian*, p. 42.

60. Howard L. Boorman, ed., *Biographical Dictionary of Republican China*, vol. 1 (New York: Columbia University Press, 1968), pp. 387–388; A. R. Burt, J. B. Powell, and C. Crow, eds., *Biographies of Prominent Chinese* (Shanghai: Biographical Publishing Co., 1925), p. 79; Feldwick, *Present Day*, pp. 578–579; Wu, *Xianggang Huaren*, pp. 4–5.

61. Dr. Arthur Wai-tak Woo: Burt, et al., *Prominent Chinese*, p. 135, and Wu, *Xianggang Huaren*, pp. 35–37; Lo Man Kam: Chen Datong, et al., *Xianggang Huaqiao tuanti zonglan* [Overseas Chinese organizations in Hong Kong] (Hong Kong: Guoji xinwenshe, 1947), n.p.; Wu Xinglian, *Xianggang Huaren*, p. 13.

62. See, for example, Stoddard, "Cricket and Colonialism," and André Odendaal, "South Africa's Black Victorian: Sport and Society in South Africa in the Nineteenth Century," in Mangan, *Pleasure, Profit, Proselytism*, pp. 183–214.

63. Chen Gongzhe, ed., *Xianggang zhinan* [Guide to Hong Kong] (Changsha: Shangwu yinshuguan, 1938), p. 96; *Nanhua tiyuhui bashi zhounian jinian tekan* [South China Athletic Association Eightieth Anniversary] (Hong Kong: n.p., 1990), pp. 26–27; *Nanhua tiyuhui liushi zhounian jinian tekan* [South China Athletic Association Sixtieth Anniversary] (Hong Kong: n.p., 1970), pp. 1–5; *Nanhua tiyuhui qishi zhounian jinian tekan* [South China Athletic Association Seventieth Anniversary] (Hong Kong: n.p., 1980), pp. 19–22. See also Xian, "Shehui zuzhi," pp. 190–191.

64. Chen, *Bainian shangye*, n.p.; Wright and Cartwright, *Twentieth Century*, p. 231; Wu, *Xianggang Huaren*, p. 28.

65. Chau Tsun-nin: Chen, *Xianggang Huaqiao*, n. p., Wu, *Xianggang Huaren*, p. 12; Lee Chi Chung: Wu, *Xianggang Huaren*, p. 53; Li Yau Tsun: Chen, *Xianggang Huaqiao*, n. p., Wu, *Xianggang Huaren*, p. 20.

66. Burt, et al., *Prominent Chinese*, p. 65; Chen Datong, *Bainian shangye*, n.p; Wu, *Xianggang Huaren*, pp. 6–8.

67. Sources for YMCA: *Hong Kong Hansard, 1932*, pp. 46–47; *Xianggang Zhonghua jidujiao qingnianhui wushi zhounian jinian tekan* [Hong Kong Chinese YMCA Fiftieth Anniversary Commemoration] (Hong Kong, 1951), pp. 2–7, 49–62; Xianggang Zhonghua jidujiao qingnianhui [Hong Kong Chinese YMCA], *Qingnianhui shiye gaiyao* [YMCA guide] (Hong Kong, 1918), pp. 15–22.

68. The literature on Ma Ying Piu, the Sincere Company, and overseas Chinese in Australia is extensive. On Ma, see Burt, et al., *Prominent Chinese*, p. 66; *Ma Yingbiao xiansheng jianshi* [Brief history of Mr. Ma Yingbiao (Ma Ying Piu)] (Guangzhou: Guangdong sheng gongansi faguanli ganbu xueyuan, 1986); and Wu, *Xianggang Huaren*, pp. 22–23. On the Sincere Company, see Wellington K. K. Chan, "The Organizational Structure of the Traditional Chinese Firm and Its Modern Reform," *Business History Review* 56.2 (Summer 1982): 229–232; "Jijia Huazi baihuo gongsi" [Several Chinese department stores], in *Xianggang shangyelu* [Hong Kong commercial directory] (Hong Kong: Zhongguo xinwenshe, 1948), p. 13; Xianggang Xianshi youxian gongsi [Sincere Company Limited, Hong Kong]; *Xianshi gongsi ershiwunian jingguoshi* [The Sincere Co., Ltd. Twenty-fifth Anniversary] (Hong Kong: Commercial Press, 1924); Yang Guoxiong, "Xianggang zaoqi baihuo gongsi," p. 114; Feng Bangyan, *Xianggang Huazi caituan, 1841–1997* [Chinese financial organizations in Hong Kong, 1841–1997] (Hong Kong: San-lian, 1997), pp. 58–62; and Zhang Xiaohui, *Xianggang Huashangshi*, pp. 72–76.

5. Nationalism and Identity

1. "Group of reformers": Paul A. Cohen, "Littoral and Hinterland in Nine-teenth Century China: The 'Christian' Reformers," in John K. Fairbank, ed., *The Missionary Enterprise in China and America* (Cambridge, Mass.: Harvard University Press, 1974), pp. 197–230, and *Between Tradition and Modernity: Wang T'ao and Reform in Late Ch'ing China* (Cambridge, Mass.: Harvard University Press, 1974), chapter 9; Sun Yatsen and Ho's theory: Lloyd E. Eastman, "Political Reformism in China before the Sino-Japanese War," *Journal of Asian Studies* 27.4 (August 1968): 698, 709; "using Western Ideals": Xiao Gongquan, *Zhongguo zhengzhi si-xiangshi* [History of Chinese political thought], vol. 6 (Taipei: Zhonghua wenhua chuban shiye weiyuanhui, 1954), pp. 795–803; Ho's Hong Kong "affiliation": For example, Immanuel C. Y. Hsu, "Late Ch'ing Foreign Relations, 1866–1905," in John K. Fairbank, ed., *The Cambridge History of China*, vol. 11 (Cambridge: Cambridge University Press), pp. 189–190, 195. Cf. Hao Chang's essay in the same volume, "Intellectual Change and the Reform Movement, 1890–8," where Ho is described on pp. 280–281 as a "leading citizen" of the colony.

2. "Comprador reformer": Ren Jiyu, "He Qi, Hu Liyuan de gailiang zhuyi sixiang" [The reformist thought of He Qi (Ho Kai) and Hu Liyuan], in Feng Youlan, ed., *Zhongguo jindai sixiangshi lunwen ji* [Essays on modern Chinese thought] (Shanghai: Renmin chubanshe, 1958), pp. 75–91; foreign investment: Hu Bin, *Zhongguo jindai gailiang zhuyi sixiang* [Reformist thought in modern China] (Beijing: Zhonghua shuju, 1964), pp. 73–75; Marxist critique of Ho: for example, Watanabe Tetsuhiro, "Ka Kei, Ko Reien no shin seiron" [Ho Kai and Hu Liyuan's discourse on new government] *Ritsu meikan bungaku* 197 (1961): 59–75.

3. Huang Yifeng, "Guanyu jiu Zhongguo maiban jieji de yanjiu" [Research on the comprador class in old China] *Lishi yanjiu* 87 (1964): 89–112 and "Diguo zhuyi qinlue Zhongguo diyige zhongyao zhizhu: maiban jieji" [One important pillar of the imperialist invasion of China: the comprador class] *Lishi yanjiu* 91 (1965): 55–70; Huang Yifeng, et al., *Jiu zhongguo de maiban jieji* [The comprador class in old China] (Shanghai: Renmin chubanshe, 1982); Nie Baozhang, *Zhongguo maiban zichan jieji de fasheng* [The emergence of the Chinese comprador class] (Beijing: Zhongguo shehui kexue chubanshe, 1979), pp. 52, 64, 119–126; Ren,

"He Qi, Hu Liyuan," pp. 88; Wang Jingyu, "Shijiu shiji waiguo qinHua qiye zhong de Huashang fugu yundong" [Investment by Chinese merchants in the foreign enterprises that invaded China in the nineteenth century], *Lishi yanjiu* 94 (1965): 39, 69–70.

4. Blurred distinctions: Yen-p'ing Hao, *The Comprador in Nineteenth Century China: Bridge between East and West* (Cambridge, Mass.: Harvard University Press, 1970), pp. 112, 217; Marie-Claire Bergère, *The Golden Age of the Chinese Bourgeoisie, 1911–1937*, trans. Janet Lloyd (Cambridge: Cambridge University Press, 1989), p. 49, and "The Role of the Bourgeoisie," in Mary C. Wright, ed., *China in Revolution* (New Haven: Yale University Press, 1968), pp. 249–250.

5. Harold Z. Schiffrin, *Sun Yat-sen and the Origins of the Chinese Revolution* (Berkeley: University of California Press, 1968), pp. 211–212; Jung-fang Tsai, *Hong Kong in Chinese History: Community and Social Unrest in the British Colony, 1842–1913* (New York: Columbia University Press, 1993), p. 160. See also Tsai's essay, "The Predicament of the Comprador Ideologists: He Qi (Ho Kai, 1859–1914) and Hu Li-yuan (1847–1916)," *Modern China* 7.2 (April 1981): 191–225; "genuine natives": *Asian Quarterly Review*, cited in *Hong Kong Daily Press*, July 22, 1890; "curious mixture": Chan Lau Kit-ching, *China, Britain and Hong Kong, 1895–1945* (Hong Kong: Chinese University Press, 1990), p. 29.

6. 1967 riots: John D. Young, "The Building Years: Maintaining a China–Hong Kong–Britain Equilibrium, 1950–71," in Ming K. Chan, ed., *Precarious Balance: Hong Kong Between China and Britain, 1842–1992* (Armonk, New York: M. E. Sharpe, 1994), p. 140; the 1970s: Gordon Mathews, "Heunggongyahn: On the Past, and Future of Hong Kong Identity," *Bulletin of Concerned Asian Scholars* 29:3 (1997): 7–9; the 1980s: Ronald Skeldon, "Hong Kong Communities Overseas," in Judith M. Brown and Rosemary Foot, eds., *Hong Kong's Transitions, 1842–1997* (London: Macmillan, 1997), p. 122; the early 1990s: Lynn White and Li Cheng, "China Coast Identities: Regional, National, and Global," in Lowell Dittmer and Samuel S. Kim, eds., *China's Quest for National Identity* (Ithaca: Cornell University Press, 1993), p. 180–190; the late 1990s: Ackbar Abbas, *Hong Kong: The Culture of Disappearance* (Minneapolis: University of Minnesota Press, 1997).

7. Bryna Goodman, *Native Place, City, and Nation: Regional Networks and Identities in Shanghai, 1853–1937* (Berkeley: University of California Press, 1995); William T. Rowe, *Hankow: Commerce and Society in a Chinese City, 1796–1889* (Stanford: Stanford University Press, 1984), p. 342.

8. Wang Gungwu, "The Study of Identities in Southeast Asia," in Jennifer Cushman and Wang Gungwu, eds., *The Changing Identities of Chinese in Southeast Asia* (Hong Kong: Hong Kong University Press, 1988), p. 10; a "site of differences": Aihwa Ong and Donald M. Nonini, "Chinese Transnationalism as an Alternative Modernity," in Aihwa Ong and Donald M. Nonini, eds., *Ungrounded Empires: The Cultural Politics of Modern Chinese Nationalism* (New York: Routledge, 1997), pp. 24–25; Stuart Hall, "Cultural Identity and Diaspora," in Padmini Mongia, ed., *Contemporary Postcolonial Theory* (London: Arnold, 1996), p. 110.

9. Philip D. Morgan, "Encounters between British and 'Indigenous' Peoples, c. 1500–c.1800," in Martin Daunton and Rick Halpern, eds., *Empire and Others: British Encounters with Indigenous Peoples, 1600–1850* (London: University College of London Press, 1999), p. 45; Sadatru Sen, "Chameleon Games: Ranjitsinhji's

Politics of Race and Gender," *Journal of Colonialism and Colonial History* 2.3 (2001): 98 (electronic journal); Australian British: Angela Woollacott, " 'All This Is the Empire, I told Myself': Australian Women's Voyages 'Home' and the Articulation of Colonial Whiteness," *American Historical Review* 102.4 (October 1997): 1003–1029.

10. Chinese politics: Stephanie Po-yin Chung, *Chinese Business Groups in Hong Kong and Political Change in South China, 1900–25* (London: Macmillan, 1998), pp. 16, 125; Helen F. Siu, "Cultural Identity and the Politics of Difference in South China," *Daedalus* 122.2 (Spring 1993): 19–43; Ho's explanation to British officials: *Report of the Special Committee Appointed by His Excellency Sir William Robinson, &c., to Investigate and Report on Certain Points Connected with the Bill for the Incorporation of the Po Leung Kuk or Society for the Protection of Women and Girls, Together with the Evidence Taken before the Committee and an Appendix Containing Correspondence, Reports, Returns, &c* (Hong Kong: Noronha, 1893), p. 95.

11. Sir Robert Ho Tung, Kt., "The Chinese in Hong Kong," in W. Feldwick, *Present Day Impressions of the Far East and Prominent Chinese at Home and Abroad: The History, People, Commerce, Industries and Resources of China, Hongkong, Indo-China, Malaya and Netherlands India* (London: Globe Encyclopaedia, 1917), pp. 527–530.

12. Great Britain, Colonial Office, Original Correspondence: Hong Kong, 1841–1951, Series 129 (CO129), Public Record Office, London, CO 129/391, July 20, 1912, May to Harcourt, p. 110.

13. May to Harcourt, pp. 107–109.

14. Public Records Office of Hong Kong, Hong Kong Record Series (HKRS), HKRS 58.1.60–71.

15. Carl T. Smith, *Chinese Christians: Elites, Middlemen, and the Church in Hong Kong* (Hong Kong: Oxford University Press, 1985), pp. 4, 7, 129–130, 186.

16. Biographical information on Ho Kai based on *Who's Who in the Far East, 1906–7* (Hong Kong: China Mail, 1906), pp. 142–143; Gerald H. Choa, *The Life and Times of Sir Kai Ho Kai* (Hong Kong: Chinese University Press, 1981); Carl T. Smith, *Chinese Christians: Elites, Middlemen, and the Church in Hong Kong* (Hong Kong: Oxford University Press, 1985), pp. 131, 160–162; Arnold Wright and H. A. Cartwright, eds., *Twentieth Century Impressions of Hongkong, Shanghai, and other Treaty Ports of China: Their History, People, Commerce, Industries, and Resources* (London: Lloyds, 1908), p. 109; Wu Xinglian [Woo Sing Lim], *Xianggang Huaren mingren shilue* [Prominent Chinese of Hong Kong] (Hong Kong: Wuzhou, 1937), pp. 2–3.

17. *Hong Kong Telegraph*, March 3, 1870.

18. *Hong Kong Telegraph*, March 11 and 25, 1912.

19. "Kangshuo shuhou" [Review of Kang Youwei's speech], in Hu Liyuan, *Hu Yinan xiansheng quanji* [Complete works of Hu Yinan (Hu Liyuan)] (Hong Kong, 1917), vol. 13, pp. 1a–20a, reprinted in Shen Yunlong, ed., *Jindai zhongguo shiliao congkan xubian* [Reprinted materials on modern Chinese history, supplementary edition] [Taipei, 1975], vol. 262, pp. 783–821.

20. Partha Chatterjee, *The Nation and Its Fragments: Colonial and Postcolonial Histories* (Princeton: Princeton University Press, 1993), p. 55; *China Mail*, Feb. 16, 1887.

21. Wu, *Xianggang Huaren*, p. 97.

22. Feng Ziyou, *Zhongguo geming yundong ershiliunian zuzhishi* [Twenty-six years of Chinese revolutionary history] (Shanghai: Commercial Press, 1948), pp. 22–23; Schiffrin, *Sun Yat-sen*, pp. 71–75, 82, 180–208; and Tse Tsan Tai, *The Chinese Republic: Secret History of the Revolution* (Hong Kong: South China Morning Post, 1924), pp. 8–9, 19.

23. Tsai, "Comprador Ideologists," p. 209; Letter from Wei Yuk to Henry May, Aug. 20, 1914, enclosed in CO 129/413, Sept. 11, 1914, May to Harcourt, pp. 272–277. An appeal to the Legislative Council: *Hong Kong Hansard: Reports of the Meetings of the Legislative Council of Hong Kong*, July 2, 1908, p. 24, and July 24, 1908, p. 90.

24. "Zenglun shuhou" [Review of Zeng Jize's essay], in Hu, *Hu Yinan*, vol. 1, reprinted in Shen, *Jindai zhongguo*, vol. 261, pp. 221–310; see also Ho's preface to "Xinzheng lunyi," in Hu, *Hu Yinan*, vol. 4, pp. 1a–2b, reprinted in Shen, *Jindai zhongguo*, vol. 216, pp. 313–316.

25. "Xinzheng lunyi" [Discourse on new government], in Hu, *Hu Yinan*, vol. 4, reprinted in Shen, *Jindai zhongguo*, vol. 261, pp. 325–379.

26. " 'Quanxue pian' shu hou" [Review of "Exhortation to Learning"], in Hu, *Hu Yinan*, vol. 15–18, reprinted in Shen, *Jindai zhongguo*, vol. 262, pp. 855–899, vol. 263, pp. 901–1049.

27. "Kangshuo shuhou" [Review of Kang's speech], in Hu, *Hu Yinan*, vol. 13, pp. 1b–15b, reprinted in Shen, *Jindai zhongguo*, vol. 262, pp. 784–812.

28. "Xinzheng shiji [Foundations of new government], in Hu, *Hu Yinan*, vol. 7–9, reprinted in Shen, *Jindai zhongguo shiliao*, vol. 262, pp. 489–647; "Xinzheng anxing" [Administration of new government], in Hu, *Hu Yinan*, vol. 10–12, reprinted in Shen, *Jindai zhongguo shiliao*, vol. 26, pp. 653–781.

29. " 'Quanxue pian' shu hou" [Review of "Exhortation to study"], in Hu, *Hu Yinan*, vol. 15–17, especially 17: 18a–19b, reprinted in Shen, *Jindai zhongguo shiliao*, vol. 263, pp. 981–984.

30. "Xinzheng lunyi" [Discourse on new government], in Hu, *Hu Yinan*, vol. 4, pp. 1a–2b, reprinted in Shen, *Jindai zhongguo shiliao*, vol. 261, pp. 325–328; Ho's prefaces to "Xinzheng anxing" [Practice of new government] and "Xinzheng shiji" [Foundations of new government], both in Hu, *Hu Yinan*, vol. 10, pp. 1a–2a, and vol. 7, pp. 1a–2b, reprinted in Shen, *Jindai zhongguo shiliao*, vol. 262, pp. 485–487, 645–648

31. Hu, *Zhongguo jindai gailiang zhuyi*, pp. 73–74; Ren, "He Qi, Hu Liyuan de gailiang zhuyi," pp. 75–91.

32. "Bourgeois interests": Tsai, "Comprador Ideologists," p. 202; merchant-intelligentsia: Tsai, *Hong Kong in Chinese History*, pp. 157–159; Chan Lau, *China, Britain, and Hong Kong*, p. 27.

33. "Xinzheng lunyi" [Discourse on new government], in Hu, *Hu Yinan*, vol. 4, p. 18b, and vol. 6, pp. 20a–21a, reprinted in Shen, *Jindai zhongguo shiliao*, vol. 261, p. 362, vol. 262, pp. 457–459; "Quanxueshuhou" [Review of "Exhortation to Study"], in Hu, *Hu Yinan*, vol. 18, pp. 4a–b, reprinted in Shen, *Jindai zhongguo shiliao*, vol. 263, pp. 991–992.

34. *Report of the Special Committee*, p. 91.

35. Chan Wai Kwan, *The Making of Hong Kong Society: Three Studies of Class Formation in Early Hong Kong* (Oxford: Clarendon Press, 1991), p. 130.

36. Defending the strikers: *Hong Kong Daily Press*, Oct. 16, 1884; the Tramways

Bill: Choa, *Life and Times*, p. 107; rickshaw rental: Chan, *Making of Hong Kong Society*, p. 160.

37. Cited in Choa, *Life and Times*, pp. 111–112.

38. "Memorial to the Registrar General (Lockhart) Respecting Gaol Extension, from Wei A Yuk, Lau Wai Chün, Seung Sz Kai, Ip Juck Kai, Ho Fook, Chan Pan Poo, Law Yam Chuen, C. Chee Bee, Poon Pong, Ho Kai, Chan A Fook, Wong Shing, Chow Peng, Chen Quan Ee, Kaw Hong Take, Woo Lin Yuen, Ho Tung," *Hong Kong Legislative Council Sessional Papers*, Jan. 6, 1893.

39. "Dr Ho Kai's Protest Against the Public Health Bill, Submitted to the Government by the Sanitary Board, and the Board's Rejoinder Thereto," *Sessional Papers, 1887*, p. 404.

40. "Dr Ho Kai's Protest," pp. 405–407.

41. Ibid., p. 404.

42. Carol Benedict, "Framing Plague in China's Past," in Gail Hershatter, et al. eds., *Remapping China: Fissures in Historical Terrain* (Stanford: Stanford University Press, 1996), pp. 27–41; anti-opium debate: Colin Criswell and Mike Watson, *The Royal Hong Kong Police (1841–1945)* (Hong Kong: Macmillan, 1982), p. 100, and Yang Sixian, *Xianggang cangsang* [Hong Kong vicissitudes] (Beijing: Youyi chubanshe, 1986), pp. 120–121.

43. "Dr Ho Kai's Protest," p. 405.

44. "Memorial Respecting Gaol Extension," p. 71.

45. Ibid., p. 72.

46. Uday S. Mehta, "Liberal Strategies of Exclusion," in Frederick Cooper and Ann Laura Stoler, eds., *Tensions of Empire: Colonial Cultures in a Bourgeois World* (Berkeley: University of California Press, 1997), p. 59.

47. "Dr Ho Kai's Protest," pp. 405–406.

48. *Hong Kong Telegraph*, April 2, 1912.

49. On the tram boycott, see Tsai, *Hong Kong in Chinese History*, chapter 10; and Ming K. Chan, "Hong Kong in Sino-British Conflict: Mass Mobilization and the Crises of Legitimacy, 1912–26," in Ming K. Chan, ed., *Precarious Balance: Hong Kong Between China and Britain, 1842–1992* (Armonk, New York: M. E. Sharpe, 1994), pp. 29–32.

50. CO 129/394, Dec. 30, 1912, May to Harcourt, pp. 175–190.

51. CO 129/403, Aug. 18, 1913, May to Harcourt, pp. 124–126.

52. Ibid., p. 127.

53. Ibid., May to Harcourt, pp. 128–129.

54. CO 129/404, Nov. 20, 1913, Severn to Harcourt, pp. 161–164.

55. CO 129/409, March 5, 1914, May to Harcourt, pp. 410–412.

56. Ibid., p. 410.

57. *Hong Kong Hansard, 1914*, pp. 28–29; also enclosed in May to Harcourt, pp. 414–415.

58. Ibid., p. 29; pp. 414–415.

59. Ibid., p. 79; also enclosed in CO 129/413, Sept. 11, 1914, May to Harcourt, pp. 269–277.

60. Letter from S. W. Tso, *South China Morning Post*, Jan. 4, 1921.

6. Preserving Hong Kong

1. Daniel Y. K. Kwan, *Marxist Intellectuals and the Chinese Labor Movement: A Study of Deng Zhongxia (1894–1933)* (Seattle: University of Washington Press, 1997), pp. 99, 111.

2. Ibid. pp. 118–119.

3. D. W. Tratman, "Report of the Secretary for Chinese Affairs for the Year 1925," in Hong Kong, *Administrative Report, 1925*, Appendix C, p. 17; Great Britain, Colonial Office, Original Correspondence: Hong Kong, 1841–1951, Series 129 (CO129), Public Record Office, London, CO 129/488, (Stubbs to Amery), June 26, 1925, pp. 468–472; July 10, 1925, pp. 580–585; July 24, 1925, pp. 646–649.

4. Alexander Grantham, *Via Ports: From Hong Kong to Hong Kong* (Hong Kong: Hong Kong University Press, 1965), p. 15; students marched out: Robert Kotewall's report on the strike, Oct. 24, 1925, enclosed in CO 129/489, Oct. 30, 1925, Stubbs to Amery, p. 432; fifty thousand left: Tratman, "Report of the Secretary for Chinese Affairs," Appendix C, p. 17; . . . rickshaw pullers: Paul Gillingham, *At the Peak: Hong Kong Between the Wars* (Hong Kong: Macmillan, 1983), p. 35.

5. CO 129/488, June 26, 1925, telegram, Stubbs to Amery, p. 455. On Stubbs's censorship and other emergency measures, see Chen Qian, "Xianggang jiushi jianwenlu (4)" [Recollections of old Hong Kong, part 4], *Guangdong wenshi ziliao* 47 (1986): 31–33.

6. Chen, "Xianggang jiushi jianwenlu (4)," pp. 31–32.

7. "Ghost town": Gillingham, *At the Peak*, p. 37; "undesirables": CO 129/488, July 10, 1925, Stubbs to Amery, pp. 580–581; trade loan: CO 129/489, Sept. 18, 1925, Stubbs to Amery, p. 212.

8. G. B. Endacott, *A History of Hong Kong*, rev. ed. (Hong Kong: Oxford University Press, 1973), pp. 289–290; Chinese labor movement: for example, Cai Luo, et al., *Shenggang da bagong* [The Canton-Hong Kong general strike] (n.p., 1980); Gan Tian, *Xianggang da bagong* [The great Hong Kong strike] (Beijing: Renmin chubanshe, 1956). The definitive study of the labor movement in this region is still Ming K. Chan's "Labor and Empire: The Chinese Labor Movement in the Canton Delta, 1895–1927," Ph.D. diss., Stanford University, 1975.

9. Chinese nationalism: Zhang Yueai, "Xianggang, 1841–1980" [Hong Kong, 1841–1980], in Lu Yan, et al., *Xianggang zhanggu* [Hong Kong anecdotes], vol. 4 (Hong Kong: Guangjiaojing chubanshe, 1981), pp. 22–26, and Yuan Bangjian, *Xianggang shilue* [History of Hong Kong] (Hong Kong: Zhongliu chubanshe, 1993), pp. 156–158; Chan Lau Kit-ching, *China, Britain and Hong Kong, 1895–1945* (Hong Kong: Chinese University Press, 1990), chapter 4; Henry J. Lethbridge, "Introduction," in Henry J. Lethbridge, *Hong Kong: Stability and Change: A Collection of Essays* (Hong Kong: Oxford University Press, 1978), pp. 21, 25.

10. Stubbs to Amery: CO129/488, July 10, pp. 580–581; July 24, 1925, pp. 645–649; July 27, 1925, telegram, p. 655; Sept. 25, 1925, telegram, p. 237; Oct. 30, 1925, pp. 428–429.

11. W. T. Southorn, "Annual General Report for 1925," in Hong Kong, *Administrative Report, 1925*, p. 2; Tratman's report, Appendix C, pp. 16–17.

12. Clementi's statement to the Legislative Council, Feb. 4, 1926, in *Hong Kong*

Hansard: Reports of the Meetings of the Legislative Council of Hong Kong, 1926–1927, pp. 1–2.

13. Ibid., p. 2.

14. Diary Letters of Sir Cecil Clementi, 1925–1927, Public Records Office of Hong Kong, microfilm, Dec. 23, 1925, Clementi to Amery, box 1, file 1, ff. 28–57.

15. Diary Letters, Dec. 30, 1925, Clementi to Amery, box 1, file 2, ff. 81–83.

16. Diary Letters, Jan. 6, 1926, Clementi to Amery, telegram, box 1, file 2, f. 2.

17. Diary Letters, Jan. 6, 1926, Clementi to Amery, box 1, file 2, f. 2.

18. Diary Letters, Feb. 2, 1926, Clementi to Amery, box 1, file 3, f. 2.

19. Diary Letters, cypher telegram, Clementi to Amery, Feb., 1926, box 1, file 3, ff. 29–35.

20. Kwan, *Marxist Intellectuals,* pp. 111, 126.

21. *Hong Kong: A Short History of the Colony and an Outline of the Present Political Situation in China* (Hong Kong: Publicity Bureau for South China, 1928), p. 68. For an autobiographical account of the Soviet presence in South China, see Vera Vladimirovna Vishnyakova-Akimova's *Two Years in Revolutionary China,* trans. Steven I. Levine (Cambridge, Mass.: Harvard University Press, 1971).

22. Kotewall's report, pp. 456–457.

23. CO 129/488, July 17, 1925, telegram, Stubbs to Amery, p. 643.

24. *Hong Kong: A Short History,* pp. 66, 68.

25. Chen Qian, "Xianggang jiushi jianwenlu (3)" [Recollections of old Hong Kong, part 3], *Guangdong wenshi ziliao* 46 (1985): 28, 56–60.

26. Lu Yan, "Xianggang Huaren shetuan de fazhanshi" [The development of a Chinese society in Hong Kong], in Lu Yan et al., *Xianggang zhanggu* [Hong Kong anecdotes], vol. 5 (Hong Kong: Guangjiaojing chubanshe, 1982), p. 50.

27. Robert S. Ward, *Asia for the Asiatics? The Techniques of Japanese Occupation* (Chicago: University of Chicago Press, 1945), p. 14; never viewed as Chinese: Ming K. Chan, review of Jung-fang Tsai's *Hong Kong in Chinese History: Community and Social Unrest in the British Colony, 1842–1913,* in *China International* 2.1 (Spring 1995): 257–258.

28. "Precarious position": Arnold Wright and H. A. Cartwright, eds., *Twentieth Century Impressions of Hongkong, Shanghai, and other Treaty Ports of China: Their History, People, Commerce, Industries, and Resources* (London: Lloyds, 1908), p. 341; Henry J. Lethbridge, "Caste, Class, and Race in Hong Kong before the Japanese Occupation," in Lethbridge, *Hong Kong,* p. 176; "disdained Eurasians": cited in Norman J. Miners, *Hong Kong under Imperial Rule, 1912–1941* (Hong Kong: Oxford University Press, 1987), p. 128; "Interview with Dr. B. Kotewall by Dr. Alan Birch," n.d., Public Records Office of Hong Kong.

29. Diary Letters, March 30, 1926, Kotewall's letter to Rt. Hon. Viscount Willington, box 3, file 4, f. 197; Kotewall's report, p. 454.

30. Kotewall's report, pp. 431–432.

31. Ibid., p. 433. Particularly in the south, Chinese often referred to foreigners, especially Europeans, as "devils."

32. Ibid., pp. 433–434.

33. Ibid., pp. 434, 435, 439–440.

34. Ibid., pp. 455–456.

35. Ibid., p. 458.

36. Ibid., pp. 455, 444–448.

37. Kotewall's report, p. 447. Also enclosed in CO 129/489, Sept. 4, 1925, Stubbs to Colonial Office, p. 167.

38. Reviving the *Daily News*: CO 129/490, Sept. 3, 1926, Clementi to Amery, pp. 125–126.

39. Kotewall's report, p. 442, CO 129/488, July 10, 1925, Stubbs to Amery: p. 582, and July 24, 1925, p. 647.

40. Kotewall's report, pp. 442–443; Stubbs to Amery: CO 129/488, July 24, 1925, p. 647, and CO 129/489, Oct. 2, 1925, p. 249.

41. Li Jiayuan, *Xianggang baoye zatan* [On the Hong Kong press] (Hong Kong: Joint Publishing, 1989), p. 67; Lin Ling, "Wo suo zhidao de Xianggang *Gongshang ribao*" [What I know about the Hong Kong *Gongshang ribao* (*Kung Sheung Yat Po*)], *Guangdong wenshi ziliao* 51 (1987): 105–111.

42. Kotewall's report, p. 444; Clementi to Amery: CO 129/498, Sept. 3, 1926, p. 125.

43. Labor conflicts: *Kung Sheung Yat Po*, May 4, 1926, section 1, p. 3; Russian influence: May 7, 1926, section 1, pp. 2–3; assassinations: May 5, 1926, section 1, p. 3; China still in chaos: May 10, 1926, section 1, p. 2.

44. CCP exploitation of workers: *Kung Sheung Yat Po*, June 12, 1926, section 1, p. 3, June 16, 1926, section 1, p. 3; student fight: June 16, 1926, section 1, p. 3; striking workers' illegal activities: June 16, 1926, section 1, p. 3; Canton authorities' involvement: June 16, 1926, section 1, p. 3; Great South Tobacco Company advertisement: Dec. 17, 1926, n.p.; Tian Yi Company advertisement: June 19, 1926, n.p.

45. Kotewall's report, p. 446; Clementi to Amery: CO 129/498, Sept. 3, 1926, p. 125.

46. Diary Letters, March 8, 1926, Clementi to Amery, box 1, file 4, ff. 37–73, and translation of Wang Jingwei's letter, box 1, file 4, f. 49; Diary Letters, March 5, 1926, copy of Chow and Kotewall's confidential report to Hallifax, box 1, file 3, pp. 50–72.

47. Copy of Chow and Kotewall's confidential report to Hallifax, ff. 50–72.

48. Chow and Kotewall's report to Hallifax, ff. 50–72.

49. Kotewall's report, pp. 439–441, 458–459.

50. Kotewall's report, p. 460.

51. Kotewall's report, pp. 435–439. On Tso's activities during the strike, see also Wu Xinglian [Woo Sing Lim], *Xianggang Huaren mingren shilue* [Prominent Chinese in Hong Kong] (Hong Kong: Wuzhou, 1937), pp. 8–11. See also Chen Datong, comp., *Bainian shangye* [A century of commerce] (Hong Kong: 1941), n.p.; and Wu, *Xianggang Huaren*, p. 32. On Kwok Chan, reservist: Chen Datong, et al., *Xianggang Huaqiao tuanti zonglan* [Overseas Chinese organizations in Hong Kong] (Hong Kong: Guoji xinwenshe, 1947), n.p.; Wu, *Xianggang Huaren*, p. 62. On the volunteer fire brigade: Kotewall's report, p. 439.

52. CO 129/489, Sept. 10, 1925, Wodehouse to Colonial Secretary, pp. 193–196.

53. CO 129/488, June 26, 1925, telegram, Stubbs to Amery, p. 455; CO 129/489, Sept. 18, 1925, Stubbs to Amery, p. 212.

54. CO 129/489, Oct. 30, 1925, Stubbs to Amery, p. 428.

55. Tratman's report, Appendix C, pp. 1–6.

56. CO 129/263, Aug. 23, 1894, Ripon to Robinson, reprinted in Steve Tsang, ed., *Government and Politics: A Documentary History of Hong Kong* (Hong Kong: Hong Kong University Press, 1995), p. 109.

57. CO 129/268, Robinson to Chamberlain, Aug. 16, 1895, reprinted in Tsang, *Government and Politics*, p. 109.

58. CO 129/74, Chamberlain to Robinson, May 29, 1896, reprinted in Tsang, *Government and Politics*, p. 110.

59. CO 129/493, June 24, 1926, telegram, Clementi to Amery, reprinted in Tsang, *Government and Politics*, p. 111.

60. Cecil Clementi, "Annual Report for 1926," in Hong Kong, *Administrative Report, 1926*, p. 2.

61. Diary Letters, March 26, 1927, Clementi to Amery, box 7, file 4, ff. 14–15; March 31, 1927, Clementi to Amery, box 7, file 4, ff. 100–102.

62. Diary Letters, March 31, 1927, Clementi to Amery, box 7, file 4, ff. 100–102.

63. Diary Letters, copy of Amery's message to Hong Kong community, box 7, file 4, ff. 92–94.

64. Robert Bickers, *Britain in China: Community, Culture and Colonialism, 1900–1949* (Manchester: Manchester University Press, 1999), pp. 3–4.

7. *Transforming the Barren Island*

1. Robert Kotewall, "Anglo-Chinese Co-operation—Past, Present & Future," in *Hong Kong Centenary Commemorative Talks, 1841–1941* (Hong Kong: World News Service, 1941), p. 30. Originally published in China Mail, *Hong Kong Centenary Number*, Jan. 20, 1941, pp. 2–18.

2. "The Jubilee Celebrations," in Hong Kong Daily Press, *Fifty Years of Progress: The Jubilee of Hongkong as a British Crown Colony, Being an Historical Sketch to Which is Added an Account of the Celebrations of 21st to 24th January, 1891* (Hong Kong: Hong Kong Daily Press, 1891), pp. 32–42; *China Mail*, Jan. 10–26, 1891. On the "throng of Chinese": "Jubilee Celebrations," p. 41. On the 1941 centenary: Chen Datong, ed., *Bainian shangye* [A Century of Commerce] (Hong Kong: Guangming wenhua shiye gongsi, 1941); Li Jinwei, ed., *Xianggang bainianshi* [Centenary History of Hong Kong] (Hong Kong: Nanzhong chubanshe, 1948).

3. On commemorations, see John Bodnar, *Remaking America: Public Memory, Commemoration, and Patriotism in the Twentieth Century* (Princeton: Princeton University Press, 1991); John R. Gillis, ed., *Commemorations: The Politics of National Identity* (Princeton: Princeton University Press, 1994); and William M. Johnston, *Celebrations: The Cult of Anniversaries in Europe and the United States Today* (New Brunswick, N.J.: Transaction Publishers, 1991).

4. Guan Lixiong, *Rizhan shiqi de Xianggang* [Hong Kong under the Japanese Occupation] (Hong Kong: Sanlian, 1993), pp. 9–10, p. 11.

5. "Neutral zone": Philip Snow, *The Fall of Hong Kong: Britain, China, and the Japanese Occupation* (New Haven: Yale University Press, 2003), p. 29; G. B. En-

dacott, *Hong Kong Eclipse*, ed. Alan Birch (Hong Kong: Oxford University Press, 1978), p. 29; Guan, *Rizhan shiqi*, p. 24.

6. Endacott, *Hong Kong Eclipse*, pp. 25, 63.

7. E. I. Wynne-Jones, "One Hundred Years of Communications Facilities in Hong Kong," in *Commemorative Talks*, p. 35.

8. "How Hong Kong Became a Colony," in *South China Morning Post/Hong Kong Telegraph, Centenary Supplement*, Jan. 25, 1941, p. 1.

9. E. F. Norton, "A Hundred Years' Growth: The Development of Hong Kong," in *Commemorative Talks*, p. 24.

10. "Low wartime tax": "Hong Kong Centenary Messages," in *Commemorative Talks*, p. 30; "preserver of freedom": "Gejie mingliu dui Xianggang bainian zhi guannian" [Local notables' observations of Hong Kong's hundred years], in *Bainian shangye*, p. 21; "maximum contribution": "Centenary Messages," p. 31.

11. Guang Zhanming, "Xianci" [Congratulatory message], in *Bainian shangye*, pp. 1–2; "assurance of loyalty": "Centenary Messages," p. 31; J. P. Braga, "Portuguese Pioneering: A Hundred Years of Hong Kong," in *Commemorative Talks*, p. 54.

12. On Parsi merchants: "Hundred Years of Commercial Activities of Parsi Merchants in Hong Kong," in *Commemorative Talks*, pp. 99, 102, 105. On "Indian pioneers": K. P. Vaida, "Indian Pioneers," in *Commemorative Talks*, p. 110; K. P. Vaida, "Pioneers," in *Centenary Number*, p. 54.

13. *Bainian shangye*, p. 37; *Centenary Number*, pp. 48–49; *Commemorative Talks*, pp. 56–57; *Centenary Supplement*, p. 3. See also "A Century of Progress: A Brief History of Watson's from 1841 to 1941," in *Centenary Number*, p. 82.

14. Small matshed shop: *Commemorative Talks*, p. 37, and *Centenary Supplement*, p. 6; first department store: *Centenary Number*, p. 71; air-raid defense equipment: *Bainian shangye*, p. 4.

15. Jocelyn Létourneau, "The Current Great Narrative of Québecois Identity," in V. Y. Mudimbe, ed., *Nations, Identities, Cultures* (Durham: Duke University Press, 1997), p. 61; Paul Connerton, *How Societies Remember* (Cambridge: Cambridge University Press, 1989), p. 1.

16. "Hong Kong in History," in China Mail, *Hong Kong Centenary Number*, Jan. 20, 1941, p. 2; Norton, "Hundred Years' Growth," p. 21.

17. "Centenary Messages," p. 32.

18. Cheng Zhi, "Xianggang jianshi" [Brief history of Hong Kong], in *Xianggang bainianshi*, p. 7.

19. "Centenary Messages," p. 33.

20. Norton, "Hundred Years' Growth," pp. 21, 28; Chow Shouson: "Centenary Messages," p. 32.

21. David Cressy, "National Memory in Early Modern England," in Gillis, *Commemorations*, p. 61.

22. Gillis, "Memory and Identity," p. 8.

23. Elizabeth Tonkin, *Narrating Our Pasts: The Social Construction of Oral History* (Cambridge: Cambridge University Press, 1992), p. 11.

24. "Hong Kong in History," p. 2.

25. This is particularly noticeable because the volume contains numerous photographs of Hong Kong's harbor and night skyline, which even then drew the admiration of visitors. The scholar Hu Shi recalled a trip to Hong Kong in the

late 1920s, insisting that the city at night was far more impressive than either New York or San Francisco. Hu Shi *Nanyou zayi* [Memories of my trip south] (Taipei: Qiming shuju, 1959), p. 2. A Chinese guidebook from 1938 noted that watching the sunset from one of Hong Kong's many peaks was "as good as seeing Mount Tai itself." Cheng Gongzhe, ed., *Xianggang zhinan* [Guide to Hong Kong] (Changsha: Shangwu, 1938), p. 23.

26. "Centenary Messages," p. 33.

27. He Dong [Ho Tung], "Shen Xianggang zaonian zhi huaiyi" [Memories of early Hong Kong], in *Bainian shangye*, p. 6.

28. Shou-son Chow, "An Octogenarian Remembers Hong Kong's Progress and Prosperity," in *Commemorative Talks*, p. 69; "Gejie mingliu," p. 21.

29. Connerton, *How Societies Remember*, p. 3.

30. "Xianggang fazhanshi" [History of Hong Kong's development], in *Bainian shangye*, p. 27.

31. Cheng Zhi, "Xianggang jianshi" [Brief history of Hong Kong], in *Xianggang bainianshi*, p. 7.

32. Chen Datong, "Xianggang gaiguan" [Overview of Hong Kong], in *Bainian shangye*, p. 19.

33. "Hong Kong in History," p. 2.

34. Abbreviating the conflicts: Chen Zhao, "Xianggang kaifoushi" [The opening of Hong Kong], in *Xianggang bainian shi*, p. 3; racial discrimination: Pan Kongyan, "Zongzu qishi de bianlun" [A debate about racial prejudice], in *Xianggang bainianshi*, p. 53.

35. "Hong Kong Jubilee: 21st–24th January, 1891," in *Fifty Years of Progress*, pp. 3–4.

36. "Hong Kong, 1841–1891," in *Fifty Years of Progress*, p. 6.

37. "The Jubilee Celebrations," in *Fifty Years of Progress*, p. 34.

38. Norton, "Hundred Years' Growth," p. 21; North's comments: "Centenary Messages," p. 29.

39. "Gejie mingliu," p. 21.

40. "Centenary Messages," p. 31.

41. Kotewall, "Anglo-Chinese Co-operation," pp. 46–47; "concerted efforts": Luo Xuhe [Lo Yuk-wo], "Zhong-Ying hezuo yu Xianggangbainian" [Anglo Chinese cooperation and Hong Kong's 100 years], in *Bainian shangye*, p. 7; integrity: "Centenary Messages," p. 45.

42. M. K. Lo, "Progress of Sport in Hong Kong," in *Commemorative Talks*, p. 88; M. K. Lo, "Chinese Turn to Sport," in *Hong Kong Centenary Number*, p. 90.

43. Kotewall, "Anglo-Chinese Co-operation," p. 47.

44. Lo, "Progress of Sport," p. 87; Norton, "Hundred Years' Growth," p. 21.

45. Lo, "Progress of Sport," pp. 84–86.

46. L. Forster, "The End of a Century: The Peaceful Progress of Hong Kong," *Hong Kong Daily Press*, Jan. 20, 1941, p. 7.

47. "Centenary Messages," pp. 31–32.

48. "Centenary Messages," p. 30.

49. Kotewall, "Anglo-Chinese Co-operation," p. 48; Li Jowson: "Gejie mingliu," p. 21.

50. "Centenary Messages," p. 31; "Gejie mingliu," p. 21.

51. "Centenary Messages," p. 31; "Gejie mingliu," p. 21.

52. Chen Datong, et al., *Xianggang Huaqiao tuanti zonglan* [Chinese organizations in Hong Kong] (Hong Kong: Guoji xinwenshe, 1947) n.p.; Norman J. Miners, *Hong Kong under Imperial Rule, 1912–1941* (Hong Kong: Oxford University Press, 1987), p. 63; Wu Xinglian [Woo Sing Lim], *Xianggang Huaren mingren shilue* [Prominent Chinese of Hong Kong] (Hong Kong: Wuzhou, 1937), p. 13.

53. Su Fuxiang, " 'Zhongxi hebi' di xianggang wenhua" [Hong Kong culture: the junction of East and West], in *Xianggang bainianshi*, pp. 168–169.

54. P. F. Cassidy, "Commercial History of Hong Kong: A Century of Trade," in *Commemorative Talks*, pp. 38–44.

55. "Hongkong, 1841–1891," p. 5.

56. "Hong Kong Jubilee," pp. 3–4.

57. Cassidy, "Commercial History," pp. 43–44.

58. Chow, "Octogenarian," p. 71; 97 percent of population: He Dong, "Shen Xianggang zaonian," p. 6; Robert Ho Tung, "Reminiscences of Hong Kong: A Personal Memory," in *Commemorative Talks*, pp. 72–73. Originally published as "Hong Kong's Grand Old Man," in *Centenary Number*, p. 32.

59. "Gejie mingliu," p. 21.

60. He Dong, "Shen Xianggang zaonian," p. 6; Ho Tung, "Reminiscences of Hong Kong," pp. 73–74.

61. Kotewall, "Anglo-Chinese Co-operation," p. 46.

62. Chow, "Octogenarian," p. 71.

63. "Centenary Messages," p. 34.

64. Kotewall, "Anglo-Chinese Co-operation," p. 49; Luo, "Zhong-Ying hezuo," p. 7.

65. "Gejie mingliu," p. 21.

66. Kotewall, "Anglo-Chinese Co-operation," pp. 47–48.

67. "Wu da Huazi gongsi shilue" [History of the five large Chinese companies], in *Xianggang bainianshi*, pp. 149–150; "Jijia Huazi gongsi shilue" [History of a few Chinese-capitalized companies], in *Bainian shangye*, n.p.

68. "Hangshang zhuanbian shi" [History of commercial changes], in *Bainian shangye*, pp. 33–42.

69. English sources: for example, "An Industrial Revolution," in *Centenary Number*, p. 54; "Colony's Premier Industry," in *Centenary Number*, pp. 44–46; negative terms: "An Industrial Revolution," p. 54.

70. Flourishing industry: "Xianggang Huazi gongye shi" [History of Chinese-capitalized industry in Hong Kong], in *Bainian shangye*, p. 42; exports: "Hangshang zhuanbianshi," p. 33.

71. "Xianggang Huazi gongyeshi," p. 42.

72. "Centenary Messages," p. 32; "Gejie mingliu," p. 21.

73. Kotewall, "Anglo-Chinese Co-operation," p. 47; Luo, "Zhong-Ying hezuo," p. 7.

74. "Centenary messages," p. 32.

75. Chen Zhao, "Guofu zai Xianggang" [The *Guofu* in Hong Kong], in *Xianggang bainianshi*, p. 29; Feng Ziyou, "Guofu zai xianggang zhi geming yundong" [Sun Yatsen's revolutionary activities in Hong Kong], in *Xianggang bainianshi*, pp. 30–31. On the 1911 revolution: Su Fuxiang, "Diyici shuangshi qingzhuhui" [The first celebration of Double Tenth], in *Xianggang bainianshi*, p. 18.

76. "Huaqiao bainian cishan shiye" [One hundred years of Huaqiao charitable and philanthropic activities], in *Bainian shangye*, p. 72.

77. "Qiaotuan shilue" [History of Chinese organizations], in *Bainian shangye*, p. 73.

78. "Gejie mingliu," p. 21.

79. Wang Xiaolai, "Gongshangye zai jinri" [Commerce and industry today], in *Bainian shangye*, p. 22.

80. Dialect: Chen Shifeng, "Xianggang fangyan de fuza" [The complexities of the Hong Kong dialect], in *Xianggang bainianshi*, p. 131. This notion of Hong Kong being culturally and linguistically different from any city in China is also borne out in Chinese guidebooks to Hong Kong. Apart from explaining the colony's laws and customs, these books often included lists of local Cantonese words and phrases. See, for example, *Xianggang daoyou* [Guide to Hong Kong] (Shanghai: Zhongguo luxing she, 1940), p. 125, and Chen Gongzhe, ed., *Xianggang zhinan* [Guide to Hong Kong] (Changsha: Shangwu, 1938), p. 179. On Laws and regulations: Su Fuxiang, "Xianggang lifaju" [Hong Kong's Legislative Council]; Yi Se, "Hunyin zhuceshu" [Wedding registration laws], both in *Xianggang bainianshi*, pp. 44, 62. On the legal system: "Falü ershiliu tiao" [Twenty-six laws], in *Xianggang bainianshi*, p. 58. On animal abuse: *Xianggang bainianshi*, p. 52.

81. Seth Harter, "Now and Then: The Loss of Coevalness Between Hong Kong and Guangdong," paper, Association for Asian Studies, Annual Meeting, Washington, DC, March 1998.

82. Bryna Goodman, "Improvisations on a Semicolonial Theme, or, How to Read Multiethnic Participation in the 1893 Shanghai Jubilee," *Journal of Asian Studies* 59.4 (November 2000): 889–926.

83. Goodman, "Improvisations," pp. 922–923.

Conclusion

1. This brief account of the Japanese occupation is based on G. B. Endacott, *Hong Kong Eclipse*, ed. Alan Birch (Hong Kong: Oxford University Press, 1978); Gao Tianqiang and Tang Zuomin, *Xianggang Rizhan shiqi* [Hong Kong under the Japanese occupation] (Hong Kong: Sanlian, 1995); Guan Lixiong, *Rizhan shiqi de Xianggang* [Hong Kong under the Japanese occupation] (Hong Kong: Sanlian, 1993); Henry J. Lethbridge, "Hong Kong under Japanese Occupation: Changes in Social Structure," in I. C. Jarvie and Joseph Agassi, eds., *Hong Kong: Society in Transition* (London: Routledge and Kegan Paul, 1969), pp. 77–127; and Philip Snow, *The Fall of Hong Kong: Britain, China, and the Japanese Occupation* (New Haven: Yale University Press, 2003).

2. Snow, *Fall of Hong Kong*, p. 161.

3. Ibid., pp. 107–108, 116.

4. Lethbridge, "Japanese Occupation," pp. 110–111.

5. Snow, *Fall of Hong Kong*, p. 130.

6. Ibid., pp. 164–165.

7. Endacott, *Hong Kong Eclipse*, p. 238.

8. North's account of the meeting with Chow and Kotewall is in *South China Morning Post*, Oct. 2, 1945.

9. Lethbridge, "Japanese Occupation," p. 99.

10. Snow, *Fall of Hong Kong*, p. 171.

11. Lethbridge, "Japanese Occupation," p. 117.

12. Snow, *Fall of Hong Kong*, p. 281.

13. Jürgen Osterhammel, *Colonialism: A Theoretical Overview*, trans. Shelley L. Frisch (Princeton: Marcus Wiener, 1997), p. 4.

14. Ibid., p. 15.

15. Ibid., pp. 45–46, 64. Original emphasis.

16. Ibid., p. 15. Original emphasis.

17. Frantz Fanon, *Black Skin, White Masks*, trans. Charles Lam Markmann (London: MacGibbon and Kee, 1952), and *The Wretched of the Earth*, trans. Constance Farrington (New York: Grove, 1961).

18. Frederick Cooper, "Conflict and Connection: Rethinking Colonial African History," *American Historical Review* 99.5 (December 1994): 1542.

19. Osterhammel, *Colonialism*, p. 111.

20. Nicholas Thomas, *Colonialism's Culture: Anthropology, Travel and Government* (Princeton: Princeton University Press, 1994), p. x.

21. For example, K. C. Fok, *Lectures on Hong Kong History: Hong Kong's Role in Modern Chinese History* (Hong Kong: Commercial Press, 1990); Huo Qichang (K. C. Fok), *Xianggang yu jindai Zhongguo* [Hong Kong and modern China] (Taipei: Shangwu yinshuguan, 1993).

22. Wong Hongzhi (Wang Wang-chi), *Lishi de chenzhong: Cong Xianggang kan Zhongguo de Xianggangshi lunshu* [The Burden of History: A Hong Kong Perspective of the Mainland Discourse of Hong Kong History] (Hong Kong: Oxford University Press, 2000), chapter 1.

23. For example, Nicholas Canny and Anthony Pagden, eds., *Colonial Identity in the Atlantic World, 1500–1800* (Princeton: Princeton University Press, 1987).

24. Robert Bickers, *Britain in China: Community, Culture and Colonialism, 1900–1949* (Manchester: Manchester University Press, 1999).

25. See, for example, Robert Bickers and Christian Henriot, eds., *New Frontiers: Imperialism's New Communities in East Asia, 1842–1953* (Manchester: Manchester University Press, 2000).

26. This point has been made by various observers, including Stephen Vines in *Hong Kong: China's New Colony* (London: Aurum Press, 1998), and William P. MacNeil in "Enjoy Your Rights! Three Cases from the Postcolonial Commonwealth," *Public Culture* 23 (1997): 381.

27. Lynn White and Li Cheng, "China Coast Identities: Regional, National, and Global," in Lowell Dittmer and Samuel S. Kim, eds., *China's Quest for National Identity* (Ithaca: Cornell University Press, 1993), p. 180.

28. Ibid., p. 183.

29. Ibid., p. 190.

Selected Bibliography

Abbas, Ackbar. *Hong Kong: The Culture of Disappearance*. Minneapolis: University of Minnesota Press, 1997.

Administrative Reports. Hong Kong: Government Printer, 1879–1939.

Allen, G. C., and Audrey G. Donnithorne. *Western Enterprise in Far Eastern Economic Development: China and Japan*. New York: Macmillan, 1954.

Altbach, Philip G., and Gail P. Kelly, eds. *Education and the Colonial Experience*. New Brunswick, NJ: Transaction, 1984.

Annual Report. Hong Kong: Government Printer, 1889–1927, 1931.

Bard, Solomon. *Traders of Hong Kong: Some Foreign Merchant Houses, 1841–1899*. Hong Kong: Urban Council, 1993.

Bayly, C. A. *Empire and Information: Intelligence Gathering and Social Communication in India, 1780–1870*. Cambridge: Cambridge University Press, 1996.

Benedict, Carol. "Framing Plague in China's Past." In Gail Hershatter, Emily Honig, Jonathan N. Lipman, and Randall Stross, eds., *Remapping China: Fissures in Historical Terrain*, pp. 27–41. Stanford: Stanford University Press, 1996.

Bergère, Marie-Claire. *The Golden Age of the Chinese Bourgeoisie, 1911–1937*. Trans. Janet Lloyd. Cambridge: Cambridge University Press, 1989.

Berncastle, Julius. *A Voyage to China: Including a Visit to the Bombay Presidency; the Mahratta Country; the Cave Temples of Western India, Singapore, the Straits of Malacca and Sunda, and the Cape of Good Hope*. 2 vols. London: William Shoberl, 1850.

Bhabha, Homi. *The Location of Culture*. London: Routledge, 1994.

Bickers, Robert. *Britain in China: Community, Culture, and Colonialism 1900–1949*. Manchester: Manchester University Press, 1999.

Bickers, Robert, and Christian Henriot, eds. *New Frontiers: Imperialism's New Communities in East Asia, 1842–1953*. Manchester: Manchester University Press, 2000.

Blue Book. Hong Kong: Noronha, 1871–1941.

Blussé, Leonard. *Strange Company: Chinese Settlers, Mestizo Women, and the Dutch in VOC Batavia*. Dordrecht, The Netherlands: Foris, 1986.

Bodnar, John. *Remaking America: Public Memory, Commemoration, and Patriotism in the Twentieth Century*. Princeton: Princeton University Press, 1991.

Bordieu, Pierre. "Sport and Social Class." In Chandra Mukerji and Michael Schudson, eds., *Rethinking Popular Culture: Contemporary Perspectives in Cultural Studies*, pp. 357–373. Berkeley: University of California Press, 1991.

Brook, Timothy, and Bob Tadashi Wakabayashi, eds. *Opium Regimes: China, Britain, and Japan, 1839–1952*. Berkeley: University of California Press, 2000.

Burt, A. R., J. B. Powell, and C. Crow, eds. *Biographies of Prominent Chinese*. Shanghai: Biographical Publishing Co., 1925.

Cai Luo, et al. *Shenggang da bagong* (The Canton-Hong Kong general strike). n.p., 1980.

Cai Rongfang [Jung-fang Tsai]. *Xianggang ren zhi Xianggang shi, 1841–1945* [The Hong Kong People's History of Hong Kong, 1841–1945]. Hong Kong: Oxford University Press, 2001.

Cannadine, David. *Ornamentalism: How the British Saw Their Empire*. Oxford: Oxford University Press, 2001.

Canton Press. 1841–1844.

Cao Shanyun boshi shizhui silu [Biography of the late Dr. Cao Shanyun (Tso Seen Wan)]. Hong Kong: Qiaosheng chubanshe, 1956.

Carnoy, Martin. *Education as Cultural Imperialism*. New York: Longman, 1974.

Carroll, John M. "Colonialism and Collaboration: Chinese Subjects and the Making of British Hong Kong." *China Information* 12.1/2 (Summer/Autumn 1997): 12–35.

Cashman, Richard. *Patrons, Players, and the Crowd: The Phenomenon of Indian Cricket*. New Delhi: Longman Orient, 1980.

Chadourne, Marc. *China*. Trans. Harry Block. New York: Covici Friede, 1932.

Chan, Ming K. "All in the Family: The Hong Kong-Guangdong Link in Historical Perspective." In Reginald Yin-Wang Kwok and Alvin Y. So, eds., *The Hong Kong-Guangdong Link: Partnership in Flux*, pp. 31–63. Armonk, New York: M. E. Sharpe, 1995.

——. "Labor and Empire: The Chinese Labor Movement in the Canton Delta, 1895–1927." Ph.D. diss., Stanford University, 1975.

——. "The Legacy of the British Administration of Hong Kong: A View from Hong Kong." *China Quarterly* 151 (September 1997): 567–582.

——. "Stability and Prosperity in Hong Kong: The Twilight of Laissez-faire Colonialism?" *Journal of Asian Studies* 42.3 (May 1983): 589–598.

Chan, Ming K., ed. *Precarious Balance: Hong Kong Between China and Britain, 1842–1992*. Armonk, New York: M. E. Sharpe, 1994.

Chan, Wai Kwan. *The Making of Hong Kong Society: Three Studies of Class Formation in Early Hong Kong*. Oxford: Clarendon Press, 1991.

Chan, Wellington K. K. "The Organizational Structure of the Traditional Chinese Firm and Its Modern Reform." *Business History Review* 56.2 (Summer 1982): 218–235.

Chan Lau, Kit-ching. *China, Britain and Hong Kong, 1895–1945*. Hong Kong: Chinese University Press, 1990.

Chang, Hao. "Intellectual Change and the Reform Movement, 1890–8." In John K. Fairbank, ed., *The Cambridge History of China*. Vol. 11, pp. 274–338. Cambridge: Cambridge University Press, 1980.

Chatterjee, Partha. *The Nation and Its Fragments: Colonial and Postcolonial Histories.* Princeton: Princeton University Press, 1993.

Chaturvedi, Vinayak, ed. *Mapping Subaltern Studies and the Postcolonial.* London: Verso, 2000.

Chen Datong, comp. *Bainian shangye* [A Century of Commerce]. Hong Kong: Guangming wenhua shiye gongsi, 1941.

Chen Datong, et al. *Xianggang Huaqiao tuanti zonglan* [Overseas Chinese organizations in Hong Kong]. Hong Kong: Guoji xinwenshe, 1947.

Chen Gongzhe, ed. *Xianggang zhinan* [Guide to Hong Kong]. Changsha: Shangwu yinshuguan, 1938.

Chen Mingqiu [Ming K. Chan]. "Gang-Ying huanghun jin, luori Xiangjiang hong: zhimindi buganyu zhuyi de moluo" [British Sunset in Hong Kong: The demise of colonial nonintervention]. *Xinbao yuekan* [Hong Kong Economic Journal Monthly] 130 (January 1988): 36–42.

Chen Qian. "Xianggang jiushi jianwen lu (1)" [Recollections of old Hong Kong, part 1]. *Guangdong wenshi ziliao* 41 (1984): 1–34.

———. "Xianggang jiushi jianwen lu (3)" [Recollections of old Hong Kong, part 3]. *Guangdong wenshi ziliao* 46 (1985): 3–76.

———. "Xianggang jiushi jianwen lu (4)" [Recollections of old Hong Kong, part 4]. *Guangdong wenshi ziliao* 47 (1986): 1–42.

Cheng, Irene. *Clara Ho Tung: A Hong Kong Lady, Her Family and Her Times.* Hong Kong: Chinese University Press, 1976.

China Directory. 1861–1874. Hong Kong: A. Shortrede, 1861–1874.

China Mail. 1845–1865.

China Mail. *Hong Kong Centenary Number.* 20 January 1941.

Chiu, Fred Y. L. "Politics and the Body Social in Colonial Hong Kong." In Tani E. Barlow, ed., *Formation of Colonial Modernity in East Asia*, pp. 295–322. Durham: Duke University Press, 1997.

Choa, Gerald H. *The Life and Times of Sir Kai Ho Kai.* Hong Kong: Chinese University Press, 1981.

Chung, Stephanie Po-yin. *Chinese Business Groups in Hong Kong and Political Change in South China, 1900–25.* Basingstoke, Eng.: Macmillan, 1998.

Clarke, Colin G. "A Caribbean Creole Capital: Kingston, Jamaica (1692–1938)." In Robert Ross and Gerald J. Telkamp, eds., *Colonial Cities: Essays on Urbanism in a Colonial Context*, p. 153–170. Leiden: Martinus Nijhoff, for Leiden University Press, 1985.

Clementi, Cecil. Diary Letters of Sir Cecil Clementi, 1925–1927. Public Records Office of Hong Kong. Microfilm.

Cohen, Paul A. *Between Tradition and Modernity: Wang T'ao and Reform in Late Ch'ing China.* Cambridge, Mass.: Harvard University Press, 1974.

———. "Littoral and Hinterland in Nineteenth-Century China: The 'Christian' Reformers." In John K. Fairbank, ed., *The Missionary Enterprise in China and America*, pp. 197–230. Cambridge, Mass.: Harvard University Press, 1974.

Cohn, Bernard S. *Colonialism and Its Forms of Knowledge: The British in India.* Princeton: Princeton University Press, 1996.

Commercial and Industrial Hong Kong: A Record of 94 Years Progress of the Colony in Commerce, Trade, Industry, and Shipping (1841–1935). Hong Kong: Bedikton, 1935.

Connerton, Paul. *How Societies Remember.* Cambridge: Cambridge University Press, 1989.

Cooper, Frederick. "Conflict and Connection: Rethinking Colonial African History." *American Historical Review* 99.5 (December 1994): 1516–1545.

Cooper, Frederick, and Ann Laura Stoler, eds. *Tensions of Empire: Colonial Cultures in a Bourgeois World.* Berkeley: University of California Press, 1997.

Cree, Edward H. *The Cree Journals: The Voyage of Edward H. Cree, Surgeon R. N., as Related in His Private Journals, 1837–1856.* Ed. Michael Levien. Exeter, Eng.: Webb and Bower, 1981.

Crisswell, Colin N. *The Taipans: Hong Kong's Merchant Princes.* Hong Kong: Oxford University Press, 1981.

Cunynghame, Arthur. *The Opium War; Being Recollections of Service in China.* London: Saunders and Otely, 1844.

Des Voeux, G. William. *My Colonial Service in British Guiana, St. Lucia, Trinidad, Fiji, Australia, Newfoundland, and Hong Kong with Interludes.* 2 vols. London: John Murray, 1903.

Ding Xinbao [Ting Sun Pao, Joseph]. "Xianggang zaoqi zhi Huaren shehui, 1841–1870" [Early Chinese Community in Hong Kong, 1841–1870]. Ph.D. diss., University of Hong Kong, 1989.

Ding You. *Xianggang chuqi shihua* [Early Hong Kong]. Beijing: Lianhe chubanshe, 1983.

Dirlik, Arif. "Chinese History and the Question of Orientalism." *History and Theory* 35.4 (December 1995): 96–120.

Dirks, Nicholas B. "Colonialism and Culture." In Nicholas B. Dirks, ed., *Colonialism and Culture*, pp. 1–25. Ann Arbor: University of Michigan Press, 1992.

Eastman, Lloyd E. "Political Reformism in China before the Sino-Japanese War." *Journal of Asian Studies* 27.4 (August 1968): 695–710.

Eitel, E. J. *Europe in China: The History of Hong Kong from the Beginning to the Year 1882.* Hong Kong: Kelly and Walsh, 1895. Reprint, Hong Kong: Oxford University Press, 1983.

Endacott, G. B. *An Eastern Entrepot: A Collection of Documents Illustrating the History of Hong Kong.* London: Her Majesty's Stationery Office, 1964.

——. *Government and People in Hong Kong, 1841–1962: A Constitutional History.* Hong Kong: Hong Kong University Press, 1964.

——. *A History of Hong Kong.* Rev. ed. Hong Kong: Oxford University Press, 1973.

——. *Hong Kong Eclipse.* Ed. Alan Birch. Hong Kong: Oxford University Press, 1978.

Evans, Dafydd Emrys. "Chinatown in Hong Kong: The Beginnings of Taipingshan." *Journal of the Hong Kong Branch of the Royal Asiatic Society* 10 (1970): 69–78.

——. "The Foundation of Hong Kong: A Chapter of Accidents." In Marjorie Topley, ed., *Hong Kong: The Interaction of Traditions and Life in the Towns*, pp. 11–41. Hong Kong: Hong Kong Branch of the Royal Asiatic Society, 1975.

Fairbank, John King. *Trade and Diplomacy on the China Coast: The Opening of the Treaty Ports, 1842–1854.* 2 vols. 1953. Reprinted as 1 vol., Cambridge, Mass.: Harvard University Press, 1964.

Fang Hanqi. "Yiba basi nian Xianggang renmin fandi douzheng" [The 1884 Hong Kong popular anti-imperialist struggle]. *Jindai shi ziliao* 6 (1957): 20–30.

Fang Meixian [Fong, Mee-yin]. *Xianggang zaoqi jiaoyu fazhan shi* [The First Hundred Years of Hong Kong Education]. Hong Kong: Zhongguo xueshe, 1975.

Feldwick, W. *Present Day Impressions of the Far East and Prominent Chinese at Home and Abroad: The History, People, Commerce, Industries, and Resources of China, Hongkong, Indo-China, Malaya, and Netherlands India.* London: Globe Encyclopaedia, 1917.

Feng Bangyan. *Xianggang Huazi caituan,* 1841–1996 [Chinese financial organizations in Hong Kong, 1841–1997]. Hong Kong: Sanlian, 1997.

——. *Xianggang Yingzi caituan,* 1841–1996 [British financial organizations in Hong Kong, 1841–1996]. Hong Kong: Sanlian, 1996.

Feng Ziyou. *Zhongguo geming yundong ershiliunian zuzhishi* [Twenty-six years of Chinese revolutionary history]. Shanghai: Commercial Press, 1948.

Fok, K. C. *Lectures on Hong Kong History: Hong Kong's Role in Modern Chinese History.* Hong Kong: Commercial Press, 1990.

Fortune, Robert. *Three Years' Wanderings in the Northern Provinces of China, Including a Visit to the Tea, Silk, and Cotton Countries: With an Account of Agriculture and Horticulture of the Chinese, New Plants, etc.* London: J. Murray, 1847.

Friend of China. 1842–1869.

Gan Tian. *Xianggang da bagong* [The great Hong Kong strike]. Beijing: n.p., 1956.

Gao Tianqiang and Tang Zuomin. *Xianggang Rizhan shiqi* [Hong Kong under the Japanese occupation]. Hong Kong: Sanlian, 1995.

Gillingham, Paul. *At the Peak: Hong Kong Between the Wars.* Hong Kong: Macmillan, 1983.

Gillis, John R., ed. *Commemorations: The Politics of National Identity.* Princeton: Princeton University Press, 1994.

Goodman, Bryna. "Improvisations on a Semicolonial Theme, or, How to Read Multiethnic Participation in the 1893 Shanghai Jubilee." *Journal of Asian Studies* 59.4 (November 2000): 889–926.

——. *Native Place, City, and Nation: Regional Networks and Identities in Shanghai, 1853–1937.* Berkeley: University of California Press, 1995.

Grantham, Alexander. *Via Ports: From Hong Kong to Hong Kong.* Hong Kong: Hong Kong University Press, 1965.

Great Britain, Colonial Office. Original Correspondence: Hong Kong, 1841–1951, Series 129 (CO129). London: Public Record Office.

——. Executive and Legislative Council Minutes: Hong Kong (from 1844), Series 131 (CO 131). London: Public Record Office.

Great Britain, Foreign Office. General Correspondence: China, 1815–1905, Series 17 (FO 17). London: Public Record Office.

——. Records of Letters between the Plenipotentiary and the High Provincial Authorities, and Proclamations by H. E. the Governor and Chief Magistrate, 1844–1849, Series 233 (FO 233). London: Public Record Office.

Great Britain, Office of the Commercial Attaché, Shanghai. *List of the Principal*

Foreign and Chinese Industrial Enterprises in China and Hong Kong. Shanghai: Kelly and Walsh, 1918.

Guan Lixiong. *Rizhan shiqi de Xianggang* [Hong Kong under the Japanese Occupation]. Hong Kong: Sanlian, 1993.

Guha, Ranajit, and Gayatri Chakravorty Spivak, eds. *Selected Subaltern Studies.* New York: Oxford University Press, 1988.

Gützlaff, Karl F. A. *Journal of Three Voyages Along the Coast of China in 1831, 1832, and 1833, with Notices of Siam, Corea, and the Loo-choo Islands.* London: Frederick Westley and A. H. Davis 1834.

Hamilton, Gary G., ed. *Cosmopolitan Capitalists: Hong Kong and the Chinese Diaspora at the End of the 20th Century.* Seattle: University of Washington Press, 1999.

Hao, Yen-p'ing. *The Commercial Revolution in Nineteenth-Century China: The Rise of Sino Western Mercantile Capitalism.* Berkeley: University of California Press, 1986.

———. *The Comprador in Nineteenth Century China: Bridge Between East and West.* Cambridge, Mass.: Harvard University Press, 1970.

Harter, Seth. "Now and Then: The Loss of Coevalness Between Hong Kong and Guangdong." Paper, annual meeting of the Association for Asian Studies, Washington, DC, 1998.

Hayes, James. "The Nam Pak Hong Commercial Association of Hong Kong." *Journal of the Hong Kong Branch of the Royal Asiatic Society* 19 (1979): 216–226.

He Wenxiang. *Xianggang jiazushi* [History of Hong Kong families]. Hong Kong: Mingbao chubanshe, 1992.

Hershatter, Gail. "The Subaltern Talks Back: Reflections on Subaltern Theory and Chinese History." *positions* 1.1 (Spring 1993): 103–130.

Hevia, James L. *Cherishing Men from Afar: Qing Guest Ritual and the Macartney Embassy of 1793.* Durham: Duke University Press, 1995.

———. *English Lessons: The Pedagogy of Imperialism in Nineteenth-Century China.* Durham: Duke University Press, 2003.

Historical and Statistical Abstract of the Colony of Hong Kong, 1841–1930. Hong Kong: Noronha, 1932.

History of the Ladies Recreation Club. Hong Kong: n.p., 1960.

Hoe, Susanna. *The Private Life of Old Hong Kong: Western Women in the British Colony.* Hong Kong: Oxford University Press, 1991.

Hong Kong Annual Administration Reports, 1841–1941. Ed. R. L. Jarman. Vol. 1: 1841–1886. Oxford: Archive Editions, 1996.

Hong Kong Centenary Commemorative Talks, 1841–1941. Hong Kong: World News Service, 1941.

Hong Kong Civil Service List. Hong Kong: Noronha, 1904–1958.

Hong Kong Government Gazette. Hong Kong: Noronha, 1853–1941.

Hong Kong Hansard: Reports of the Meetings of the Legislative Council of Hong Kong. Hong Kong: Noronha, 1890–1941.

Hong Kong Legislative Council Sessional Papers. Hong Kong: Noronha, 1884–1941.

Hong Kong: A Short History of the Colony and an Outline of the Present Political Situation in China. Hong Kong: Publicity Bureau for South China, 1928.

Hong Kong Almanack and Directory for 1846. Hong Kong: China Mail, 1846.

Hong Kong Club. *Articles of Association of the Hongkong Club.* Hong Kong: Noronha, 1924.

Hong Kong Daily Press. 1857–1941.

Hong Kong Daily Press. *Fifty Years of Progress: The Jubilee of Hongkong as a British Crown Colony, Being an Historical Sketch to Which is Added an Account of the Celebrations of 21st to 24th January, 1891.* Hong Kong: Hong Kong Daily Press, 1891.

Hong Kong Register. 1844–1863.

Hostetler, Laura. *Qing Colonial Enterprise: Ethnography and Cartography in Early Modern China.* Chicago: Unversity of Chicago Press, 2001.

Hsu, Immanuel C. Y. "Late Ch'ing Foreign Relations, 1866–1905." In John K. Fairbank, ed., *The Cambridge History of China.* Vol. 11, pp. 71–141. Cambridge: Cambridge University Press, 1980.

Hu Bin. *Zhongguo jindai gailiang zhuyi sixiang* [Reformist thought in modern China]. Beijing: Zhonghua shuju, 1964.

Hu Liyuan. *Hu Yinan xiansheng quanji* [Complete works of Hu Yinan (Hu Liyuan)]. 60 vols. Hong Kong: n.p., 1917. Reprinted in Shen Yunlong, ed., *Jindai Zhongguo shiliao congkan xubian* (Reprinted materials on modern Chinese history, supplementary edition), vols. 261–266. Taipei: Wenhai chubanshe 1975.

Hu Shi. *Nanyou zayi* [Memories of my trip south]. Taipei: Qiming shuju, 1959.

Huang Yifeng. "Diguo zhuyi qinlue Zhongguo diyige zhongyao zhizhu: maiban jieji" [One important pillar of the imperialist invasion of China: the comprador class]. *Lishi yanjiu* 91 (1965): 55–70.

———. "Guanyu jiu Zhongguo maiban jieji de yanjiu" [Research on the comprador class in old China]. *Lishi yanjiu* 87 (1964): 89–116.

Huang Yifeng, et al. *Jiu zhongguo de maiban jieji* [The comprador class in old China]. Shanghai: Renmin chubanshe, 1982.

Hughes, Richard. *Hong Kong: Borrowed Place, Borrowed Time.* London: André Deutsch, 1968.

Hunter, William C. *The "Fan Kwae" at Canton before Treaty Days, 1825–1844.* London: Kegan Paul, Trench, and Co., 1882.

Huo Qichang. "Xianggang Huaren zai jindaishi dui Zhongguo de gongxian shixi" [The contributions of Hong Kong Chinese to modern China]. *Haiwai Huaren yanjiu* 1 (1989): 81–88.

———. *Xianggang yu jindai Zhongguo* [Hong Kong and modern China]. Taipei: Shangwu yinshuguan, 1993.

Hurley, R. C. *Picturesque Hong Kong: A British-Crown-Colony and Dependencies.* Hong Kong: Commercial Press, 1925.

"Interview with Dr. B. Kotewall by Dr. Alan Birch." N.d., Public Records Office of Hong Kong.

Irish University Press Area Studies Series. *British Parliamentary Papers, China, 24: Correspondence, Dispatches, Reports, Ordinances, Memoranda, and Other Papers Relating to the Affairs of Hong Kong, 1846–60.* Shannon: Irish University Press, 1971.

Irish University Press Area Studies Series. *British Parliamentary Papers, China, 25: Correspondence, Dispatches, Reports, Returns, Memorials, and other Papers Re-*

specting the Affairs of Hong Kong, 1862–81. Shannon: Irish University Press, 1971.

Jiang Zulu and Fang Zhiqian, eds. *Jianming Guangdongshi* [Concise history of Guangdong]. Guangzhou: Guangdong renmin chubanshe, 1993.

"Jijia Huazi baihuo gongsi" [Several Chinese department stores]. In *Xianggang shangyelu* [Hong Kong commercial directory], p. 13. Hong Kong: Zhonghua xinwenshe, 1948.

Jingji ziliaoshi, comp. *Xianggang gongshang shouce* [Hong Kong commercial and industrial guide]. Hong Kong: n.p., 1947.

Johnson, James D. *China and Japan: Being a Narrative of the Cruise of the U.S. Steam Frigate Powhatan, in the Years 1857, '58, '59, and '60*. Philadelphia: Charles DeSilver, 1860.

Kennedy, Dane. "Imperial History and Post-Colonial Theory." *Journal of Imperial and Commonwealth History* 24.3 (September 1996): 345–363.

———. *Islands of White: Settler Society and Culture in Kenya and Southern Rhodesia, 1890–1939*. Durham: Duke University Press, 1987.

———. *The Magic Mountains: Hill Stations and the British Raj*. Berkeley: University of California Press, 1996.

King, Anthony D. "Culture, Social Power and Environment: The Hill Station in Colonial Urban Development." *Social Action* 26.3 (July–September 1976): 195–213.

King, Frank H. H. *The History of the Hongkong and Shanghai Banking Corporation*. 4 vols. Cambridge: Cambridge University Press, 1987–1990.

———. *Survey our Empire! Robert Montgomery Martin (1801?–1868): A Bio-Bibliography*. Hong Kong: Centre of Asian Studies, University of Hong Kong, 1979.

Kratoska, Paul H., ed. *Honourable Intentions: Talks on the British Empire in South-East Asia Delivered at the Royal Colonial Institute, 1874–1928*. Singapore: Oxford University Press, 1983.

Kung Sheung Yat Po (Gongshang ribao [Commercial Press]). 1925–1926.

Kwan, Daniel Y. K. *Marxist Intellectuals and the Chinese Labor Movement: A Study of Deng Zhongxia (1894–1933)*. Seattle: University of Washington Press, 1997.

The Ladies' Recreation Club, 1883–1983. Hong Kong: Ladies' Recreation Club, 1983.

Larson, Pier M. " 'Capacities and Modes of Thinking': Intellectual Engagements and Subaltern Hegemony in the Early History of Malagasy Christianity." *American Historical Review* 102.4 (October 1997): 969–1002.

Lau, Siu-kai. *Society and Politics in Hong Kong*. Hong Kong: Chinese University Press, 1982.

———. *Utilitarianistic Familism: An Inquiry into the Basis of Political Stability in Hong Kong*. Hong Kong: Chinese University of Hong Kong Social Research Centre, 1977.

Leeming, Frank. "The Earlier Industrialization of Hong Kong." *Modern Asian Studies* 9.3 (1975): 337–342.

Lethbridge, Henry J. *Hong Kong: Stability and Change: A Collection of Essays*. Hong Kong: Oxford University Press, 1978.

———. "Hong Kong under Japanese Occupation: Changes in Social Structure." In I. C. Jarvie and Joseph Agassi, eds., *Hong Kong: Society in Transition*, pp. 77–127. London: Routledge and Kegan Paul, 1969.

Létourneau, Jocelyn. "The Current Great Narrative of Québecois Identity." In V. Y. Mudimbe, ed., *Nations, Identities, Cultures,* pp. 59–73. Durham: Duke University Press, 1997.

Levine, Philippa. "Modernity, Medicine, and Colonialism: The Contagious Diseases Ordinances in Hong Kong and the Straits Settlements." *positions* 6:3 (Winter 1998): 675–705.

Li Jiayuan. *Xianggang baoye zatan* [On the Hong Kong Press]. Hong Kong: Joint Publishing, 1989.

Li Jinwei, ed. *Xianggang bainianshi* [Centenary history of Hong Kong]. Hong Kong: Nanzhong chubanshe, 1948.

Li Minren. "Yiba basi nian Xianggang bagong yundong" [The 1884 Hong Kong strike movement]. *Lishi yanjiu* 3 (March 1958): 89–90.

Li Zhaohuan. "Huaqiao ziben de wujia yinhang" [Five overseas Chinese-capitalized banks]. *Guangdong wenshi ziliao* 8 (1963): 133–138.

Lin Ling. "Wo suo zhidao de Xianggang *Gongshang ribao*" [What I know about the Hong Kong *Gongshang ribao* (*Kung Sheung Yat Po*)]. *Guangdong wenshi ziliao* 51 (1987): 105–111.

Lin Youlan. *Xianggang shihua, zengding ben* [Stories of Hong Kong, revised edition]. Hong Kong: Shanghai shudian, 1985.

Liu Fuzong, et al. *Liugong Zhubo xingshu* [Biography of the late Mr. Liu Zhubo (Lau Chu Pak)]. Hong Kong: n.p., 1922.

Liu Shuyong, ed. *Jianming Xianggangshi* [Concise history of Hong Kong]. Hong Kong: Joint Publishing, 1998.

Lo, Hsiang-lin. *Hong Kong and Its External Communications Before 1842: The History of Hong Kong Prior to the British Arrival.* Hong Kong: Institute of Chinese Culture, 1963.

———. *The Role of Hong Kong in the Cultural Interchange Between East and West.* Tokyo: Centre for East Asian Studies, 1963.

Loomba, Ania. *Colonialism/Postcolonialism.* London: Routledge, 1998.

Lu Yan, et al. *Xianggang zhanggu* [Hong Kong anecdotes]. 12 vols. Hong Kong: Guangjiaojing chubanshe, 1977–1989.

Luk, Bernard Hung-kay. "Chinese Culture in the Hong Kong Curriculum: Heritage and Colonialism." *Comparative Education Review* 35.4 (November 1991): 650–668.

Luo Xianglin. *Xianggang yu Zhong-Xi wenhua zhi jiaoliu* [The Role of Hong Kong in the Cultural Interchange Between East and West]. Hong Kong: Zhongguo xueshe, 1961.

———. *Yiba siyi nian yiqian zhi Xianggang ji qi duiwai jiaotong* [Hong Kong's overseas relations before 1841]. Hong Kong: Zhongguo xueshe 1963.

Lutz, Jessie G. "Karl F. A. Gützlaff: Missionary Entrepreneur." In Suzanne Wilson Barnett and John King Fairbank, eds., *Christianity in China: Early Protestant Missionary Writings,* pp. 61–87. Cambridge, Mass.: Harvard University, Council on East Asian Studies, 1985.

Ma Hongshu, and Chen Zhenming. *Xianggang Huaqiao jiaoyu* [Chinese education in Hong Kong]. Taipei: Haiwai chubanshe, 1958.

Ma Yinchu. "Zhongguo zhi maiban zhidu" [The comprador system in China]. *Dongfang zazhi (Eastern Miscellany)* 20.6 (March 1923): 129–132.

Ma Yingbiao xiansheng jianshi [Brief history of Mr. Ma Yingbiao]. Guangzhou: Guangdongsheng gongansi faguanli ganbu xueyuan, 1986.

MacKenzie, John M. *Orientalism: History, Theory and the Arts.* Manchester: Manchester University Press, 1995.

———. *Propaganda and Empire: The Manipulation of British Public Opinion, 1880–1960.* Manchester: Manchester University Press, 1984.

MacNeil, William P. "Enjoy Your Rights! Three Cases from the Postcolonial Commonwealth." *Public Culture* 23 (1997): 377–393.

Mangan, J. A. *The Games Ethic: Aspects of the Diffusion of an Ideal.* New York: Viking, 1986.

Mangan, J. A., ed. *Pleasure, Profit, Proselytism: British Culture and Sport at Home and Abroad, 1700–1914.* London: Frank Cass, 1988.

Marshall, J. F. *Whereon the Wild Thyme Flows: Some Memoirs of Service with the Hongkong Bank.* Surrey, England: Token, 1986.

Mathews, Gordon. "Heunggongyahn: On the Past, Present, and Future of Hong Kong Identity." *Bulletin of Concerned Asian Scholars* 29.3 (1997): 3–13.

Mayers, William Fred, N. B. Dennys, and Charles King. *The Treaty Ports of China and Japan: A Complete Guide to the Open Ports of those Countries, Together with Peking, Yedo, Hongkong, and Macao.* Hong Kong: A. Shortrede, 1867.

Mei, June. "Socioeconomic Origins of Emigration: Guangdong to California, 1850–1882." *Modern China* 5.4 (October 1979): 463–501.

Mills, Lennox A. *British Rule in Eastern Asia: A Study of Contemporary Government and Economic Development in British Malaya and Hong Kong.* London: Oxford University Press, 1942.

Millward, James A. *Beyond the Pass: Economy, Ethnicity, and Empire in Qing Central Asia, 1759–1864.* Stanford University Press, 1998.

Miners, Norman J. *Hong Kong under Imperial Rule, 1912–1941.* Hong Kong: Oxford University Press, 1987.

Mitchell, Timothy. *Colonising Egypt.* Berkeley: University of California Press, 1988; Cambridge: Cambridge University Press, 1991.

Mongia, Padmini, ed. *Contemporary Postcolonial Theory.* London: Arnold, 1996.

Morgan, Philip D. "Encounters between British and 'Indigenous' Peoples, c. 1500–c.1800." In Martin Daunton and Rick Halpern, eds., *Empire and Others: British Encounters with Indigenous Peoples, 1600–1850*, pp. 42–78. London: University College of London Press, 1999.

Morris, Jan. *The Spectacle of Empire: Style, Effect, and the Pax Brittanica.* London: Doubleday, 1982.

Munn, Christopher. *Anglo-China: Chinese People and British Rule in Hong Kong, 1841–1880.* Richmond, Surrey, Eng.: Curzon Press, 2001.

———. "The Chusan Episode: Britain's Occupation of a Chinese Island, 1840–46," *Journal of Imperial and Commonwealth History* 25.1 (January 1997): 82–112.

Murray, Dian. *Pirates of the South China Coast, 1790–1810.* Stanford: Stanford University Press, 1987.

Nanbeihang gongsuo chengli yibai zhounian jinian tekan [Commemorative edition of the hundredth anniversary of the Nam Pak Hong]. Hong Kong: n.p., 1968.

Nanbeihang gongsuo xinxia luocheng ji chengli bashiliu zhounian jinian tekan [Commemorative edition of the completion of the new building and the eighty-sixth anniversary of the Nam Pak Hong]. Hong Kong: 1954.

Nanhua tiyuhui bashi zhounian jinian tekan[South China Athletic Association Eightieth Anniversary]. Hong Kong: n.p., 1990.

Nanhua tiyuhui qishi zhounian jinian tekan [South China Athletic Association Seventieth Anniversary]. Hong Kong: n.p., 1980.

Nanhua tiyuhui liushi zhounian jinian tekan [South China Athletic Association Sixtieth Anniversary]. Hong Kong: n.p., 1970.

Ng, Alice Lun Ngai Ha. *Interactions East and West: Development of Public Education in Early Hong Kong*. Hong Kong: Chinese University Press, 1984.

Ng, Peter Y. C., and Hugh D. R. Baker. *New Peace County: A Chinese Gazetteer of Hong Kong Region*. Hong Kong: Hong Kong University Press, 1983.

Ngo, Tak-Wing, ed. *Hong Kong's History: State and Society under Colonial Rule*. London: Routledge, 1999.

Nie Baozhang. "Cong Meishang Qichang lunchuan gongsi de chuangban yu fazhan kan maiban de zuoyong" [The function of the comprador seen though the history and development of the American Shanghai Steam Navigation Company]. *Lishi yanjiu* 86 (1964): 91–110.

———. *Zhongguo maiban zichanjieji de fasheng* [The emergence of the Chinese comprador class]. Beijing: Zhongguo shehui kexue chubanshe, 1979.

Norton-Kyshe, James William. *The History of the Laws and Courts of Hong Kong*. 2 vols. Hong Kong: Noronha and Company, 1898.

Ong, Aihwa. *Flexible Citizenship: The Cultural Logics of Transnationality*. Durham: Duke University Press, 1999.

Ong, Aihwa, and Donald M. Nonini. "Chinese Transnationalism as an Alternative Modernity." In Aihwa Ong and Donald M. Nonini, eds., *Ungrounded Empires: The Cultural Politics of Modern Chinese Nationalism*, pp. 3–33. New York: Routledge, 1997.

Osterhammel, Jürgen. *Colonialism: A Theoretical Overview*. Trans. Shelley L. Frisch. Princeton: Marcus Wiener, 1997.

Ouchterlony, John. *The Chinese War: An Account of All the Operations of the British Forces from the Commencement to the Treaty of Nanking*. London: Saunders and Otley, 1844.

Pennycook, Alastair. *The Cultural Politics of English as an International Language*. London: Longman, 1994.

Pope-Hennessy, James. *Half-Crown Colony: A Hong Kong Notebook*. London: Jonathan Cape, 1969.

Porter, Jonathan. *Macau: The Imaginary City*. Boulder: Westview Press, 1996.

Rabushka, Alvin. *Hong Kong: A Study in Economic Freedom*. Chicago: University of Chicago Press, 1979.

Ren Jiyu. "He Qi, Hu Liyuan de gailiang zhuyi sixiang" [The reformist thought of He Qi and Hu Liyuan]. In Feng Youlan, ed., *Zhongguo jindai sixiang shi lunwen ji* [Essays on modern Chinese thought]. Shanghai: Renmin chubanshe, 1958.

Report of the Special Committee Appointed by His Excellency Sir William Robinson, &c., to Investigate and Report on Certain Points Connected with the Bill for the Incorporation of the Po Leung Kuk, or Society for the Protection of Women and Girls, Together with the Evidence Taken before the Committee and an Appendix Containing Correspondence, Reports, Returns, &c. Hong Kong: Noronha, 1893.

Richards, Thomas. *The Imperial Archive: Knowledge and the Fantasy of Empire.* London: Verso, 1993.

Robinson, Ronald. "Non-European Foundations of European Imperialism: Sketch for a Theory of Collaboration." In Roger Owen and Bob Sutcliffe, eds., *Studies in the Theory of Imperialism*, pp. 117–142. London: Longman, 1972.

Rowe, William T. *Hankow: Commerce and Society in a Chinese City, 1796–1889.* Stanford: Stanford University Press, 1984.

———. *Hankow: Conflict and Community in a Chinese City, 1796–1895.* Stanford: Stanford University Press, 1989.

Ruan Rou. *Xianggang jiaoyu: Xianggang jiaoyu zhidu zhi shi de yanjiu* [Historical study of the educational system of Hong Kong]. Hong Kong: Jinbu jiaoyu chubanshe, 1948.

Said, Edward. *Orientalism: Western Conceptions of the Orient.* New York: Pantheon, 1978.

Sayer, Geoffrey Robley. *Hong Kong: Birth, Adolescence, and Coming of Age, 1841–1862.* London: Oxford University Press, 1937.

———. *Hong Kong 1862–1919: Years of Discretion.* Hong Kong: Hong Kong University Press, 1975.

Schiffrin, Harold Z. *Sun Yat-sen and the Origins of the Chinese Revolution.* Berkeley: University of California Press, 1968.

Sen, Sadatru. "Chameleon Games: Ranjitsinhji's Politics of Race and Gender." *Journal of Colonialism and Colonial History* 2.3 (2001): 1–98 (electronic journal).

Sha Weikai. *Zhongguo zhi maiban zhi* [The comprador system in China]. Shanghai: Shangwu yinshuguan, 1927.

Sinn, Elizabeth. "Fugitive in Paradise: Wang Tao and Cultural Transformation in Late Nineteenth Century Hong Kong." *Late Imperial China* 19.1 (1998): 56–81.

———. *Growing with Hong Kong: The Bank of East Asia, 1919–1994.* Hong Kong: Bank of East Asia, 1994.

———. *Power and Charity: The Early History of the Tung Wah Hospital, Hong Kong.* Hong Kong: Oxford University Press, 1989.

Siu, Helen F. "Cultural Identity and the Politics of Difference in South China." *Dædalus* 122.2 (Spring 1993): 19–43.

Skeldon, Ronald. "Hong Kong Communities Overseas." In Judith M. Brown and Rosemary Foot, eds., *Hong Kong's Transitions, 1842–1997*, pp. 121–148. London: Macmillan, 1997.

Smith, Carl T. *Chinese Christians: Elites, Middlemen, and the Church in Hong Kong.* Hong Kong: Oxford University Press, 1985.

———. "The Chinese Settlement of British Hong Kong." *Chung Chi Bulletin* 48 (May 1970): 26–32.

———. "Compradores of The Hongkong Bank." In Frank H. H. King, ed. *Eastern Banking: Essays in the History of The Hongkong and Shanghai Banking Corporation*, pp. 93–111. London: Athlone Press, 1983.

Smith, George. *A Narrative of an Exploratory Visit to Each of the Consular Cities of China and to the Islands of Hong Kong and Chusan, In Behalf of the Church Missionary Society in the Years 1844, 1845, 1846.* London: Seely, Burnside and Seeley, 1847.

Snow, Philip. *The Fall of Hong Kong: Britain, China, and the Japanese Occupation.* New Haven: Yale University Press, 2003.

South China Morning Post. 1904–1941.

South China Morning Post/Hong Kong Telegraph, Centenary Supplement, 25 January 1941.

Stokes, Gwenneth G. *Queen's College, 1862–1962.* Hong Kong: Queen's College, 1962.

Sweeting, Anthony. *Education on Hong Kong, Pre-1841 to 1941, Fact and Opinion: Materials for a History of Education in Hong Kong.* Hong Kong: Hong Kong University Press, 1990.

Thomas, Nicholas. *Colonialism's Culture: Anthropology, Travel, and Government.* Princeton: Princeton University Press, 1994.

Thomas, Nicholas. *In Oceania: Visions, Artifacts, Histories.* Durham: Duke University Press, 1997.

Tobin, Beth Fowkes. *Picturing Imperial Power: Colonial Subjects in Eighteenth-Century British Painting.* Durham: Duke University Press, 1999.

Tonkin, Elizabeth. *Narrating Our Pasts: The Social Construction of Oral History.* Cambridge: Cambridge University Press, 1992.

Tronson, John M. *Personal Narrative of a Voyage to Japan, Kamtschatka, Siberia, Tartary, and Various Parts of the Coast of China; in H. M. S. Barraracouta, 1854–1856.* London: Smith, Elder & Co., 1859.

Tsai, Jung-fang. *Hong Kong in Chinese History: Community and Social Unrest in the British Colony, 1842–1913.* New York: Columbia University Press, 1993.

———. "The Predicament of the Comprador Ideologists: He Qi (Ho Kai, 1859–1914) and Hu Li-yuan (1847–1916)." *Modern China* 7.2 (April 1981): 191–225.

Tsang, Steve, ed. *Government and Politics: A Documentary History of Hong Kong.* Hong Kong: Hong Kong University Press, 1995.

Turnbull, C. Mary. "Hong Kong: Fragrant Harbour, City of Sin and Death." In Robin W. Winks and James R. Rush, eds., *Asia in Western Fiction*, pp. 117–136. Honolulu: University of Hawaii Press, 1990.

Vines, Stephen. *Hong Kong: China's New Colony.* London: Aurum Press, 1998.

Vishnyakova-Akimova, Vera Vladimirovna. *Two Years in Revolutionary China, 1925–1927.* Trans. Steven I. Levine. Cambridge, Mass.: Harvard University Press, 1971.

Viswanathan, Gauri. *Masks of Conquest: Literary Study and British Rule in India.* London: Faber and Faber, 1990.

Wakeman, Frederic, Jr. "*Hanjian* [Traitor]! Collaboration and Retribution in Wartime Shanghai." In Wen-hsin Yeh, ed., *Becoming Chinese: Passages to Modernity and Beyond*, pp. 298–341. Berkeley: University of California Press, 2000.

———. *Strangers at the Gate: Social Disorder in South China, 1839–1861.* Berkeley: University of California Press, 1966.

Wakeman, Frederic, Jr., and Wen-hsin Yeh, eds. *Shanghai Sojourners.* Berkeley: Institute of East Asian Studies, 1992.

Wang Chuying, ed. *Xianggang gongchang diaocha* [Survey of Hong Kong factories]. Hong Kong: Nanqiao xinwen qiye gongsi, 1947.

Wang, Gungwu. "The Study of Identities in Southeast Asia." In Jennifer Cushman and Wang Gungwu, eds., *The Changing Identities of Chinese in Southeast Asia*, pp. 1–31. Hong Kong: Hong Kong University Press, 1988.

Wang Hongzhi [Wong Wang-chi]. *Lishi de chenzhong: Cong Xianggang kan Zhongguo de Xianggangshi lunshu* [The Burden of History: A Hong Kong

Perspective of the Mainland Discourse of Hong Kong History]. Hong Kong: Oxford University Press, 2000).

Wang Jingyu. "Shijiu shiji waiguo qinHua qiyezhong de Huashang fugu yundong" [Investment by Chinese merchants in the foreign enterprises that invaded China in the nineteenth century]. *Lishi yanjiu* 94 (1965): 39–74.

Ward, Robert S. *Asia for the Asiatics? The Techniques of Japanese Occupation.* Chicago: University of Chicago Press, 1945.

Watanabe Tetsuhiro. "Ka Kei, Ko Reien no shin seiron" [Ho Kai and Hu Liyuan's discourse on new government]. *Ritsu meikan bungaku* 197 (1961): 59–75.

Welsh, Frank. *A Borrowed Place: The History of Hong Kong.* New York: Kodansha, 1993.

Wesseling, H. L., ed. *Expansion and Reaction: Essays in European Expansion and Reactions in Asia and Africa.* Leiden: Leiden University Press, 1978.

White, Barbara-Sue, ed. *Hong Kong: Somewhere Between Heaven and Earth.* Hong Kong: Oxford University Press, 1996.

White, Lynn, and Li Cheng. "China Coast Identities: Regional, National, and Global." In Lowell Dittmer and Samuel S. Kim, eds., *China's Quest for National Identity,* pp. 154–193. Ithaca: Cornell University Press, 1993.

Who's Who in the Far East, 1906–7. Hong Kong: China Mail, 1906.

Williams, Patrick, and Laura Chrisman, eds. *Colonial Discourse and Post-Colonial Theory.* New York: Columbia University Press, 1994.

Wilson, Dick. *Hong Kong! Hong Kong!* London: Unwin Hyman, 1990.

Woollacott, Angela. " 'All This Is the Empire, I told Myself': Australian Women's Voyages 'Home' and the Articulation of Colonial Whiteness." *American Historical Review* 102.4 (October 1997): 1003–1029.

Wang Qile [Wong Chai-lok]. *Xianggang zhongwen jiaoyu fazhan shi* [History of the Development of Chinese Education in Hong Kong]. Hong Kong: Po Wen Book Co., 1982.

Wong, J. Y. *Anglo-Chinese relations, 1839–1860: A Calendar of Chinese Documents in the British Foreign Office Records.* Oxford: Oxford University Press, for the British Academy, 1983.

Wong, Siu-lun. *Emigrant Entrepreneurs: Shanghai Industrialists in Hong Kong.* Hong Kong: Oxford University Press, 1988.

Wright, Arnold, and H. A. Cartwright, eds. *Twentieth Century Impressions of Hongkong, Shanghai, and other Treaty Ports of China: Their History, People, Commerce, Industries, and Resources.* London: Lloyds, 1908.

Wright, Gwendolyn. *The Politics of Design in French Colonial Urbanism.* Chicago: University of Chicago Press, 1991.

Wu Hao. *Huai jiu Xianggang di* [Longing for old Hong Kong]. Hong Kong: Boyi, 1988.

Wu Xinglian [Woo Sing Lim]. *Xianggang Huaren mingren shilue* [Prominent Chinese in Hong Kong]. Hong Kong: Wuzhou, 193.

Xian Yuyi [Elizabeth Sinn]. "Shehui zuzhi yu shehui zhuanbian" [Social organization and social change]. In Wang Gengwu [Wang Gungwu], ed., *Xianggangshi xinbian* [Hong Kong History: New Perspectives], vol. 1, pp. 157–210. Hong Kong: Sanlian, 1997.

Xianshi gongsi ershiwu nian jingguo shi [The Sincere Co., Ltd., Twenty-fifth Anniversary]. Hong Kong: Commercial Press, 1924.

Xianggang Donghua sanyuan bainian shilue [One Hundred Years of the Tung Wah Group of Hospitals]. 2 vols. Hong Kong, 1971.

Xianggang Donghua yiyuan liushi zhounian jinian ji [Hong Kong Tung Wah Hospital sixtieth anniversary commemoration]. Hong Kong: n.p., 1931.

Xianggang Huaqiao gongshangye nianjian [Hong Kong commercial and industrial yearbook]. Hong Kong: Xiequn, 1940.

Xianggang Xianshi youxian gongsi [Sincere Company Limited, Hong Kong]. *Jinzanxi jinian ce* [Diamond Jubilee]. Hong Kong: n.p., 1975.

Xianggang yongan youxian gongsi [The Wing On Co, Ltd.]. *Ershiwu zhounian jinian lu* [In Commemoration of 25th Anniversary]. Hong Kong: n.p. 1932.

Xianggang Zhonghua jidujiao qingnianhui [Hong Kong Chinese YMCA]. *Qingnianhui shiye gaiyao* [YMCA guide]. Hong Kong: n.p., 1918.

———. *Xianggang Zhonghua jidujiao qingnianhui wushi zhounian jinian tekan* [Hong Kong Chinese YMCA Fiftieth Anniversary Commemoration]. Hong Kong: n.p., 1951.

Xianggang Zhonghua youle hui [Chinese Recreation Club Hong Kong]. Hong Kong: Chinese Recreation Club, 1987.

Xianggang Zhonghua youle hui qishinian jinian tekan [Hong Kong Chinese Recreation Club seventieth anniversary commemoration]. Hong Kong: Chinese Recreation Club, 1982.

Xianggang Zhonghua zongshanghui chengli bashi zhounian jinian tekan [Commemorative edition of the eightieth anniversary of the Hong Kong Chinese General Chamber of Commerce]. Hong Kong: Zhonghua zongshanghui, 1980.

Xianggang Zhonghua zongshanghui chengli liushi zhounian jinian tekan [Special edition in commemoration of the sixtieth anniversary of the Hong Kong Chinese General Chamber of Commerce]. Hong Kong: Zhonghua zongshanghui, 1960.

Xiao Gongquan. *Zhongguo zhengzhi sixiangshi* [History of Chinese political philosophy]. Vol. 6. Taipei: Zhonghua wenhua chuban shiye weiyuanhui, 1954.

Xiao Guojian. *Xianggang qiandai shehui* [Early Hong Kong society]. Hong Kong: Zhonghua shuju, 1990.

Yang Sixian. *Xianggang cangsang* [Hong Kong vicissitudes]. Beijing: Youyi chubanshe, 1986.

Yen, Ching-hwang. "Ch'ing Changing Images of the Overseas Chinese (1644–1912)," *Modern Asian Studies* 15.2 (1981): 261–285.

———. "Ch'ing's Sale of Honours and the Chinese Leadership in Singapore and Malaya (1877–1912)," *Journal of Southeast Asian Studies* 1.2 (September 1970): 20–32.

Yeoh, Brenda S. A. *Contesting Space: Power Relations and the Urban Built Environment in Colonial Singapore*. Kuala Lumpur: Oxford University Press, 1996.

Yu Shengwu and Liu Cunkuan, eds. *Shijiu shiji de Xianggang* [Nineteenth-century Hong Kong]. Hong Kong: Qilin shuye, 1994.

Yuan Bangjian. *Xianggang shilue* [History of Hong Kong]. Hong Kong: Zhongliu chubanshe, 1993.

Zeng Wu. "Xianggang Baoliangju shilue" [History of the Baoliangju (Po Leung Kuk)]. *Guangdong wenshi ziliao* 61 (1990): 212–224.

Zhang Xiaohui. *Xianggang Huashangshi* [History of Hong Kong Chinese merchants]. Hong Kong: Mingbao, 1996.

Zhongguo lüxingshe. *Xianggang daoyou* [Guide to Hong Kong]. Shanghai: Zhongguo lüxingshe, 1940.

"Zhongguo zhi maiban zhidu" [The comprador system in China]. *Dongfang zazhi* 20.6 (March 1923): 129–132.

Zhou Hong. "Origins of Government Social Protection Policy in Hong Kong, 1842–1941." Ph.D. diss., Brandeis University, 1991.

Index